Edited by

George S.
McGovern

Donald C.
Simmons, Jr.

Daniel M.
Gaken

Leadership and Service

An Introduction

KENDALL/HUNT PUBLISHING COMPANY
4050 Westmark Drive   Dubuque, Iowa 52002

Cover images courtesy of (clockwise from top left) Dave and Cindy Baar,
Daniel M. Gaken, Darrell and Jarid Hartmann, and Diana Goldammer

Dedication

To Rachelle, my love, whose support and patience knows no bounds—DS

To my father, Coach Gaken, whose example showed me what it means to be a leader—DG

To Eleanor, always my most dependable and inspirational guide—GM

Contents

Preface

Leadership is a relatively new academic course of study at most universities but it has long been a topic of great interest to intellectuals, military professionals, people of faith, and kings, just to name a few. Ancient texts from around the globe addressed the topic long before the first European universities emerged during the Middle Ages. Today bookstore shelves are filled with texts that offer advice on how to succeed in almost any career field. Magazines provide endless "top ten" and "top twenty-five" lists and articles on how to be a better employee, boss, or parent. Television news and talk shows tantalize viewers by offering similar quick fixes to the complex challenges we face daily in our personal and professional lives. True students of the discipline know that nothing in life is that simple. Leadership is a complex interdisciplinary course of study, involving much self-reflection, constant review of individual and organizational strengths and weaknesses, and the desire to help others accomplish common goals and objectives.

Many people express concern that the youth of today are not interested in anything but watching television and playing with the latest electronic gadget. At first glance, that might appear to be true. However, if you take the time to get to know them on a personal level, it becomes apparent that many are as concerned about what is happening around the world as we are but feel helpless to do anything about it. The new global economy and challenges of importance to all of humanity, such as global warming, poverty, the loss of ecosystems, political extremists, pandemics, and world hunger, will require much of the emerging leaders who are now enrolled at colleges and universities around the world. They must be prepared intellectually and possess the leadership skills to tackle challenges that were unimaginable only a generation ago. We believe the students of today can and will be the greatest generation. They just need guidance as they prepare themselves to face the challenges ahead.

The inspiration for this textbook was a chance conversation between Donald Simmons and Dan Gaken, two of the co-editors. While attending the International Leadership Conference in Chicago during the fall of 2006, Simmons and Gaken discussed textbook options for upcoming leadership classes at their respective universities. Both expressed a desire for a leadership textbook written specifically for emerging leaders that not only introduced the student to basic leadership history and theory but also incorporated service and emphasized throughout the importance of leadership for the common good. When they approached Senator George McGovern, one of the world's most respected public servants, a former presidential candidate, and the first United Nations Global Ambassador on Hunger, he enthusiastically signed on to help with the project.

This textbook is the result of the work of many educators and leadership practitioners who are committed and passionate about preparing future leaders of the world for a life dedicated to leadership and service. The associate editors, contributing authors, photo contributors, supporters, and all who helped us along the way are the ones who made this textbook a reality. We would especially like to thank the wonderful staff at Kendall/Hunt Publishing Company, particularly David Tart, Amanda Smith, Amanda Kennedy, Jay Hay, Karen Hoffmann, and Colleen Zelinsky for believing in us and our idea and helping us make it a reality.

To the students who are about to begin their studies in leadership and service, our hope is that these essays, exercises, and case studies, in combination with their instructor's lectures and required service related activities, compel them to become leaders who are truly dedicated to leading with integrity and service to others above all else.

George S. McGovern
Donald C. Simmons, Jr.
Daniel M. Gaken

Editors

Daniel M. Gaken serves as the coordinator of leadership at Central Michigan University, where he develops leadership programming and teaches leadership studies. Gaken also coordinates the unique Leader Advancement Scholarship program, a residential cohort of forty scholars who complete an academic and co-curricular leadership protocol, and works with the CMU LEAD Program and the LeaderShape Institute. He is also a contributing author for this text.

George S. McGovern is a prolific author who has lectured at colleges and universities around the world. After completing his undergraduate studies at Dakota Wesleyan University, he enrolled at Northwestern University in Chicago, where he earned his M.A. and Ph.D. degrees in American history and government. He has also received many honorary degrees and distinguished awards, including the Presidential Medal of Freedom, the United States' highest civilian honor. A war hero, twenty-two-year member of Congress and the US Senate, and 1972 Democratic presidential nominee, McGovern will long be remembered for his courage in speaking out against US involvement in the Vietnam War and his work on behalf of hungry children throughout the world. He is also a contributing author for this text.

Donald C. Simmons, Jr., serves as associate professor and founding executive director of the George and Eleanor McGovern Center for Leadership and Public Service at Dakota Wesleyan University. Simmons holds a Ph.D. in history and international studies from the University of Denver. Prior to joining the DWU faculty, he founded the South Dakota Center for the Book and the South Dakota Festival of the Book, he was twice elected a city councilman, and he served as the executive director of the South Dakota Humanities Council. A former recipient of the Association of Third World Studies Presidential Award for his work related to third world development, Simmons currently serves on the editorial board of *White House Studies*. He is also a contributing author for this text.

Associate Editors

Jeremy Christensen is an assistant professor of speech and assistant director of debate at Hillsdale College, where he teaches courses in public speaking and argumentation. He is currently pursuing a doctoral degree in English at the University of South Dakota.

Robert P. Watson is the director of American studies at Lynn University in Boca Raton, Florida. The author or editor of more than twenty-five books on American politics and history and a frequent media commentator, he serves as a member of the board of several scholarly journals, academic associations, and presidential foundations, including the McGovern Center for Leadership and Public Service. Watson is also a contributing author for this text.

Contributing Authors

Jenell Barnard serves as the coordinator of leadership development for K–12 students at Central Michigan University. In this role, she helps CMU fulfill its commitment to serve the public good by providing leadership training and development for the youth of Michigan. Barnard also teaches communication courses and introduction to leadership.

John S. (Jack) Burns is professor of leadership studies and management in the School of Global Commerce and Management at Whitworth University in Spokane, Washington, where he coordinates the interdisciplinary undergraduate minor in leadership studies. He has been teaching leadership studies since 1985 and has developed leadership studies programs at two universities. He has been a director of an Eisenhower Leadership Program Grant and has published several articles on leadership education. Burns received his Ph.D. in higher education administration from Washington State University.

Kate Cadenhead is the chair of the Department of Language Arts and Humanities at Iowa Central Community College. A former member of the faculty at the University of Texas and Cuyahoga Community College in Ohio, Cadenhead has been the recipient of numerous awards for academic excellence. She has written extensively about the role of women and leadership and the importance of diversity as a leadership strategy. Cadenhead received her Ph.D. in The Community College Leadership Program from the University of Texas and her undergraduate degree in history from Rutgers University.

Gregory E. Christy currently serves as the president of Northwestern College in Orange City, Iowa. Prior to assuming that position, he worked in higher education in a variety of capacities, most recently as vice president for institutional advancement at Dakota Wesleyan University. During his career, he has committed his life to improving the study of leadership and service. Christy is a graduate of Simpson College in Indianola, Iowa, where he played intercollegiate baseball and basketball, and Western Illinois University, where he completed graduate study in sports management.

Robert G. Duffett is president of Dakota Wesleyan University in Mitchell, South Dakota. A graduate of Princeton Theological Seminary, he received his Ph.D. in organizational theory/management and historical theology from the University of Iowa. One of the longest serving presidents in the Midwest, Duffett led the largest fundraising campaign and building expansion in the university's history. He also played a significant role in increasing student diversity at DWU, which now has the most ethnically diverse student body in the region. Prior to joining DWU, Duffett served as provost and academic dean at Ottawa University.

Beverly Wade Hogan is president of Tougaloo College in Jackson, Mississippi. Hogan has extensive experience in organizational and community leadership. She has been a mental health administrator, state government official, and college administrator, and she has served as board chair for nonprofit organizations and a community foundation. Hogan holds degrees in psychology, public policy, and administration and is currently engaged in doctoral studies in human and organizational development at Fielding Graduate University. She has also studied at Harvard University and Oxford University in England.

Daniel N. Huck holds the W. R. Gruver Chair of Leadership Studies at Berea College and serves as the co-director of the Entrepreneurship for the Public Good Program. He began his career as a lawyer, a businessman, and an entrepreneur after graduating from Bucknell University and the Northeastern University School of Law. He has served in the West Virginia attorney general's office as deputy attorney general, director of the Antitrust and Complex Litigation Division, and later as legal counsel to the governor of West Virginia. He left the practice of law to complete his doctorate in Leadership Studies at West Virginia University. Prior to his current appointment, Huck served on the faculty of the McDonough Center for Leadership at Marietta College in Ohio.

Karla Larson Hunter serves as assistant professor of communication at Dakota Wesleyan University. Her independent communication consulting, motivational speeches, *Empowerment Through Service,* and experiential college pedagogy empower others to serve their communities optimally through the development of key leadership communication skills.

John A. Kline, a former university provost, has led large organizations and is now the distinguished professor of leadership and director of the Institute for Leadership Development at Troy University in Alabama. He has written many books and essays on communication and leadership and regularly conducts leadership training for corporate, military, and religious audiences. He has two websites: www.klinespeak.com and http://troy.troy.edu/leadership.

Curtina Moreland-Young is currently the CEO of Pathfinders and Associates Inc., a management consulting firm located in Jackson, Mississippi. She is the retired founding chair of the Department of Public Policy and Administration at Jackson State University. Moreland-Young began her study of leadership as a research interest while writing her dissertation and since that time she has authored several articles and monographs on leadership. Additionally, she was selected as a Kellogg National Leadership Fellow and has consulted on leadership at the local, regional, national, and international levels. Moreland-Young received her Ph.D. from the University of Illinois in Champaign–Urbana in political science.

Kellie Pickett is the director of student leadership and civic engagement at Georgia Southern University. Previously, she worked developing student leaders in orientation at Georgia Southern and in Admissions at Duke University. She earned her B.A. from Ball State University and M.S. from Miami University (OH).

Amy Radford-Popp is the residence life assistant director for staff selection and development at Michigan State University. She has over sixteen years of experience in student and academic affairs at MSU, as well as other public and private institutions. In 2006, Radford-Popp earned her Ph.D. in higher education from Michigan State University.

Abrina Schnurman-Crook is the executive director of the Batten Leadership Institute at Hollins University. She received her undergraduate degree from the University of North Carolina at Greensboro and her master's and doctoral degrees from Virginia Tech. She is a licensed professional counselor with a broad range of clinical experience, having spent a number of years working in crisis services. Schnurman-Crook has experience working in two university counseling centers and has taught undergraduate courses at Hollins University, as well as graduate courses at Virginia Tech.

Raymond D. Screws is an assistant professor of history and assistant coordinator of the MA program in public history at the University of Arkansas at Little Rock. Previously, Screws was the senior program officer at the Nebraska Humanities Council. In 2003, he earned a Ph.D. in history from the University of Nebraska.

Annemarie Seifert is the associate vice president for student affairs and enrollment management at Georgia Southern University, where she also teaches leadership. Most recently she spent nine professional years at The University of Texas at Austin where she also earned a Ph.D. in educational administration. Seifert is committed to educating and challenging the whole student, and is always interested in engaging students in the leadership and service dialogue in and outside of the classroom.

John R. Shoup serves as the associate dean of the School of Education at California Baptist University in Riverside, California. He teaches leadership and educational history and policy at the graduate level and has presented and conducted research and workshops on leadership development and best practices and educational policy. Shoup has also served as a school principal and in various social service settings. He has a Ph.D. in education with an emphasis in institutional leadership and policy studies from the University of California, Riverside. He also has a Master of Divinity and a Master of Arts in counseling psychology from Trinity Evangelical Divinity School in Deerfield, Illinois.

Michael J. C. Taylor, a Los Angeles native, earned his Ph.D. from the University of Missouri, Kansas City, in 2001, under the mentorship of Herman M. Hattaway. Taylor's publications include articles for *The Journal of Supreme Court History* and *White House Studies,* along with several book chapters and reviews. His current project is a constitutional re-examination of *Scott v. Sandford* (1857).

Bruce Tucker is the coordinator of the Santa Fe Community College Leadership Institute, the acting director of student development programs, and an associate professor in the Student Development Instruction Department. He has designed several courses on leadership for Santa Fe Community College, conducted leadership seminars and training for the college and community, and authored several books and articles. He is a certified instructor for the Phi Theta Kappa Leadership Curriculum and holds a Ph.D. from Purdue University in instructional research and development.

Katherine Walker is the founding director of the Batten Leadership Institute at Hollins University. She received her undergraduate degree at the University of Virginia and her master's and doctoral degrees at Virginia Tech. Walker is a licensed professional counselor and a licensed marriage and family therapist. Her clinical work focused on adolescent development and female identity formation. This experience, combined with her ongoing academic interest in leadership studies, led her to develop the institute's focus on personal growth and skill development.

Donald A. Watt is vice president for academic affairs and dean of the faculty at Dakota Wesleyan University. Previously, he was associate professor of political science and geography at Southern Arkansas University, where he also served as dean of the College of Liberal and Performing Arts. Prior to working full-time in higher education, Watt served in leadership positions within the United Methodist Church. He holds degrees from Mount Union College and Pacific School of Religion, as well as a Ph.D. in conflict analysis and peace research from the University of Pennsylvania.

Introducing Leadership and Service

College

A Foundation for Living a Life of Leadership and Service

Kellie
Pickett

Annemarie
Seifert

■ WHAT IS LEADERSHIP?

Leadership is a complex and intricate phenomenon. Do a search for "Leadership" on the Internet and you will find many definitions, examples, and options for framing your definition of leadership. For example, a search may lead you to any one of the following definitions:

> "Leadership is a matter of how to be, not how to do. We spend most of our lives mastering how to do things, but in the end it is the quality and character of the individual that defines the performance of great leaders" (Hesselbein, 1999, introduction, p. xii).

> "Leadership requires orchestrating . . . conflicts among and within the interested parties . . ." (Heifetz, 1994, p. 22).

> "Effective Leadership addresses problems that require people to move from a familiar but inadequate equilibrium—through disequilibrium—to a more adequate equilibrium" (Daloz Parks, 2005, p. 9).

> "An act or instance of leading; guidance; direction" (Dictionary.com, 2007).

> "A leader takes people where they want to go. A great leader takes people where they don't necessarily want to go, but ought to be" Rosalynn Carter, US First Lady.

> "Leadership is a combination of strategy and character. If you must be without one, be without the strategy" General H. Norman Schwarzkopf.

> "Leadership is the art of mobilizing others to want to struggle for shared aspirations" (Kouzes & Posner, 1995, p. 30).

Leadership is not black and white. Your challenge, as you explore leadership, is to define what leadership means to you and characterize it in the framework of your values, experiences, and discussions spurred from this text.

There are many lenses from which you can view leadership, and throughout this chapter and others to follow, you will be

introduced to several of these approaches. From the many different theories and new research on leadership to its different styles, this chapter will challenge you to analyze and apply your own style of leadership and the leadership of others with whom you interact.

While defining leadership and exploring different approaches to leadership, you will also need to consider the function service and civic engagement play in your role as a leader. Additionally, the examination of your college or university environment for unique, hands-on experiences to test, study, and challenge your perceptions of leadership and service will be critical as you search for the role leadership and service will play in your life. This chapter will introduce you to all of these concepts and encourage you to participate in some of the challenges posed and experiences suggested, as well as to read some of the examples listed as you define leadership for yourself. The chapter will end with a discussion of civic responsibility and examine the role leaders have to give back to their community.

To begin our discussion of leadership, it is important to provide a definition to serve as a foundation for the remainder of the chapter. While we provide you with the following definition to use as a framework, we challenge you to develop one that reflects the importance of leadership to you as you continue through your search for the meaning of leadership throughout your life. **Leadership** is the process by which a leader facilitates change. It is the function of three elements: leaders, followers, and situation. Leadership occurs when all three of these elements interact and work together, while respecting the role each piece plays in the process. When the personality, position, and expertise of the leader(s) work in combination with the values, norms, and cohesiveness of followers and interact and respect the environment, history, and task of the situation, leadership occurs (Hughes, Ginnett, & Curphy, 2006). A **leader** is someone who is able to lead others to effect change. While leaders often improve conditions for others within society, not all leaders facilitate positive change.

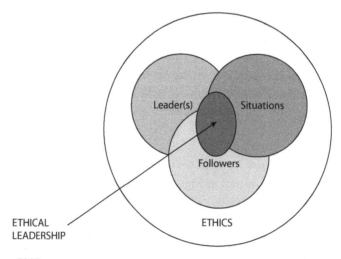

Source: Prince, 2007.

Adolph Hitler, for example, was the undisputed leader of Germany but few people today would argue that the changes he brought to Germany were positive. **Followers** are individuals who come together to support the vision of a leader(s) and use their personal strengths, knowledge, and skills to assist in reaching a common goal. **Situation** is defined as the environment in which a task is undertaken, in combination with knowledge and human interaction.

When these three elements act with a foundation of **ethics,** a system of moral values and principles that guides behavior, **ethical leadership** occurs (Prince, 2007). Having a foundation of ethics is critical, as our society has seen how unethical leaders can cause the demise of an organization, others, and themselves. Think of some examples you have seen in recent news. Whether it is a politician or a business executive, unethical behavior has an impact on all levels of leadership, creating distrust and a lack of productivity.

While many texts and courses may focus on developing leaders, the focus of this chapter will concentrate on developing your understanding of the leadership process. Developing personal leadership skills, understanding active followership, and gaining an understanding of the situation will be the focus of this discussion on leadership.

■ WHY EXPLORE LEADERSHIP DURING COLLEGE?

College is likely the first time you are on your own. It can be an opportunity for you to explore who you are and allow you to shape who you would like to become as an individual, apart from a family or community. The college environment usually encourages students to take advantage of time, access, and opportunity to engage in leadership and service. Approach all of your college experiences with the hope of learning something new about yourself and the world around you. College and university campuses are the perfect environment to examine, practice, and critically think about leadership and service, as you are exposed to a wide range of people, ideas, and experiences, thereby increasing your understanding of the world and society.

Furthermore, the study of leadership and the practice of being a leader are a great match in the college setting. For this reason, make sure you link your academic study of leadership to your co-curricular involvement by applying what you learn in the classroom to your college leadership involvement: Don't leave that exploration in the classroom! Your ability to connect the intellectual with the practical will reinforce the concepts and theories you learn and strengthen your leadership skills during college and beyond.

Today, more people are entering the workforce with a college degree, so it is important to consider what will make you stand out after you complete your undergraduate degree and begin to explore your chosen field of study. Leadership and service experiences are one way to stand out. Employers are seeking well-rounded candidates to join the ranks of their organizations, and leadership and service involvement often fit this bill. You can gain a great deal of knowledge and skills from leadership and service experiences at the college level that can help you with your future career. Additionally, you will be more successful during the interview process if you are able to articulate your skills and abilities and connect them to practical experiences.

Among many transferable skills, leadership allows you to practice verbal and nonverbal communication, recognize and manage ethical issues, delegate responsibility, deal with multiple tasks, lead a team, resolve conflicts, motivate people into action, establish and attain goals, and work with people from diverse backgrounds.

College offers the opportunity for you not only to study leadership but also to observe and engage others practicing leadership as you define your personal leadership style and fine-tune your skills. College is one of the few times in your life when you can immerse yourself in organizations and programs that are time consuming. Take advantage of the multitude of programs and services offered on your campus. For many, college will be a time when you will have the most access to diverse lectures, movies, panel discussions, musicians, leadership workshops, and conferences.

For some students, the numerous opportunities to engage with the campus community can be overwhelming. Enjoy and explore this exciting environment. Developing leadership skills begins with involvement, so focus on learning and participating, not just obtaining a position. Some of the best leaders you'll meet do not hold a formal leadership position but lead through their actions. To explore the involvement possibilities, consider attending a student organization fair, visiting the Dean of Students' office, participating in a leadership conference, getting behind an issue that you are passionate about, attending a lecture sponsored by your multicultural student services office, or further exploring your passion in an area of campus life.

Student Organizations

Student organizations are often the most accessible route to leadership on a college campus. Student organizations allow you to manage a broad scope of issues related to leadership and service. Challenge yourself to think beyond leadership position goals and to consider what experiences would be most valuable to you as a person and your campus community. Possible types of student organizations on your campus include:

- Academic
- Cultural
- Educational
- Greek
- Honorary
- International
- Media
- Political
- Professional
- Recreational/athletic

- Religious
- Service
- Social
- Special interest
- Student governance

Leadership and Service Opportunities

Everyone has the capacity to lead. As you begin your exploration, adopt the idea that you are a leader, and recognize the skills you have and then decide where you want to go. Find programs, services, and departments on campus that promote interdisciplinary leadership development and service opportunities. These offices or organizations might also provide some of the following resources to you:

- Workshops
- Conferences
- Leadership libraries
- Volunteer opportunities/programs

Leadership Employment Opportunities

Your campus has many opportunities for employment, including work-study, internships, and paraprofessional opportunities. Campus employment provides you not only with extra income but also with the convenience of working on campus and flexible scheduling. On-campus employment may also afford you opportunities to network with faculty, staff, and other students and increase your knowledge of university resources. Moreover, your on-campus work experience will allow you to practice interpersonal skills, make greater contributions to the university community, and grow personally and professionally. Consider some of the following options:

- Resident advisors
- Peer academic advisors
- Orientation leaders/advisors
- Residential community coordinators
- Student affairs interns
- Student ambassadors
- Peer leaders/mentors

Although there are a multitude of reasons to engage with your campus community, you will be more successful if you have the drive to make a difference and are passionate about something. Passion will afford you the persistence to follow through with your initiative or involvement. Furthermore, it is important to consider "fit" as you make decisions to participate. For example, consider whether it would be more valuable for you to explore many offerings or narrow your involvement experiences to those that align with your academic discipline. Whatever your chosen involvement path, just remember that a collegiate environment is a unique laboratory that allows you to observe, study, and practice in a controlled environment. We encourage you to take leadership risks during college, as it is a place that celebrates and embraces educational growth. The lessons you learn can create a foundation for future growth and learning in leadership.

■ LEADERSHIP PHILOSOPHIES AND STYLES

Now that you have a foundation of what leadership is, why college represents a dynamic arena to practice it, and some activities you can become involved with, let us explore some philosophies and styles that guide the current practice of leadership. While many philosophies of leadership exist, this chapter will focus on five. An in-depth look at each of these philosophies, in combination with your exploration into leadership styles, will aid you in the development of your personal philosophy of leadership. Over the next few pages, you will gain insight into the situational, transformational, authentic, social change, and servant-leadership philosophies of leadership. Look for elements with which you agree, question, disagree, or want to further explore. These insights can provide a great discussion.

The Situational Leadership Model

The situational leadership model was first introduced by Hersey and Blanchard as a way to analyze leader behaviors using two broad categories: initiating structure and consideration. These two categories have evolved over the years to become task structures and relationship behaviors. Task structures describe how the leader gives information about responsibilities, including what is to be accomplished, how, when, and who is to accomplish the task. Relationship behaviors involve how much the leader engages in communication and relationship building, including listening, encouraging, and giving support (Hersey, 1984; Hersey & Blanchard, 1995; Hughes, Ginnett, & Curphy, 2006).

The situational leadership model is a good way to look at leadership from the lens of being flexible. It communicates the importance of not acting toward all people in the same way. Hersey and Blanchard's situational leadership model describes how leadership varies based on the interactions of task and relationship behaviors. The interaction of these behaviors creates the following four quadrants on a graph (see next page).

An important element of the model addresses how the success of behaviors is impacted by follower readiness, defined as the ability and willingness of followers to complete a task (Hersey, 1984; Hersey & Blanchard, 1995). As you can see from the graph, follower readiness plays an important role in the connection between the task and relationship behavior. The curved line added on the graph represents the leadership behavior that is most effective, depending on the level of follower readiness. To apply the model, leaders assess the readiness level of the followers. Draw a vertical line from the center of the readiness level up to the point where it intersects with the curved line in the graph. Where this intersection occurs is the quadrant that represents the best opportunity to produce the most successful results in leadership (Hersey, 1984; Hughes, Ginnett, & Curphy, 2006).

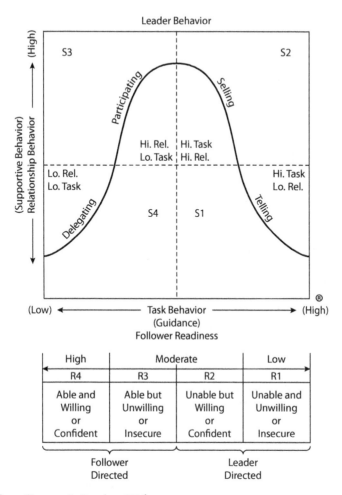

Source: Hughes, Ginnett, & Curphy, 2006.

   The situational leadership model highlights the importance of your skills and abilities as a leader, while focusing on the importance of knowing your followers. As a leader, you will be able to apply many of these skills and abilities in a variety of situations, and this model is a good representation of how you can transfer skills from one area of leadership to other areas of your life.

Transformational Leadership Theory

The transformational leadership theory, made popular by political sociologist James MacGregor Burns (1978) links the roles and values of leaders and followers. Burns defined leaders as those who seek to understand the drive of followers to better reach the goals of both leaders and followers (Burns, 1978). Transformational leadership serves to change the status quo by appealing to followers' values and their sense of high purpose. They articulate problems in the current systems and create a compelling vision for what is possible (Hughes, Ginnett, & Curphy, 2006). Transformational leaders reframe issues, ignite enthusiasm for change within followers, and encourage and develop followers to become leaders in the change movement. Transformational leaders inspire followers to see the impact they can have on society.

Transformational leaders do the following (Hughes, Ginnett, & Curphy, 2006):

- Focus on building trust, admiration, loyalty, and respect among their followers
- Convey a strong vision and form emotional connections/bonds with followers to help followers meet their goals and needs
- Be willing to embrace controversy, make self-sacrifices, and remain strong and focused to reach their vision, despite criticism
- Possess a strong standard of moral and ethical conduct and can be counted on to do the right thing
- Communicate a direction that transforms the values and norms of the organization
- Maintain a consistent emphasis on individual and organizational learning

Followers who work with transformational leaders are motivated, are inspired, and are transformed by the relationship with their leaders. It is the goal of transformational leaders to impact each follower, and in the end, to ensure that followers become leaders. Transformational leaders seek to engage the whole person by focusing on followers' motives, strengths, and values to empower them to act. They use this passion within their followers to mobilize and change social systems while building up those around them.

Authentic Leadership Theory

Authentic leadership is described as a root concept (Avolio & Gardner, 2005) that underlies positive approaches to leadership, such as transformational, charismatic, and servant-leadership. The foundation of authentic leadership is developing authenticity and increasing self-awareness.

In the book *True North: Discover Your Authentic Leadership,* Bill George and Peter Sims (2007) wrote the following about authentic leaders:

> [T]hese leaders recognize that leadership is *not* about their success or about getting loyal subordinates to follow them. They know the key to a successful organization is having empowered leaders at all levels, including those that have no direct reports.

> Authentic leaders not only inspire those around them, they empower them to step up and lead. Thus, we offer the new definition of leadership: *The authentic leader brings people together around a shared purpose and empowers them to step up and lead authentically in order to create value for all stakeholders* (introduction, pp. xxx–xxxi).

Authentic leaders know themselves. They serve others through their leadership and are more interested in empowering people than gaining power for themselves. They learn from their and others' mistakes and successes to build a positive strength initiative within their organizations (Avolio & Luthans, 2005).

Authentic leaders know their strengths and weaknesses. They recognize their shortcomings and work to overcome them. They are consistent, self-disciplined, and committed to life-long learning. The key to becoming an authentic leader is to develop one's own style. A leader who imitates the leadership styles of others is not being authentic and will most likely not succeed. A leader's style must be congruent with his or her own personality and character; the style must also be consistent with who he or she is.

There are five essential qualities of being an authentic leader (George, 2003; George & Sims, 2007). Authentic leaders must:

- Understand their purpose
- Practice solid values
- Lead with heart
- Establish connected relationships
- Demonstrate self-discipline

Authentic leadership has received much more attention since the recent ethical failures of leaders in the demise of well-known corporations, such as Enron and WorldCom, and George (2003) argues it is the way to restore confidence among followers in such corporations. While the research in this area is still ongoing, there is much to be learned by studying and engaging in the practice of authentic leadership.

Social Change Model of Leadership Development

The social change model is based on the research of college students and the influence of peer groups. Alexander Astin (1993) discovered that peer influence and interaction impact leadership development among college students more than any other factor.

The social change model is designed to use student peer groups to enhance individual leadership development in students. The model strives to prepare leaders to effect positive change both in and out of traditional leadership roles. The social change model views the leader as a change agent who influences change through collective action with followers.

The following are the key assumptions and primary goals of the social change model (Higher Education Research Institute, 1996):

- Leadership is concerned with effecting change on behalf of others and society.
- Leadership is collaborative.
- Leadership is a process rather than a position.
- Leadership should be value-based.
- All students (not just those holding formal leadership positions) are potential leaders.
- Service is a powerful vehicle for developing student leadership skills.

The two primary goals of the model are to enhance student learning and to develop self-knowledge and leadership competence in order to facilitate positive social change.

The model examines leadership development through three levels: the individual, group process, and community/societal levels. Within those three levels are seven values: (1) consciousness of self, (2) congruence, (3) commitment, (4) collaboration, (5) common purpose, (6) controversy with civility, and (7) citizenship. These levels and values constantly interact to produce leadership.

All the levels of the social change model are concerned with impacting growth and change in the other levels of the model, thereby producing a dynamic interaction of values and people within leadership development (Higher Education Research Institute, 1996).

Servant-Leadership

The servant-leadership theory was developed by Robert K. Greenleaf, a retired AT&T executive. He developed the theory out of his growing concern for college students' attitudes. Servant-leadership is a practical philosophy that describes leaders who choose to serve first and then lead as a means of extending service to others. Servant-leaders may or may not hold formal leadership positions. They emerge from all parts of the organization, depending on the situation and need. Servant-leaders operate through collaboration, trust, foresight, listening, and the ethical use of power and empowerment (Greenleaf, 1995).

Greenleaf wrote *The Servant as Leader* in 1977; in it, he described servant-leadership:

> The servant-leader is servant first . . . It begins with the natural feeling that one wants to serve, to serve *first*. Then conscious choice brings one to aspire to lead. He or she is sharply different from the person who is *leader* first, perhaps because of the need to assuage an unusual power drive or to acquire material possessions. For such it will be a later choice to serve—after leadership is established. The leader-first and the servant-first are two extreme types. Between them there are shadings and blends that are part of the infinite variety of human nature.
>
> The difference manifests itself in the care taken by the servant-first to make sure that other people's highest priority needs are being served. The best test, and difficult to administer, is this: Do those served grow as persons? Do they, *while being served,* become healthier, wiser, freer, more autonomous, more likely themselves to become servants? And, what is the effect on the least privileged in society? Will they benefit or at least will they not be further deprived? (1977, pp. 13–14)

Larry Spears, former CEO of the Greenleaf Center, has identified ten critical principles of servant-leadership: (1) listening, (2) empathy, (3) healing of relationships, (4) awareness, (5) persuasion, (6) conceptualization, (7) foresight, (8) stewardship, (9) commitment to the growth of people, and (10) building community (Baker, 2001).

■ LEADERSHIP STYLES

In addition to the models and theories previously presented, it is important to have an understanding of the different types of leadership styles that can be demonstrated and utilized. Three of the most common styles of leadership are autocratic/authoritarian, democratic/participatory, and laissez-faire/delegative (Bass, 1990; Lewin, Lippit & White, 1939). Being able to recognize different leadership styles can assist you in becoming an active member in the leadership process, both as a leader and as a follower. As you learn to integrate, with equal importance, the roles of leader, follower, and situation, your knowledge of appropriate styles will be key to your success. Additionally, these styles may assist you in creating your personal definition of leadership. As you read the descriptions of the styles, think about a time when you or someone you have worked with has exhibited each of the following styles.

Autocratic/Authoritarian

An autocratic, or authoritarian, leader makes decisions without consulting followers. An autocratic leader maintains all control, giving no power to followers. The decision is made without any form of consultation and is often used when a determination needs to be made quickly or decisions need to be made that have little to no impact on others. Since the autocratic leader does not seek input from others, this style, if used frequently, can lead to low morale among followers and feelings of distrust.

Democratic/Participatory

The democratic leader is also referred to as the participatory leader. A democratic leader involves followers in decision making and focuses on group consensus. This style of leadership is effective in making people feel valued and appreciated. However, if there are multiple opinions, it can be time consuming and cumbersome. Decisions that need to be made quickly may not be best served by this leadership style. Decisions that require commitment and investment from people within a group may be best served with a democratic style.

Laissez-Faire/Delegative

The laissez-faire, or delegative, style of leadership minimizes the leader's involvement in decision making. A laissez-faire leader steps back to "let it be," allowing people to make their own decisions. This style of leadership works best when followers are skilled, capable, and motivated to make sound decisions. The laissez-faire style gives followers freedom to determine goals, make decisions, and resolve problems on their own. The leader provides feedback to followers but allows them to chart their own course.

This chapter references only three of the more common styles of leadership, but there are many other styles, and variations of styles, of leadership. Some of the others will be discussed later in other chapters.

■ APPLYING WHAT YOU KNOW ABOUT LEADERSHIP ON YOUR CAMPUS

During college, you will have many opportunities to observe and analyze leadership and service in action. Using the previous discussions on definitions, philosophies, and styles of leadership, it is now your responsibility to take action! As you observe and interact with individuals and constituent groups on your campus, it will be valuable for you to have an understanding of the organization and community culture. Take the time to study your college campus and understand how it operates. This is important because a leader's success often depends, to a great extent, on his or her understanding of an organization's culture. In evaluating your institution, the following questions will help guide you to a better understanding of the structure, operation, and culture of your campus community.

- ■ How is leadership exhibited on your college campus?
- ■ Who holds the power on campus and who influences decision-making processes?
- ■ What is your institution's mission or strategic plan?
- ■ How effective is your student governance structure?
- ■ Which student organizations or student leaders have access to the administration?
- ■ How do the administration, faculty, and staff consider the student voice?
- ■ How do students communicate their interests and needs to the administration?
- ■ What institutional policies and resources are available that empower students in the campus decision-making process?

After you have a foundational understanding of your campus, you will be able to better understand your leadership and service observations. Many faculty, staff, and students engage in leadership and service every day. The campus community engages in classroom teaching and leadership, service through campus committees, teamwork and collaboration with colleagues and peers, administrative responses to issues facing the campus community, role modeling of appropriate behavior, and good stewardship of money.

As you interact with your campus community you should critically examine and process all that is going on around you. As you observe people in the campus environment, ask yourself questions that will help you better understand what leadership skills, techniques, and attitudes you would like to replicate.

- ■ Who is authentic in their interactions with others?
- ■ Who excites you when you hear him or her speak?
- ■ Who considers others?
- ■ Who leads with integrity?
- ■ Who is consistent in decision making and policy development?

When considering leadership roles on your college campus, remember that leaders may be defined as positional or nonpositional, depending on the situation. Positional leaders are given authority on a college campus. These leaders are able to control and command different aspects of the higher education system. Exam-

Leadership Challenge

Identify one positional leader and one nonpositional leader on your campus. Compare and contrast their impact on the campus community. From your perspective, who has more power and influence? Do you know someone on campus who is a nonpositional leader who has more power and influence than someone who is a positional leader?

ples of positional leaders you will find on your campus are the governing board/board of trustees, college president, provost, vice president for student affairs, chair of the faculty senate, president of the student government association, and college deans. Positional leaders often have power and authority derived from their formal roles. Successful positional leaders balance their power and authority with ethical actions and inclusive behaviors.

Nonpositional leaders are people at all levels of an organization who lead but lack authority or power derived from a formal position. They can also be individuals who do not aspire to positions of leadership. Nonpositional leaders often act as facilitators to help groups reach a common goal.

■ RESPONSIBILITIES OF LEADERS IN ACTION

As a student interested in leadership, you have many responsibilities. As you represent yourself, consider if your words and actions align with your goals, values, and beliefs. As an organization leader, consider how your organization communicates its goals and priorities. Do members' actions and words align with organization values? In addition to asking these questions, elevate your intellect by surrounding yourself with people who have ideas that are different from yours and people who will intellectually engage and challenge your beliefs and values. Also, reading is a great way to expose yourself to different concepts and ideas. Make sure that you comprehend the material and know the source of what you are reading. Read not only what aligns with your beliefs but also that which conflicts. Challenge narrow-minded thinking and encourage yourself and others to examine situations and people from a broad, nonjudgmental basis.

When exploring and experiencing your college environment, it is important to remember that the current philosophies, styles, and theories of leadership are a critical component of your growth as an emerging leader, in conjunction with discovering your personal strengths and weaknesses. All leaders are a reflection of their previous experiences, leadership mentors, beliefs, values, and other important elements of self. Identifying what is most important to you will create a support network and will help you create change-powered leadership.

The next section of the chapter explores the responsibilities you have as a leader. These responsibilities include personal responsibility, responsibility to others, and the responsibility to give back to society. These responsibilities all combine to formulate **civic-based leadership,** which is using your skills, knowledge, and passion for leadership and service. The examination of this topic will continue throughout the chapter.

You have probably heard the phrase "With leadership comes much responsibility." This responsibility can be explored in many ways, and through the next section, you will examine ways successful leaders interact with their followers and will consider the situations in which they find themselves.

Spirituality and Understanding Yourself

Gaining an understanding of who you are and reflecting your core values and beliefs within your everyday actions are key to strong leadership. This idea of consciousness of self and congruence was also introduced in the social change model of leadership (Higher Education Research Institute, 1996). Hagberg (1994) charges leaders to participate in a soul leadership process by discovering passion, practicing vulnerability, experiencing solitude regularly, letting go of control, facing fear, and participating in the spiritual journey of continual change and deepening of self-understanding that takes you to your core. Embracing and sharing this self-awareness only makes the connections among leader, follower, and situation stronger. As these connections increase and the leader is honest with self and others about what drives him or her, leadership becomes more dynamic.

Critical Thinking

Leaders have a responsibility to critically evaluate their environments, their strengths and weaknesses, and all the situations they encounter. Leaders don't simply accept the status quo, or "the way it has always been"; rather, leaders challenge the process and think outside the box. When thinking about how actions can impact others, leaders think about the short- and long-term outcomes. They also consider the effects decisions may have on all stakeholders, not just the people close at hand. Critical thinking demands knowledge of the strengths and weaknesses you have, and it requires you to step outside of your own experiences to see what the experiences of others may look like.

Global Awareness

It is clear that the world is becoming smaller and smaller. That is, people from all parts of the world are interacting with one another more frequently than in the past. A responsible leader is one who embraces the differences that exist among people. Leaders must be aware of their own cultural selves as well as the cultural identities of all possible followers. What is a multicultural or global leader? A multicultural leader plays the same role in leadership that any good leader should. As a leader who is interacting with followers and/or a situation or environment that is different from your own, it is your responsibility to adapt your leadership style to incorporate your followers and environment. It is true that leadership is viewed differently across the world, so what works in one culture may not work in another culture or area of the world. Your commitment to understanding others will lead you to success.

Your Influence as a Leader

As a leader, you live in a fish bowl! This silly metaphor is a great way to picture your level of influence on the people around you. As a leader, you constantly have eyes on you, even if you are not formally in a position or a setting that defines you as a leader. People around you will notice your every move, both good and bad. You must constantly be aware of how congruent your behaviors and actions are with your values and beliefs. You are influencing your followers and your situation even when you do not know it. You have power and responsibility with this influence. Consider this influence as you examine your role as a leader and as you study leadership.

Professionalism and Presentation of Self

A professional is someone who engages in an activity with knowledge of the area and within ethical standards. Being a professional and leader requires you to think about your responsibilities to yourself and others with whom you interact. Think about the many environments and people you have seen act professionally and unprofessionally.

Additionally, how you present yourself, both in words and appearance, can have a large bearing on how you are perceived. As a leader, you need to be concerned with being approachable and well informed. Using correct grammar and paying attention to details in written and spoken presentations will send a message of professionalism to those around you. In addition to what you say, how you dress sends a message of professionalism. As a leader, you need to understand the expectations of your situation and followers, then meet those needs with your attire. Wearing a business suit to a student organization meeting may not be necessary, but wearing flannel pajama pants to the same meeting may also be inappropriate. Know your environment and respect it, so that the people within it will give you the respect you deserve.

Technology

Proper use of technology is a responsibility of all, but particularly of leaders. As a leader, you must stay abreast of new technology that will positively or negatively impact your followers or environment. Additionally, the use and misuse of technology should be at the forefront of your mind. For example, burning copies of copyrighted materials may be helpful for your organization and a great new discovery in technology, but it is clearly unprofessional, unethical, and illegal.

As a leader, it is important to think about the implications that the accessibility of information via technology will have on your followers. Much more information is available through technology and it can be obtained much more quickly, so educating yourself and others about safety and ethics regarding the information that is so readily accessible is key.

Leadership Challenge

Visit an on-line community of someone you consider to be a leader. Write down a few things you learned about this person. What was negative? Positive?

Whether it is Facebook, MySpace, or some other on-line community, as a leader, you must take responsibility for the image you portray both in person and through cyberspace. Pictures, comments, hobbies, events you attend, people you connect yourself with, and much more are all a reflection on your professionalism or lack thereof.

Make sure you do not misrepresent yourself, and consider that these sites are public domains where people can view information and form opinions about you without even knowing you.

Leaders Balance Responsibilities

As a leader, you will be charged with balancing the role of being practical, visionary, and strategic. How you balance competing tasks from day to day with providing a strategic plan to being visionary is a delicate balance that leaders face daily. All three responsibilities are important. If you don't have a vision of where you are going, your followers will have a difficult time following you and sharing a purpose. If you don't have a blueprint that outlines the long-term goals and details of how adopting specific strategies and approaches will help you reach these goals, your vision will not be realized. And if you do not pay attention to the day-to-day needs of your organization and followers, including meeting agendas, payroll, and recognition, you will not be as successful in meeting your goals to reach your vision. Thus, how do you prioritize these responsibilities on a daily basis? It depends on the situation. If you constantly put off the big picture vision and strategic plan while focusing only on the practical needs, you'll never reach your potential. If you focus only on your vision, without setting goals, the vision will be too far away and out of reach. You must plan time to balance the needs of all three and include your followers in all areas of planning. Their investment in all aspects of the process only makes the process stronger.

There is no simple formula for effective leadership. Leadership is a dynamic and complex process by which you need to explore your own strengths, values, and beliefs and watch how they interact with the people and environments around you. Leaders constantly need to be aware of the world around them and learn to use their leadership experiences and studies of leadership to make the best decisions in given situations. Leaders must recognize that leadership is not about the leader, but about the impact a leader can have on others and society. Humility and focus on what changes can be made, as opposed to one's specific role in making those changes, make for a lasting imprint on society.

■ SERVICE AND CIVIC-BASED LEADERSHIP

A responsibility all leaders share is to give back to their communities. What is service? And how does it relate to leadership? **Service** is defined as work done by an individual or a group that benefits others. We are going to take service to the next level and challenge you to think about civic engagement when you think about leadership. "**Civic engagement** means working to make a difference in the civic life of our communities and developing the combination of knowledge, skills, values and motivation to make that difference. It means promoting the quality of life in a community, through both political and non-political processes" (Ehrlich, 2000, preface, p. vi). When leaders commit to giving back to society, civic engagement goes a step beyond service and opens the doors into many additional learning and growth opportunities for all involved.

Simply participating in service projects does not open up the possibilities to explore how service relates to leadership and how a leader can use skills, values, and knowledge to serve as a change agent in society. As you participate in service and

Volunteering your time, as an active learner, to help build a home for a family in need is one way to serve as a change agent.

Photo courtesy of Dave and Cindy Baar.

challenge others to join you, it is critical that you frame the service experience for yourself and others. This process is often referred to as service-learning. The Campus Compact National Center for Community Colleges defines service-learning as

> A teaching method which combines community service with academic instruction as it focuses on critical, reflective thinking and civic responsibility. Service-learning programs involve students in organized community service that addresses local needs, while developing their academic skills, sense of civic responsibility and commitment to the community. (Kendall and Associates, 1990, p. 10)

As a leader, you have a role in making service to your community meaningful, not only for yourself but also for those around you. Your campus will most likely have many structures set up to connect you with service opportunities, but you can always create experiences for yourself that will fit your personal needs. First, select an area of service that reflects a commitment or passion that you hold. The higher the level of commitment you have for an issue, the more passion you will take and exude to others around you. Additionally, prior to going into the field, research the history of the cause or issue at hand, understand the population served, read about any legislation or community efforts to address the issue, and hold pre-service meetings with others who will attend with you. Share with others the information you have found and encourage a lively discussion about what role your peers can play in addressing the issue during their service and after.

Why should you use service-learning as a leader? Service-learning promotes learning through active participation, provides an opportunity to use skills and knowledge in real-life situations, fosters a sense of caring for others, and improves critical thinking skills (Reiff, 2006). During the service experience, don't just be a participant—be an active learner by observing and questioning things you see. Consider the relationships between your followers, and think about the role you may continue to play in the understanding of this service. After participating in service-related activities, create opportunities for dialogue between participants. This reflection time about their experiences allows them to take the service experience beyond the act and into action that will follow. Encourage your peers to think about ways they can become more involved and serve as change agents in society. Just as important as the service experience itself is that service be authentic. Authentic and successful service-learning is positive, meaningful, and real to the participants. It encourages cooperative rather than competitive experiences, thereby promoting teamwork and citizenship; assists students in identifying the most important issues within a real-world situation through critical thinking; and promotes deeper learning, stressing that there are no "right answers" (Reiff, 2006).

When service-learning or civic engagement and leadership are combined, you have civic-based leadership—the kind of leadership that serves as a change agent in society. Civic-based leadership is the kind of leadership you should be exploring in college and challenging others to explore with you. Engaging in these types of opportunities will strengthen your knowledge, relationships with others, and leadership skills while positively impacting society and others you encourage to join you.

■ SERVICE LEARNING

Donald A. Watt, Contributing Author

Service learning can take many forms. After a trip to Africa, these South Dakota students marketed crafts in partnership with a women's cooperative in Tanzania to raise money for community improvement projects.

Photo courtesy of Diana Goldammer.

The formal structure of a college professor lecturing a group of students has been a standard of education for centuries. In the early twentieth century, however, new educational methodologies were attempted. For example, in several Appalachian schools, cooperative or experiential education was initiated, where employment was an integral aspect of the educational experience. As experiments with new ideas were tried, new programs developed.

One of the most successful experiments was service learning. According to the National Service-Learning Clearinghouse, the term *service learning* was first used during the 1966–1967 academic year in eastern Tennessee.[1] Since that time, it has evolved into a nationwide movement.

Service learning is the process whereby learning outcomes are designed into outreach programs of service. Thus, it differs from traditional service projects in that it has a dual purpose. The service performed is also designed as an opportunity for student growth and learning. Due to the nature of the program, students participate in various stages of planning, although often the service is pre-selected by the instructor or advisor. Participation in the planning process and reflection is integral to leadership development among the students.

Mandatory aspects of service learning include the following. (1) The project must address a real need within the community. (2) Planning must include a student analysis of the problem, including steps that might be taken to change the situation or alleviate the problem. (3) Students must work through any special aspects as to how interaction should take place. The best service learning takes place through a partnership developed between the students and those served. (4) If the service project occurs within a curricular setting, skills being developed should relate to the learning outcomes of the class. For co-curricular groups, the skills should relate to the mission of the organization. (5) After completion, all aspects of the project should be assessed. Planning, the activity, the impact on those served, and the impact on those doing the service should all be examined. Reflection by each participant on what has been learned is a key component of the assessment activity.

True service learning should be structured so that the students use critical thinking, ideas, and skills learned from the class or the organization and communication skills, in addition to planning and assessment techniques. When done properly, service learning results in positive learning experiences and a stronger sense of community. Leadership skills are at the heart of service learning. Examining the situation, planning tasks to affect the situation, adapting when initial plans do not seem to be working, communicating with others, and assessing outcomes are all important aspects of successful leadership. Thus, service learning can be an important component of leadership education.

1. See http://www.servicelearning.org/what_is_service-learning/history/index.php.

▨ CONCLUSION

This chapter is meant to be a foundation for your exploration of leadership and service in the college environment—don't stop here! The examination of leadership and service should be a life-long learning process. As you continue to reevaluate your leadership philosophy, expose yourself to diverse individuals and ideas, question your current systems of thinking, and challenge yourself to move beyond the status quo. Get involved with something that supports your passion, take your role to the next level, and be an agent of change for the betterment of society. With your knowledge about leadership and service, you now have power! Use your power to influence positive change on your campus or another community of which you are a member. Create support networks that will propel you and your vision to success and that will make a difference in the lives of others.

▨ KEY TERMS

Civic-Based Leadership—The combination of leadership and civic engagement with a commitment to serve as a change agent in society.

Civic Engagement—Working to make a difference in the civic life of the community and developing the combination of knowledge, skills, values, and motivation to make a difference.

Ethical Leadership—Leadership guided by a system of moral values and principles that guides behavior.

Ethics—A system of moral values and principles that guide behavior.

Followers—Individuals who come together to support the vision of a leader(s) and use their personal strengths, knowledge, and skills to assist in reaching a common goal.

Leader—Someone who is able to lead others, known as followers, to effect change.

Leadership—The process by which a leader facilitates change. It is the function of three elements: leaders, followers, and the situation. Leadership occurs when all three of these elements interact and work together, while respecting the role each piece plays in the process.

Service—Work done by a group or an individual that benefits others.

Situation—The environment in which a task is undertaken, in combination with knowledge and human interaction.

■ SUGGESTED READINGS

Arbinger Institute, Inc. 2002. *Leadership and Self-Deception: Getting Out of the Box*. San Francisco: Berrett-Koehler.

Collins, J. 2001. *Good to Great: Why Some Companies Make the Leap and Others Don't*. New York: HarperCollins.

George, B. & Sims, P. 2007. *True North: Discover Your Authentic Leadership*. San Francisco: Jossey-Bass.

■ REFERENCES

Astin, A. W. 1993. *What Matters in College: Four Critical Years Revisited*. San Francisco: Jossey-Bass.

Avolio, B. J. & Gardner, W. L. 2005. "Authentic leadership development: Getting to the root of positive forms of leadership." *Leadership Quarterly, 16(3),* 315–338.

Avolio, B. J. & Luthans, F. 2005. *The High Impact Leader: Moments Matter in Accelerating Authentic Leadership Development*. New York: McGraw-Hill.

Baker, J. H. 2001. "Is Servant Leadership Part of Your Worldview?" *weLEAD Online Magazine*. Retrieved from http://www.leadingtoday.org/Onmag/jan01/hb-jan01.html.

Bass, B. M. 1990. *Bass and Stogdill's Handbook of Leadership: Theory, Research and Management Applications* (3rd ed.). New York: Free Press.

Burns, J. M. 1978. *Leadership*. New York: Harper & Row.

Daloz Parks, S. 2005. *Leadership Can Be Taught*. Boston: Harvard Business School.

Dictionary.com Unabridged (v 1.1). Retrieved September 30, 2007, from http://dictionary.reference.com/browse/leadership.

Ehrlich, T. 2000. *Civic Responsibility and Higher Education*. Westport, CT: The American Council on Education and The Oryx Press.

George, B. 2003. *Authentic Leadership: Rediscovering the Secrets to Creating Lasting Value*. San Francisco: Jossey-Bass.

George, B. & Sims, P. 2007. *True North: Discover Your Authentic Leadership*. San Francisco: Jossey-Bass.

Greenleaf, R. K. 1977. *Servant Leadership: A Journey into the Nature of Legitimate Power and Greatness*. Mahwah, NJ: Paulist Press.

Greenleaf, R. K. 1995. "Servant Leadership." In J. T. Wren (Ed.), *The Leader's Companion: Insights on Leadership Through the Ages* (pp. 18–23). New York: Free Press.

Hagberg, J. 1994. *Real Power*. Salem, WI: Sheffield.

Heifetz, R. A. 1994. *Leadership Without Easy Answers*. Cambridge, MA: The Belknap Press of Harvard University Press.

Hersey, P. 1984. *The Situational Leader*. Escondido, CA: Center for Leadership Studies.

Hersey, P. & Blanchard, K. H. 1995. "Situational Leadership." In J. T. Wren (Ed.), *The Leader's Companion: Insights on Leadership Through the Ages* (pp. 207–221). New York: Free Press.

Hesselbein, F. 1999. "Introduction." In F. Hesselbein & P. M. Cohen (Eds.), *Leader to Leader* (p. xii). San Francisco: Jossey-Bass.

Higher Education Research Institute. 1996. *A Social Change Model of Leadership Development.* Los Angeles: University of California, Los Angeles.

Hughes R. L., Ginnett R. C., & Curphy G. J., 2006. *Leadership: Enhancing the Lessons of Experience.* New York: McGraw-Hill.

Kendall, J. C. and Associates. 1990. *Combining Service and Learning: A Resource Book for Community and Public Service, Volume 1.* Raleigh, NC: National Society for Experiential Education.

Kouzes, J. & Posner, B. 1995. *The Leadership Challenge.* San Francisco: Jossey-Bass.

Lewin, K., Lippit, R., & White, R. K. 1939. "Patterns of Aggressive Behavior in Experimentally Created Social Climates." *Journal of Social Psychology, 10,* 271–301.

Prince, Howard T. II. 2007. "Ethical Leadership." Retrieved August 24, 2007, from http://www.utexas.edu/lbj/research/leadership/slc2007/.

Reiff, J. Feb. 15, 2006. *Leadership Development Through Service Learning.* NSLC associates. Web Seminar.

Service-Learning Faculty Manual. 2002. Colorado State University Service Integration Project Office for Service-Learning and Volunteer Programs: Fort Collins, CO.

CHAPTER ONE REVIEW QUESTIONS

1. Leadership is presented in this chapter as an interaction between individuals at many levels. Cite three examples of leadership that you have observed on your campus. Identify the interaction between individuals for each example cited.

_____

_____

_____

2. Why is it important to include ethics when discussing leadership?

_____

_____

_____

3. What is unique about a college or university campus that makes it the perfect environment to examine, practice, and critically think about leadership and service?

_____

_____

_____

4. Discuss two leadership theories or styles and which aspects most connect with your current philosophy of leadership. Additionally, explain why it is important that leaders have an understanding of self and their personal philosophy.

_____

_____

_____

5. What are the personal and societal benefits of participation in service? What impact does service have on leadership?

_____

_____

_____

CHAPTER ONE SELF-TEST

1. _____ behavior has an impact on all levels of leadership, creating distrust and a lack of productivity.

2. _____ is the process by which a leader facilitates change.

3. _____ are individuals who come together to support the vision of a leader.

4. _____, _____, and _____ are three types of student organizations on a typical college campus.

5. Transformational leadership theory was made popular by political sociologist James McGregor _____.

6. _____ leaders make decisions without consulting followers.

7. The democratic leader is also referred to as the _____ leader.

8. A _____ leader steps back to "let it be," allowing people to make their own decisions.

9. _____ demands knowledge of the strengths and weaknesses you have.

10. A _____ is someone who engages in an activity with knowledge of the area and within ethical standards.

Leadership as a Reflection of Self

No leader sets out to be a leader. People set out to live their lives, expressing themselves fully. So the point is not to become a leader. The point is to become yourself, to use yourself completely—all of your skills, gifts, and energies—in order to make your vision manifest. You must withhold nothing. You must, in sum, become the person you started out to be, and enjoy the process of becoming.—*Warren Bennis* (1989, p. 104)

Abrina
Schnurman-
Crook

Katherine
Walker

■ THE IMPORTANT WORK THAT IS LEADERSHIP

When they engage in rigorous leadership programs, students quickly realize leadership is hard, constant work wrapped in the mess of change, struggle, and uncertainty. Some students decide they don't want to actively pursue the role of leader and their departure is certainly no surprise, given the challenge that leadership presents. Perhaps it is more surprising that so many stay. Why do they work so hard on their process of becoming a leader? Why will you? The argument can easily be made that leadership is important for all of us to understand. We do, after all, live in a democracy and elect our leaders, and the more we understand leadership as democratic citizens the better leaders and society we will have. Perhaps you and other students developing their leadership potential appreciate the importance of our role as citizen followers—that as citizens, we all need to make wise choices in selecting our leaders. Others may have the sense that they may unexpectedly be called to leadership. What if someday they have a child with an illness or a disability requiring they advocate on the child's behalf, only to realize the system they are navigating is broken? Or they recognize a glaring need in the local community that others have not addressed. Maybe they will find parts of federal government broken and decide to change it. Or they become deeply concerned about our planet's health and future and become determined to save it. Let's hope, if that call comes, they have not stopped their process of becoming. Will you be ready if you are called? This work of leadership is important, and it affects all of us.

For work that is so important, it's remarkable how little we know about it. Just as we are always in the process of becoming, the art and practice of leadership will also always be in the process of becoming. Can a leader today engage in the same practices as those a century ago and still be effective? The answer is not a simple one; in some ways yes, and in other ways no. A more authoritative, command and control style was generally considered the most effective form of leadership in the last century. While still very much in practice and arguably useful in a few specific situations, it is not reflective of the current trend in theory or practice. It may appear that the rules and practices of leadership are in constant flux, changing with the tide and the times. Cutting-edge leadership styles and practices must evolve to accommodate the ever-changing environment of merging generations and cultures. One thing is certain. Along the road to success, any given leader's efforts to get it just right will surely fail over and over again.

With all of this change afoot, as you practice leadership, you must know who you are while recognizing you can't stay exactly as you are. You also can't be everything to everyone at all times. This is a particularly hazardous view of novice leaders, who attempt to bolster their organization by appearing to have all the answers. The authors of the article "In Praise of the Incomplete Leader" (Ancona, Malone, Orlikowski, & Senge, 2007) render the sage advice that it is wise to identify one, perhaps two, areas of strength on which you can build and focus on becoming a true expert in these areas. Then it is important to actively surround yourself with others whose strengths are different from yours in ways that can really complement each other. Leadership requires more than you are or will ever be.

Still, who you are is very important in the practice of leadership. Who you are influences how you lead. We can't separate you from your leadership, nor would we want to. We also can't separate others from your leadership. Otherwise, you would be working alone and affecting no one. You would not be leading. In this chapter, we offer a framework to help organize the complex work of your leadership development. We approach leadership development through intrapersonal growth (values, resilience, strengths, weaknesses, persistence, self-discipline), interpersonal skill development (listening, conflict management, motivation, influence, general interpersonal), experiential work (practice, projects, videotaped simulations), intellectual development (critical thinking, integrative thinking, problem solving, creativity), and adaptive work (vision, change, process). As you read, we hope that you will select at least several of the skills described to further develop your leadership and focus your process of becoming.

■ INTRAPERSONAL GROWTH

Intrapersonal growth is improvement that is the result of heightened self-awareness, personal reflection, and self-discipline. In 2006, *Harvard Business Review* displayed a cover page announcing *Leadership's 1st Commandment: Leader Know Thyself*. This cover highlights the fact that not only is who you are at the core of your leadership but also understanding yourself is a foundation of your practice. Leaders must possess and apply enough self-awareness to understand themselves and their values to stay focused and persist through difficult times. This self-awareness includes knowledge of emotions, values, and beliefs, along with an accurate assessment of strengths and weaknesses (Gardner & Schermerhorn, 2004) and is essential for intrapersonal growth.

"I am so glad that I am not as judgmental
as those self-righteous, pig-headed
do-gooders I have to work with."

www.CartoonStock.com

Values

Values are the why of what we do. They are a culmination of the experiences that we have accumulated through multiple contexts of interactions with families of origin, our peer group, our educational system, our government, religion, and the media. Values are often guided by powerful constructs, such as societal norms and taboos, shifts in popular cultural trends, and high-impact events, such as natural disasters, wars, and all manner of violence enacted by humans. And they reside in the core of our being. Whether we house our values in our conscious or unconscious, they drive our actions and ultimately steer the direction of our leadership development as individuals. Because of their power and importance, it is essential

---

Leadership Challenge

What is important to you? What do you value? What inspires you? How can you best communicate your values to others? What do people around you value? Are their values in conflict or compatible with yours?

---

to know and understand your values, to move them from the basement of your unconscious to the lighter, more open space of your conscious mind—where you can access and understand them. Kouzes and Posner (2002) help us with this shift by explaining that it is our actions and how we allocate our time that most accurately demonstrates to the world the things that are most important to us. As leaders, it is important to monitor what we do with our time in relation to our goals, both short-term and long-term (Kouzes & Posner, 2002) and make sure that these actions are aligned with our values.

In this quest for understanding, however, it is also important to note that values are not static. They evolve as we develop. We must continuously redefine and reevaluate our beliefs and, in particular, our ethical and moral views. Self-evaluation, thus, must be the cornerstone of a realistic and grounded approach to the development of a personal leadership style. Before leaders can be truly effective, they must get in touch with their values. Once that practice has begun, they can then begin the work of communicating their values and connecting them to a vision for the organization, project, team, and so on. The most effective leaders also understand that the biggest leaps in a team happen because the leader is in touch with what constituents/team members value as well. It is impossible to motivate or inspire others without tapping into and connecting with the values of the team.

Resilience

Resilience is the ability to withstand or recover from challenges. Within the context of leadership, resilience allows the leader to negotiate the storms and battles that will inevitably ensue in the course of creating and navigating change. Resilience can be likened to flexibility. When designing the towering superstructures that become our modern-day skyscrapers, architects carefully plan the amount of sway that a building must accommodate, so that it is not destroyed by a strong wind. It must be supple enough to bend and shift in accordance with the forces of the winds that strike it. Rigid leaders, like rigid structures, collapse completely when faced with the winds of change. Resilience allows us to dance with the forces of nature and not to be overwhelmed by them.

It's easy to describe resilience and understand its importance, but as developing leaders, we also need to know how to cultivate that quality. Resilience is derived from an individual's interconnectedness to multiple support networks, as well as a globally optimistic perception that disciplined action and effort on the part of individuals and teams can render positive results. It's the idea that you can (and will) fail and things can still work out well. In order to develop resilience, it is important to encourage your optimism.

A leader also nurtures a core sense of well-being through interpersonal relationships supported by a self-esteem based on accomplishment and connectedness with others. Resilience is to be shared by all members of the team. It is not the exclusive domain of the leader. The building of a resilient team, family, organization, system, and so on requires a consistent positive flow of authentic feedback and praise to build efficacy. In the same way that the human immune system requires vitamins, minerals, and nutrients to defend against sources of disease and infection, so, too, must individuals within the workplace be nourished with information that allows them to see themselves as important contributors to the whole effort. "Resilience involves the willingness to accept or reach out for support from others as a coping mechanism" (Gardner & Schermerhorn, 2004, p. 278). Connect with others. Plug in. Get involved and grow roots, so that when the storms come they can't keep you down for long.

Strengths and Weaknesses

The most effective leaders carefully assess both their strengths and their limitations. No one is exceptional at everything. It is the leader's job to surround him- or herself with people whose strengths compliment his or her own in a way that allows for diversity in thoughts and ideas. This is vital to create a comprehensive and competent team (Ancona, Malone, Orlikowski, & Senge, 2007). Hone your strengths. There aren't enough days in a week or years in a lifetime for you to master everything with equal proficiency, so carefully choose where to place your time and energy. Go back to your values to help you discern what is most important. You may be competent in a variety of areas but exhibit strengths in one or two key areas. While we encourage your improving some weaknesses toward competency, it is equally if not more important to refine and improve your skills within those key areas of strength in a way that can really contribute to propelling forward a vision and a team.

One example to illustrate the notion of finding others who complement your strengths is to be found in the authors of this chapter. Abrina's drive for excellence, attention to detail, and operations leadership are the foundation of our organization. She has developed an important area of expertise in the area of conflict and negotiation and has a great willingness to challenge people in order to help them reach the next level. This balances Katherine's sometimes overly supportive style. Katherine's conceptual ability is strong and in the course of a morning she can generate multiple ideas. She is passionate about leadership development and inspirational when she talks about the possibilities of a program, making her a terrific lecturer as well. Both possess talents and skills that balance and support each other. While one functions as the creative spark that fuels forward momentum, the other steers the vehicle through more detailed operations. It is this tandem set of strengths in coordination and the ability to recognize the value of the different strengths that each contributes that help make the collaborative effort successful.

Leadership Challenge

What are key areas of strength for you? What are some weaknesses? What can you do to further develop your strengths?

Persistence

We started writing this section but got tired and gave up.

In all seriousness, disciplined persistence is what it takes to succeed as a leader. Ongoing training and education can hone and refine one's leadership skills and it is a life-long process (Witzel, 2005). In "What It Takes to Be Great" (Colvin, 2006), we learn that, on average, ten years of hard work is what it takes to be a master or an expert in an area. "Years?" you say. About now, you are probably thinking that a decade seems like a lifetime. Why so long? It takes time and diligent practice with clear and specific feedback to be competent enough in an area that some decisions can be intuitive, leaving room for higher-order decision making and thought processes once that experience has been earned. The number ten, however, isn't magic and doesn't imply that once you have been at it for a decade you can tell the world you are the foremost expert on the subject. There is always a higher and better goal. If you are doing it right, you never really feel as if you have arrived. In that respect, the destination remains just out of reach.

Fortunately, it isn't just the destination with which you need be concerned. According to business guru Bill George, who has a reputation for transforming failing enterprises into multibillion-dollar organizations, it is the journey to becoming an authentic leader where you find your true self and the purpose of your life's work (George, 2003). George's experience provides evidence of how prioritizing the practice of authenticity and connecting work with meaning and purpose translate into real returns. Persistence requires constant commitment to the process, despite the unpredictability of your environment and obstacles that seem to defy resolution.

There are countless stories of leaders who defied the odds and overcame major obstacles. They also had to overcome failures. Abraham Lincoln lost almost every time he ran for public office, except, of course, his bid for president of the United States. Both Walt Disney and Theodore Geisel (Dr. Seuss) went through years of rejection before they were famous. In our attempts to land human beings on the moon, many failures occurred before success was achieved. Some failures tragically cost the lives of brave astronauts. As we worked through the complexities inherent in the development of space travel, the loss of the space shuttle *Challenger* is a reminder that diligent persistence brings us nearer to our goal but setbacks, even ones with grave consequences, must not be impediments that block our vision and determination but opportunities to learn from mistakes along our path to success.

Leadership Challenge

How self-disciplined are you? What impact does your self-discipline (or lack thereof) have on your daily life? How would making more decisions that prioritize the long-term consequences over the short-term benefit improve your life?

Self-Discipline

The concept of self-discipline can be best described by the following popular business example. What kind of organization would you have if everyone approached their work just as you do? This is an invitation for the slackers to feel guilty and make a mental note to amp up their productivity. We are all important cogs in the organizational wheel. There will be no follow-through on a vision in the absence of self-discipline. Research and life experience show us over and over again that short-term suffering or hard work on the front end usually pays off in the long run and in almost every domain. For college students, this can mean choosing to study longer for that midterm or to edit the first or second draft of a research paper instead of the constant lure of TV or video games.

■ INTERPERSONAL SKILLS

Interpersonal growth is improvement that occurs as a direct result of interaction with others and the positive influence of others. All things being equal, the person who possesses better interpersonal skills and who understands and appropriately adjusts to social cues within a variety of contexts will be deemed the leader in most situations (Cronshaw & Ellis, 1991). Those who focus only on their own perspective without concern for adjusting their behavior based on situational cues do not connect with others in a meaningful way (Cronshaw & Ellis, 1991). Without this vital connection, it is nearly impossible to motivate, influence, or inspire others. And leadership requires others. In short, if you are interested in leadership, you must be interpersonally skilled.

While the environments in which we labor differ greatly, no single trait or capacity is as sought after and required in the modern world as the individual with well-developed interpersonal skills. It doesn't matter whether you are the president of a bank or a lemonade vendor by the side of the road, the tasks before you are equally affected by your ability to interact respectfully and tactfully as you attempt to engage others in your work environment.

If a leader has developed interpersonal skills, he or she realizes how important it is to be the most interesting person in the room. It is also important to be able to connect with others to find out and bring out into the open what makes them interesting. Become the most interested person in the room. Finding a legitimate connection and building on it validates others, and the art of seeking and spotlighting this is a key interpersonal skill for leaders. The emotionally intelligent leader will search until he or she finds a point of connection.

Within the world of leadership theories and research on what makes a leader effective, the most popular approach in recent decades is called transformational leadership (Judge & Bono, 2000). This conceptualization of leadership began in the 1970s as one theorist, James MacGregor Burns (1978), sought to distinguish how some leaders were transforming in their efforts to inspire followers with a vision that transcends anyone's self-interest, while other leaders were transactional in their focus on getting people to cooperate by setting up some kind of exchange system (giving something to get something) and then monitoring those exchanges (Judge & Bono, 2000). Burns thought you had to subscribe to one or the other, but later Bass (1985) arrived on the scene and asserted that transformational and transactional leadership can be integrated. The most basic example of this is receiving a paycheck for work done well and actively contributing more and more to an organization that encourages the practice of transformational leadership. The most effective leader in this scenario ascribes to Bass' (1985) four dimensions of transformational leadership and every one of them demands stellar interpersonal skills. These skills include idealized influence, in which the leader conveys charisma. Charisma isn't everything in leadership, but we must give it its due—it exists and it requires a honed self-awareness and confidence. The second skill, inspirational motivation, requires the leader to convey a vision with passion and clarity such that others can see themselves in that future picture. Intellectual stimulation occurs when the leader encourages followers to question the status quo and generate creative solutions. Because there is no punitive action for mistakes, morale and creativity remain high. Using the final skill, individual consideration, leaders attend to what each individual needs to develop according to his or her goals and ability.

The most effective way to inspire others is to understand what motivates them—in other words, what they value (Kouzes & Posner, 2002). This requires creating and maintaining an authentic connection with them. Developing your interpersonal skills within the following domains is a critical part of your leadership development.

Listening

Of all the skills to be addressed in this chapter, listening is probably the most important skill in the world of leadership. Quick, what did we just say?

A leader may possess passion, vision, self-determination, charisma, intelligence, or even brilliance, but if he or she has these and cannot hear and understand the needs, ideas, and concerns of those around him or her, in essence that leader has very little. Of the greatest military leaders in the history of the world, Napoleon Bonaparte was viewed as a brilliant tactician and commander. For all of his ability to lead his men, however, his stubborn unwillingness to listen to the council of others left him marooned on an island, disenfranchised from the nation he loved so dearly. Similarly, the great polar explorer Sir Ernest Shackleton provides us with one of the great stories of leadership through his brave voyage to Antarctica. When his ship was caught and crushed by the ice in the frigid Antarctic Ocean, Shackleton's quest for glory had to be revised into a two-year trial for survival for his twenty-eight-man crew. Only through Herculean effort, a fair amount of luck, and Shackleton's devotion to his crew did everyone survive the terrible ordeal. His refusal to listen to the whalers who warned that it was the worst iceberg situation in many years, however, put them in great peril. Ego-driven in his efforts to be the first explorer at his destination and refusing to wait for better conditions before embarking on the voyage put others in grave danger and prevented Shackleton and his crew from realizing their vision.

Listening can be the difference between life and death. Firefighters who fail to listen not only risk their own lives but the lives of others.

Photo courtesy of Darrell & Jarid Hartmann.

In contrast, the Internet giant Google shows us how listening very carefully and developing a work culture that appeals to smart, creative, highly skilled employees results in tremendous growth and productivity. On the surface this company's practice may seem excessive and strange, with job perks that include a casual dress code that allows pajamas, on-site massage therapists, yoga instructors, a game room, an on-site chef with free healthy gourmet meals, and on-site child-care centers for working parents. By doing these things Google has developed a workforce with unparalleled devotion to their employer and the highest reported levels of job satisfaction in the country. The leadership at Google listened carefully and took into consideration the suggestions made by its employees to improve morale in the workplace. The payoff is obvious. Listening is one skill that a leader can always call upon that will consistently have impact.

In *The Experience Economy,* B. Joseph Pine II asserts that "the experience of being understood, versus being interpreted, is so compelling, you can charge admission" (Pine & Gilmore, 1999). How can it be that most of us believe we listen perfectly well and understand what others are saying, yet there are multiple pages in the phonebook of counselors who are kept in business largely due to miscommunications and related misperceptions? For one, most of us actually don't listen particularly well. In an effort to save you any unnecessary trips to the counselor's office, we'd like to give a nod to the importance of active listening for understanding without interpretation.

Because you are clearly in good company, we hope you will open yourself up to the idea that you may not be listening well. Admit to silently constructing what you will say next while another person is speaking or, worse, recognize going completely off topic and mentally adding items to your grocery list, ticking off errands, or thinking of that giant research paper you still need to start as a major listening violation. Within the first couple of minutes of meeting people, we decide we have a basic handle on them. If our attention is not immediately captivated, we stop listening and sometimes feign attentiveness while they rattle on (Scott, 2004). Such a dismissal translates into a missed opportunity and can lead to cynicism and disaffection. Susan Scott, author of *Fierce Conversations* (2004), asserts that the antidote is to endeavor to connect fully with each person in our lives by really asking and really listening, even if only briefly, and refusing to be distracted.

The Journal of the American Medical Association (Hickson, Clayton, Entman, Miller, Githens, Whetten-Goldstein, & Sloan, 1994) highlights the importance of listening through a study of whether malpractice suits were filed against physicians involved in the same tragedy, the death of a child during childbirth. The authors found that the decision to sue the doctor overwhelmingly hinged on the extent to which the bereaved parents felt their doctor had deeply listened to them.

Given the established power and importance of listening, let's examine some ways you can become a better listener. A great place to start is through active listening. **Active listening** is nonverbal body language, including eye contact and facial expressions that indicate a person is listening. When using active listening skills you can begin by being aware of your nonverbal communication. Remember, whether or not you are speaking, you are always communicating. Using great eye contact (unless speaking with someone from a culture in which averting eyes is a show of respect), leaning forward slightly, using facial expressions that indicate interest, nodding appropriately, and taking a more open stance help indicate that you are listening.

In addition to nonverbal skills, there are some verbal forms of communication for you to consider:

1. *Ask open-ended questions (e.g., what or how).* Closed questions seek monosyllabic answers (yes/no). Open-ended questions, particularly those that begin with *what* or *how,* invite dialogue.

2. *Paraphrase.* Capturing the essence of what the person just said in a sentence or two demonstrates that you are listening carefully

3. *Clarify Meanings.* Stating what you think is the meaning of the other person's comments provides an opportunity to correct misunderstandings—for example, "I hear you saying that you are frustrated with XYZ; is that right?" or "What did you mean when you said . . . ?"

4. *Encourage Elaboration.* Asking for more information will give you more detail and shows interest. "What happened next?" or "How did that affect you?" or "Tell me more—for example, about that."

5. *Express empathy.* Sincerely validating and acknowledging the speaker's experience and understanding it from his or her point of view can be a transformative experience for both in a conversation. (You can express empathy without agreement or endorsement of support. You can help someone feel validated even if you disagree with his or her words or behavior.)

While practicing active listening, avoid making judgments, making evaluations, or giving advice. It is true that most of us want to be helpful *and* show what we know. But this is not about imparting your great wisdom. People have a remarkable knack for asking for advice when they want it. Take care not to shift the direction from the speaker to you and your experience with a similar issue or situation.

A real and present conversation requires bravery. When you listen deeply for understanding, you risk challenging your perceptions, beliefs, and interpretations as well as hearing things you have been pretending not to know. When, not if, you forget to reflect and clarify and instead jump to interpret a message without investigating, you will likely misinterpret someone's intentions and have an opportunity to engage your skills in conflict management.

Leadership Challenge

How well are you listening to those around you? What person in your life is the most in need of your listening? What might happen if you took a few minutes every day to listen more carefully to others?

Written, Nonverbal, and Oral Communication

While listening is the most important skill in this section, it is still important to develop other strong communication skills and present yourself and your ideas to others in a way that accurately reflects who you are and tells what you have to say in a manner they can hear. Through nonverbal skills, or body language, you communicate more than half of your intent to the listener. If you have your arms crossed in front of you it could really mean that you are cold, but if you pair it with a bored look or scowl and interrupt the speaker often, then you are conveying annoyance or defensiveness and are unlikely to be well received. With the combined scowl and closed body posture, you can create a divide even if you state a benign, beautifully crafted message. Your nonverbal communication should be congruent with your verbal message. Because we are often unaware of our body language and how it affects others, check yourself often. If your goal is to really connect with the person opposite you in the conversation, go back to the basics listed in the section on listening. Observing carefully can also help your communication. Consider the fascinating work of Paul Ekman and Erik Rosenberg (1997) on the meaning of our facial expressions.

Ekman has worked for the last several decades on subtle and microexpression recognition. Reading microexpressions is a particularly powerful skill because microexpressions cannot be suppressed. As soon as you can think to try to hide any emotion on your face, it has already occurred (Ekman & Rosenberg, 1997). John Gottman, a renowned researcher on marital satisfaction, applied Ekman's research to his own work to study marriage. Using these tools, Gottman studied couples discussing a point of relational contention. Even if he observed for less than fifteen minutes, he could predict with approximately 94 percent accuracy whether a couple would be divorced in the next ten years. Contemptuous expressions, among other things, were present in the couples whose relationships later dissolved (Gottman, 1994). Clearly reading certain micro, or subtle, facial expressions indicative of emotions that are universal to all cultures can be a powerful tool for understanding and prediction. While most of us won't choose to study microexpressions as carefully as Ekman or Gottman, we can certainly hone our observational skills to learn as much as we can about how to communicate effectively with any given person.

Written communication is also very important. A few tips for enhancing written communication skills include pay attention to details, such as organizing your thoughts with an outline or a quick list of main points before you write; write for the audience you have and clearly explain terms that some may not understand; be concise and get to the point right away; and reread all of your emails before you send them—you never know who will read them later. If you have a presentation, it pays to prepare and practice and work to make a personal connection with the participants via content, eye contact, and enthusiasm for the topic (Hughes, 2003).

Leadership Challenge

What are your strongest communication skills? What skills need development? In what settings are you most comfortable communicating? Least comfortable? Of the people you know, who is a particularly good communicator? What can you learn from him or her that will advance your own skills?

Feedback

Feedback is the evaluation and assessment of performance by others as part of the learning process and an ongoing effort to improve. The ability to give and receive timely feedback is a vital skill for leaders. In our fast-paced culture driven by instant gratification and quests for immediate results, people need information about how they are doing. Most want to do at least reasonably well in their jobs or assigned tasks. Providing accurate, specific, and descriptive feedback about the impact of their actions and behavior on you, the team, and the quality of the overall task is critical to building up strengths and shoring up weaknesses in leaders and followers alike (Buron & McDonald-Mann, 1999). In the most effective leadership programs, students spend time learning to give and receive feedback in a direct and diplomatic manner. It feels awkward because giving constructive feedback is not a typical social form of communication. Most conversations stay on the surface.

As with any new behavior, learning to give feedback effectively takes time and practice. Initially, it is helpful to examine early messages about feedback and how internal tapes dictate default communication. For example, invalidating early messages—such as "If you can't say anything nice," "Don't be angry," or "What will other people think?"—create lasting impact within an individual who suppresses thoughts and ideas for feedback that could prove to be valuable to another person (Hathaway, 2006). These individuals might be so focused on getting everything perfect and keeping up appearances by looking happy and saying niceties all day long that very little substantive work can take place. Additionally, learning to communicate in an environment where feelings are denied and constructive feedback is withheld does not allow for the practice of communicating in the real world of improvement and change. When such a person finally gets feedback that is substantive, he or she is likely to feel off-balance until the information can be assimilated. As we will repeat often in this chapter, no one is great at everything. When we are good at something, praise is the best tool for continued motivation. When we need to learn to do better, appropriate feedback is the tool that will allow us to grow and develop in necessary directions. Don't be afraid to ask for feedback from your peers, your professors, and others. Each group will likely see you in a different context, so more feedback will allow you to piece together the puzzle of how you are being perceived.

Conflict Management

Ask the head of any organization to identify some of the biggest challenges he or she faces as a leader and he or she will invariably bring up the issue of conflict management. Leaders spend up to 40 percent of their workdays dealing with conflict in the workplace (Runde & Flanagan, 2007). The effects of unmanaged conflict are so severe on employee productivity that leaders must take steps to make sure that they and their employees are skilled in being able to navigate difficult issues with confidence and skill. When leaders cannot or will not take those steps, employees quit because of the stress and a desire to avoid the situation, take off work via sick leave to avoid the stress temporarily, or show up but don't accomplish anything worthwhile (Runde & Flanagan, 2007). Given the damage poorly handled conflict inflicts, leaders clearly must understand what to do in different conflict situations, learn new skills, and practice those constructive conflict management skills. Inviting those difficult conversations and refusing to avoid the elephant in the room are good leadership practices that should be intentionally stated and lived as part of the organizational culture.

One obstacle to developing a culture of effective conflict management is conflict avoidance. Diffusing the energy around an issue deprives the person accused (or from your perspective, the villain) from setting the record straight on his or her intentions and desires for the conversation. For example, when you are upset at someone else and tell all your friends, your close family members, the postman, and the telemarketer who happens to randomly dial your number that day the intimate details of how someone failed you, you may get a sense of relief. You haven't, however, addressed the conflict. The best way to start is by staying quiet and listening. Despite what you may have told yourself about the offending person—aka, the villain—you really know only what you were thinking and feeling. You have absolutely no idea about that person's intentions to harm or irritate you. Start by getting the other side of the story. If you can't do this without getting upset and verbally sparring until the entire situation becomes toxic, then disengage and stay away from the topic until you can approach it with genuine curiosity and a determination to gain insight into the other person's perspective. More often than not, we derail the whole process by deciding we know the whole story, that our story is the one and only truth, and that the other person requires us to set him or her straight. From this low place in the conflict, you will likely go on to lecture the person until he or she agrees that you are all-knowing and express a heaping dose of shame and guilt at having crossed you, the king or queen.

A willingness to give up your moral high ground and need to be right will not be easy, but it will be worth it. If you can lead without punishing upfront or retaliating later, you will be ahead of the game at work and in life. Pay attention to your conflict management abilities and start honing them today. Leading yourself and others through painful conversations in a caring and competent manner *is* leadership in action.

Motivation

Aspiring leaders often seek to find the mysterious holy grail of motivation, so that they might inspire others to put forth their best effort at all times. What they don't

Leadership Challenge

How does your behavior during conflict impact your relationship with others? How safe do others feel in coming to you with their problems? Have you proven yourself trustworthy? Are you a good listener?

realize is that, when it comes to motivation, one size does not fit all. Applying a superficial motivator from the latest pop leadership fad that doesn't take into account others' interests is ultimately futile. Fortunately, people are motivated by something all the time. Tapping into motivation requires understanding another's values and meaningfully connecting each person involved to something about the mission, vision, or project that is important.

Influence

There will be few followers and little progress made for a leader who lacks the ability to influence. Robert Cialdini (1998), a leading researcher in influence, distills effectively influencing others into six factors that encourage others to comply with what we want. Liking is the most influential of these six factors. People like those who like them. People also follow those whom they like. The most effective way to establish liking is to seek an authentic reason to like those around you. If you try to fake a reason, you miss an important opportunity to grow and connect with another human. Once you have mastered authentically connecting with others, you can build their confidence through attention to verbal supports in which you express confidence in their abilities and encourage their continued development. Liking others is important leadership work. A leader without liking may lose followers because over time it becomes easier to leave rather than tolerate working for a leader they don't like (Demorest & Grady, 2002).

Sincere validation is very powerful and influential. Think about someone who has gone out of his or her way to mentor you and help bring you along in terms of confidence, ability, and a perception that you can be great. Chances are, there isn't much that you wouldn't do for such a person. There is a self-fulfilling prophecy about how we treat others and the likely corollary of what will occur. Motivational speaker and branding expert Karen McCullough advises that if we "treat others as if they are poets, geniuses, and artists . . . they will be." Don't wait to start practicing this concept. Apply it today. Help others understand the extent to which you value them and their contributions and you will find that your influence increases exponentially.

■ EXPERIENTIAL WORK

Activities conducted for the purpose of improving competency in the skills necessary for success are known as **experiential work.** From time to time, we may hear the following statement: "You can't learn leadership from a book." In light of the fact that this statement may be disheartening as you wade through this tome, we would like to share our response. We believe you can't learn leadership only from a book. Leadership is a complex process and deserves a complex process for its development. Books are a part of the process, so you are not wasting your time right now. They certainly cannot, however, substitute for experience.

Practice

Leadership can be taught, even in a book, but it is learned only if the student of leadership pays close attention to the lessons. Almost all successful leaders in history benefited from a tutor or served apprenticeships to gain competency in necessary skills (Witzel, 2005). Disciplined practice in multiple domains over time serve the leader well. Continuous focus on the development of the self and knowledge of one's own motivations and reinforcers allow for a clearer perspective when interacting with others and their agendas, motivations, and perspectives. Warren Bennis (1989) also believes that personal qualities, such as vision, meaning, trust, and self-knowledge, can only be nurtured and developed over time and with significant practice.

Life is short and the constraints of time dictate that there just isn't enough of it for you to be equally proficient at everything. Real competency demands concentrated attention on just a few things. Perhaps this is a time in your life when you can begin to examine what is worthy of your energy and attention.

Videotaped Simulations

Have you ever experienced watching yourself on video? It's a strange feeling to think we look and act in a certain way and then have that perception challenged as we see ourselves for a moment as others do. When this happens, chances are you can identify at least something you would like to have done differently. If you are involved in a program that makes use of video for training purposes, take advantage of it. Of course, it will seem awkward and uncomfortable at first. You may find that you are distracted by how you looked, what you wore, what your hair looked like, what your voice sounded like, whether you inserted "um" or some other filler word after every thought or waved your hands about wildly as if gesturing an airplane onto the landing strip. But somewhere between the third and eighth sessions, you will start honing in on more substantial concerns without being distracted by the camera pointed at you. You can watch your development and keep track of your progress. It will be even better if there is a stable group of other students with whom you can work, so that everyone's victories can be observed and celebrated.

In some leadership programs, students prepare for structured scenarios or role-plays on camera. These leadership labs allow students to work alone or with others not only to communicate in a more articulate, professional, and influential manner but also to practice other interpersonal skills. In order to keep sessions productive, they must be based in high-quality content and thoughtful, careful evaluation. All participants receive feedback on the performance and leave with

Leadership Challenge

What resources are available at your school for you to practice your leadership skills using a videotaped lab setting? What would be helpful about practicing your leadership skills by recording them on video? What fears do you have about that practice?

two kinds of information. First, they recognize what they did well and their areas of strength. Second, they identify one or two things to work on for the next week. Areas for improvement can encompass a wide range of behaviors, both verbal and nonverbal. In videotaped practice sessions, students have a unique opportunity to get specific feedback from others and take a bird's-eye view of their own skills and development.

Projects

An intense focus on intrapersonal and interpersonal skill development provides a foundation for leadership project work. With the groundwork in skill development, students examine who they are, understand how they are becoming, and develop skills to connect effectively with others. Projects provide an opportunity for practical application of the skills that we insist matter so much. At the undergraduate level, students might identify an existing leadership role to fill that can benefit the campus or surrounding community, or they can devise an entirely new initiative. Projects allow students to succeed, and perhaps more important, to sometimes fail. Some of the best learning experiences in life are born of failure, and failure in this context is a resilience-building opportunity. There are always challenges along the way, unforeseen pitfalls, bureaucratic procedures that stifle progress, changes in the course of the project, and any number of other hoops and ditches that require redirection, adaptation, or disappointment. Spending at least a semester focused on contributing to the greater good calls your values to action and lends perspective to your leadership development as you make a difference in the world around you.

Even if you aren't involved in a formalized leadership program, we encourage and challenge you to take on such a project. Ideally, you can engage in this important practice in an environment of diverse and committed individuals willing to support, challenge, and hold you accountable to finish what you start (win, lose, or draw). You may be tempted to talk yourself into the notion that you have done projects in the past, even leading people along the way. The reality is, however, that, once you start delving into the hard intrapersonal and interpersonal work of leadership, you *will* lead differently and your projects will be qualitatively different from past endeavors.

■ INTELLECTUAL DEVELOPMENT

Critical Thinking

Intellectual development occurs when one engages in activities that improve critical thinking skills, integrative thinking, problem-solving skills, and creative abilities. The ability to think through complex problems is critical for leadership. There is a joke that education is defined as what remains of your knowledge after you subtract all that you have forgotten. If you haven't learned to write thorough critiques or work through problems using critical thinking skills, take more classes that allow you to learn and practice this quality. Philosophy majors and those in law school learn to do this really well. Systems theory classes are great for teaching critical thinking by examining systemic successes and failures. If you gain proficiency in this vital area and maintain your skill level, you will appreciate it probably more than your other classes (even the popular and entertaining ones!) years after you graduate. Even if you decide you don't want to be a leader in the world at work or at home, it is still important that you learn to be a good citizen who can vote qualified leaders into office who will be making decisions that impact you. Whether a leader or a follower, you don't want to take the risk of relying on someone else's logic to break down a complex problem and deal with it. His or her particular slant may not be aligned with your own. Why risk it?

Integrative Thinking

When faced with a problem or an issue requiring attention, most of us tend to generate one or two possible solutions and go with the best one. Often, we choose the first idea generated because it represents a quick solution, and we are keenly motivated to return to homeostasis. There is a new line of thought on the horizon about methods to work toward better solutions. The idea of integrative thinking doesn't allow for single thought generation and application. It requires us to stretch our minds. Nobel Prize–winning chemist Linus Pauling believed that "the best way to get a good idea is to get lots of ideas." This illustrates an important element of integrative thinking. Better decision making and creative problem solving can occur if you let your mind relax and brainstorm and then hold multiple ideas or possible solutions to a problem in your head at once. While this is a difficult concept to put into practice, you can train your brain to get in the habit of keeping several possibilities in the air, much like juggling. At some point, these ideas and solutions will link together in a meaningful way, and your mind will be able to work out a way to place the best of all options into one integrative solution.

Creativity, Innovation, and Problem Solving

Leaders, by virtue of the title, are expected to be good problem solvers. More and more in organizations, it is becoming apparent that, with fewer budgetary allowances and lean staffing, problems require a creative, innovative approach. While creativity and innovation are related constructs, they are not the same. Creativity is looking elsewhere for new ideas, and innovation is implementing those ideas, thereby changing the current structure. By fostering a collaborative and reflective culture where creativity is valued and innovation is expected, everyone in an organization can make important contributions and become a part of the success of the team. Improvisational actors teach an effective technique to foster this practice. For an effective improvisation, saying "no" to someone's ideas and shutting them down early is forbidden. Leaders can learn from this practice and understand that saying "no" or "yes, but" (which is a well-disguised "no") is a sure way to stifle enthusiasm and the generation of new ideas. Improvisational actors have shared the secret of the genius of their practice and use it as a rule to guide their brilliant and entertaining interplay during scenes. Everything spoken is accepted and built upon—nothing is ever shot down. "Yes" becomes "yes, and," never "no, that won't work" or "yes, but."

We challenge you to look for ways to foster innovation and start seeing others' ideas as gifts rather than second-rate solutions for you to find flaws. Instead, commit to taking ideas to the next level by applying the improvisational rule. If you consistently acknowledge others' contributions and give them credit whenever you can, you will continue to get the best they have to offer.

Vision

Leadership is an art that requires seeing the whole. A manager's role is to attend to the day-to-day details, while a leader must be looking to the future, setting and refining the vision for the future of the organization. Once you are clear on the vision, it is imperative to communicate it to others in a way that they can see how their contributions will be important for the big picture (Kouzes & Posner, 2002). Use stories and metaphors to paint a vivid picture of how the end result of the vision will look, even if all the details aren't yet in place (Ancona, Malone, Orlikowski, & Senge, 2007). To do this effectively, you must be passionate about the direction in which you wish to go and think about how you can communicate this vision in an enthusiastic manner while maintaining confidence and humility (tall order, huh?).

■ CHANGE AND ADAPTIVE WORK

When we see the need for deep change, we usually see it as something that needs to take place in someone else. In our roles of authority, such as parent, teacher, or boss, we are particularly quick to direct others to change. Such directives often fail, and we respond to the resistance by increasing our efforts. The power struggle that follows seldom results in change or brings about excellence. One of the most important insights about the need to bring about deep change in others has to do with where deep change actually starts.—Robert E. Quinn (1996, p. 11)

Faced with the choice between changing one's mind and proving that there is no need to do so, almost everyone gets busy on the proof.—John Kenneth Galbraith (2001, p. 241)

Copyright Grantland Enterprises; www.grantland.net.

Because leadership involves forward movement, change is an essential element. In our role as leaders, we must be clear on our own relationship with change. You can even rate your comfort with leadership on a continuum with an enthusiastic embrace on one end and dread on the other. While it may seem to be best to find yourself on the end toward an enthusiastic embrace, and having a positive relationship with change is helpful, it is also important to recognize that you still need to lead others who have more difficulty with change. No matter where you fall on the continuum, remember that there are people on the opposite extreme who have a very difficult time understanding your perspective on change. Change creates stress, stress that some find exhilarating and others find horrifying. When those who react closer to the latter face major change, perfectly normal adults can begin to act like children as the psychological stress builds. They also are more apt to focus on potential losses than on what they might gain. This shift in focus is important because not only are we at risk for focusing on loss but we also tend to overestimate loss. Tversky and Kahneman (1991) won the 2002 Nobel Prize in economics for their research impacting consumer behavior and the psychology behind losses and gains. Through their work, they identified loss aversion, which indicated that, on average, humans overvalue loss by a factor of three (Gourville, 2006).

Loss aversion is the tendency to reject change and embrace the status quo due to an unreasonable fear of loss, even when better alternatives present themselves. In times of change, leaders must anticipate that people may hang on tightly to what they perceive they will lose even if the thing taking its place will likely be better. Understanding this phenomenon and how your life has been impacted by loss aversion (think material possessions, relationships, etc.) will enable you to more effectively assist others through difficult periods of change and adjustment.

Process

According to Heifetz and Laurie (1998, pp. 173–74), "Leadership is the activity of mobilizing people to address adaptive challenges." Because adaptive work is at the core of the leadership process as defined by Heifetz, it is important to understand it.

Bridging the gap between the present state or culture and the desired state that meets the needs and aspirations of the social system is adaptive work. Heifetz describes six principles for leading people through the adaptive challenges that must take place for any organization to thrive. They include *getting on the balcony, identifying the adaptive challenge, regulating distress, maintaining disciplined attention, giving the work back to people,* and *protecting voices of leadership from below.*

Adaptive work is stressful for those who are dealing with it; as a result, leaders are prone to shield constituents from it. In their efforts to lead the organization through major changes, they identify the threat and devise a plan to address the adaptive challenge, but others in the organization may not have a clear understanding of those threats and challenges. Heifetz admonishes leaders to refrain from attempts to overprotect constituents from outside threats. Otherwise, they may feel that change has been levied upon them without sufficient explanation from their leadership. In order to face adaptive challenges effectively, leaders can help the entire organization by allowing reality to charge everyone in the organization to accept the threat as a reality, accept that something must be done, and begin the process of adapting.

One of the keys to beginning this work is "getting on the balcony." By getting on the balcony, leaders can observe larger interactive patterns as if they were on a balcony, as opposed to being caught up in the day-to-day action. Moving back and forth between the field of action and the balcony provides the understanding necessary to create the context for change. This can be a reminder for you to step back periodically and look at the big picture, including patterns that are emerging for you.

An **adaptive challenge** is a situation, or a set of challenges, that requires individuals and/or organizations to accept that a new approach or direction must be undertaken. Because change can create dramatic emotions in people, leaders need to strike a careful balance between people feeling the need to change and people feeling overwhelmed by change by regulating distress. Too little emphasis on change fosters a stagnant environment that leads to dying organizations. Too much change at once shuts people down. The formula to this balance and a "holding environment" consists of pacing and sequencing work, making initiatives without stopping other activities, and taking care not to start too many initiatives at once (Heifetz & Laurie, 1998). If you are seeing signs of people being overwhelmed or burned out, look to these tips to restore the appropriate balance for adaptive work.

The process of adaptive work requires connecting with others in a compassionate, trustworthy, and inspiring manner. By doing so, leaders can encourage followers to take initiatives to define and solve problems. Giving the work back to the people requires delegating problem solving, as opposed to simply assigning tasks. Members take responsibility. At times, adaptive work meets resistance in the form of work avoidance. When avoiding adaptive work, people may scapegoat to relieve themselves of the difficult responsibility and find someone to blame. Sheer denial is another option, as is the temptation to focus only on the technical work that can easily fill anyone's workday.

During adaptive work, the leader cannot ignore the vital information from every level of the organization, even entry-level positions. Everyone has a valuable perspective. In order to protect voices from below, Heifetz and Laurie (1998) state that the leader must listen well. Have you heard this before? Because important information may lie within poorly expressed and ill-timed comments and concerns, adaptive leaders resist the tendency to ignore the entire message if the delivery is poor. The content may contain an important truth. Finally, as the leader, you must resist the urge to restore social equilibrium and prevent yourself from silencing someone too quickly. While it's easier to avert a conflict to keep everyone comfortable, a lack of thorough exploration into the discontent leads to a superficial solution to a much deeper problem. Nobody said leadership is easy.

■ CONCLUSION

Given that leadership requires addressing the difficult adaptive challenges, intellectual capacity, experiential work, interpersonal skill development and intrapersonal growth, it is easy to get overwhelmed. Leadership is ultimately a humbling enterprise, and all of us who are students of it ultimately embrace this leadership paradox: We are all that we bring to our leadership and we are never enough. Don't get discouraged that you haven't perfected all of these qualities. None of us have. We don't actually have to. But we do have to constantly become better. Targeting our efforts to become better by using the framework provided will increase our effectiveness. We are convinced that fully engaging our process of becoming and working in tandem with others to address a need, create a new way, or help right a wrong are exhilarating. They will fill you with energy, purpose, and determination, so keep striving for who you can become and lead with your best self in all situations. As you weather your own trials, tribulations, and unfortunately for some even tragedies in your life and leadership, we hope that you will be prepared. After the April 16, 2007, shooting massacre at Virginia Tech, poet Nikki Giovanni lifted the hearts of her grieving university community with an important truth by declaring that "we are better than we think and not quite who we hope to be."—another paradox we hope will always be true for you.

■ KEY TERMS

Active Listening—Nonverbal body language, including eye contact and facial expressions that indicate a person is listening.

Adaptive Challenge—A situation, or set of challenges, that requires individuals and/or organizations to accept that a new approach or direction must be undertaken.

Experiential Work—Activities conducted for the purpose of improving competency in skills necessary for success.

Feedback—Evaluation and assessment of performance by others as part of the learning process and an ongoing effort to improve.

Intellectual Development—Development that occurs when one engages in activities that improve critical thinking skills, integrative thinking, problem-solving skills, and creative abilities.

Interpersonal Growth—Improvement that occurs as a direct result of interaction with others and the influence of others.

Intrapersonal Growth—Improvement that is the result of heightened self-awareness, personal reflection, and self-discipline.

Loss Aversion—The tendency to reject change and embrace the status quo due to an unreasonable fear of loss, even when better alternatives present themselves.

Resilience—The ability to withstand threats and challenges.

■ SUGGESTED READINGS

Collins, J. 2001. *Good to Great: Why Some Companies Make the Leap and Others Don't.* New York: HarperCollins.

Heifetz, R. A. & Linsky, M. 2002. *Leadership on the Line: Staying Alive Through the Dangers of Leading.* Boston: Harvard Business School Press.

Jones, D. 2005. "Business Leaders Can Learn from Pope." *USA Today,* April 5, 2005, 3B.

Kouzes, J. M. & Posner, B. Z. 2002. *The Leadership Challenge* (3rd ed.). San Francisco: Jossey-Bass.

Runde, C. & Flanagan, T. A. 2007. *Becoming a Conflict Competent Leader: How You and Your Organization Can Manage Conflict Effectively.* San Francisco: Jossey-Bass.

Schein, E. 2006. "Leadership Competencies: A Provocative New Look." In F. Hesselbein and M. Goldsmith, *Leader of the Future 2: Visions, Strategies and Practices for the New Era.* San Francisco: Jossey-Bass.

■ REFERENCES

Ancona, D., Malone, T. W., Orlikowski, W. J., & Senge, P. 2007. "In Praise of the Incomplete Leader." *Harvard Business Review, 85(2)*, 92–100.

Bass, B. M. 1985. *Leadership and Performance Beyond Expectations.* New York: Free Press.

Bennis, W. 1989. *On Becoming a Leader.* Reading, MA: Addison-Wesley, p. 104.

Burns, J. M. 1978. *Leadership.* New York: Harper & Row.

Buron, R. J. & McDonald-Mann, D. 1999. *Giving Feedback to Subordinates.* Greensboro, NC: Center for Creative Leadership.

Cialdini, R. B. 1998. *The Psychology of Persuasion* (rev. ed.). New York: Collins.

Colvin, G. 2006. "What It Takes to Be Great." *Fortune, 154(9)*, 88–96.

Cronshaw, S. F. & Ellis, R. J. 1991. "A Process Investigation of Self-Monitoring and Leader Emergence." *Small Group Research, 22(4)*, 403–420.

Demorest, L. S. & Grady, D. 2002. "In Search of a Leader." *Women in Business, 54(2)*, 11–12.

Ekman, P. & Rosenberg, E. L. 1997. *What the Face Reveals: Basic and Applied Studies of Spontaneous Expression Using the Facial Action Coding System (FACS).* New York: Oxford University Press.

Galbraith, J. K. 2001. *The Essential Galbraith.* New York: Houghton-Mifflin.

Gardner, W. L. & Schermerhorn, Jr. J. R. 2004. "Unleashing Individual Potential: Performance Gains Through Positive Organizational Behavior and Authentic Leadership." *Organizational Dynamics, 33(3)*, 270–281.

George, B. 2003. *Authentic Leadership: Rediscovering the Secrets to Creating Lasting Value.* San Francisco: Jossey-Bass.

Gottman, J. 1994. *Why Marriages Succeed or Fail.* New York: Fireside.

Gourville, J. T. 2006. "Eager Sellers & Stony Buyers: Understanding the Psychology of New-Product Adoption." *Harvard Business Review, June,* 99–106.

Hathaway, P. 2006. *Feedback Skills for Leaders: Building Constructive Communication Skills Up and Down the Ladder.* (3rd ed). Boston: Thomson Learning.

Heifetz, R. A. & Laurie, D. L. 1998. "The Work of Leadership." *Harvard Business Review on Leadership,* 171–197.

Hickson, B., Clayton, E. W., Entman, S. S., Miller, C. S., Githens, P. B., Whetten-Goldstein, K., & Sloan, F. A. 1994. "Obstetricians' Poor Malpractice Experience and Patients' Satisfaction with Care." *Journal of the American Medical Association, 272,* 1583–1587.

Hughes, L. 2003. "Enhancing Communication Skills." *Women in Business, 55(5),* 21–22.

Judge, T. A. & Bono, J. E. 2000. "Fine Factor Model of Personality and Transformational Leadership," *Journal of Applied Psychology,* v. 69, pp. 751–65.

Karen McCullough & Co. Branding expert with leadership skills. http://www.karenmccullough.com/articles/article_may04.htm.

Kouzes, J. M. & Posner, B. Z. 2002. *The Leadership Challenge.* San Francisco: Jossey-Bass.

Pine II, B. J. & Gilmore, J. H. 1999. *The Experience Economy: Work Is Theatre and Every Business a Stage.* Boston: Harvard Business School Press.

Quinn, R. E. 1996. *Deep Change: Discovering the Leader Within.* San Francisco: Jossey-Bass.

Runde, C. & Flanagan, T. A. 2007. *Becoming a Conflict Competent Leader: How You and Your Organization Can Manage Conflict Effectively.* San Francisco: Jossey-Bass.

Scott, S. 2004. *Fierce Conversations: Achieving Success at Work & in Life, One Conversation at a Time.* New York: Berkley Books.

Tversky, A. & Kahneman, D. 1991. "Loss Aversion in Riskless Choice: A Reference Dependent Model." *Quarterly Journal of Economics, 106,* 1039–1061.

Witzel, M. 2005. "Vision and Ethics at the Heart of Training." *Business Life Management, Financial Times,* April 4, p. 12.

CHAPTER TWO REVIEW QUESTIONS

1. What is the most powerful influence technique?

_____

_____

_____

2. What are some of the effects of unmanaged conflict?

_____

_____

_____

3. What are the five components of active listening?

_____

_____

_____

4. Discuss the concept of *loss aversion* and provide an example.

_____

_____

_____

5. What does the term *getting on the balcony* mean?

_____

_____

_____

6. What are the steps a leader must take to regulate the distress of followers during adaptive work?

_____

_____

_____

CHAPTER TWO SELF-TEST

1. In 2006, *Harvard Business Review* displayed a cover page announcing *Leadership's 1st Commandment:* _____.

2. _____ are why we do what we do.

3. _____ is the ability to withstand or recover from challenges.

4. The building of a resilient organization or team requires a consistent positive flow of authentic _____ and _____.

5. All things being equal, the person who possesses better _____ skills and understands and adjusts to _____ will be deemed the leader.

6. Of all the skills, _____ is the most important skill in the world of leadership.

7. Leaders spend up to _____ percent of their workday dealing with conflict in the workplace.

8. According to researcher Robert Cialdini, people are most likely to follow a person they _____.

9. Change always creates _____, which some will find exhilarating and others find horrifying.

10. According to researchers who study consumer behavior and psychology, humans overvalue loss by a factor of _____.

A Brief History of Leadership and Service as an Academic Field of Study

Robert G.
Duffett

Raymond D.
Screws

Donald C.
Simmons, Jr.

■ INTRODUCTION

Since the beginning of human history, men and women have been obsessed with the notion of leadership. For the earliest of nomadic peoples who followed the herds, identifying qualities of those who might be best suited to lead the hunt was of vital importance because failure might mean starvation and death. The Greeks, Romans, and Mali surely obsessed over what virtues a great warrior leader should possess because failure might mean defeat and enslavement. Leaders have always been entrusted with life and death issues, and they still are to this day. What might happen if the CEO of a Fortune 500 company or a university president miscalculates or makes a big mistake? People might lose their jobs, their homes, their health insurance, and their pensions. Leadership has always been, and it always will be, serious business. Service, at the most basic level, is also keeping others alive, protected, and healthy. Given these facts, it should be no surprise that some of the earliest and most studied texts were about leadership and service—specifically, how one maintains control and thus keeps the group alive.

Hammurabi's Codes, which originated from one of the earliest human civilizations in the Middle East, focused on how to maintain authority and order. Early religious texts likewise took a similar approach to leadership. In Deuteronomy 16:19 (*Holy Bible,* 1994) appointed judges and officers were warned not to "take a gift: for a gift doth blind the eyes of the wise, and pervert the words of the righteous." Very specific guidelines for conduct were clearly spelled out for Hebrew leaders in the religious texts. Punishments for those who broke codes of conduct, what to allow followers to eat as well as which foods to avoid, and how to resolve domestic issues and business disagreements were all spelled out in great detail. To students of today, some of these laws may appear a bit odd, or make no sense at all, but the texts were specifically authored and in line with the culture of the day in order to maintain accepted societal norms and ensure the success of the leader, as well as the survival of the community of followers.

Some other early texts that focused on leadership offered surprisingly insightful lessons, and several are still used in college classrooms even today. In *The Art of War,* for example, Chinese general and philosopher **Sun Tzu** wrote, in the fifth century B.C., that military leaders stand "for the virtues of wisdom, sincerity, benevolence, courage and strictness" (Tzu, 2003, p. 87). Sun Tzu defined the "consummate leader" as one who "cultivates the moral law, and strictly adheres to method and discipline" (p. 115). Today, *The Art of War* is considered one of the most important works ever written, one that is read in classrooms around the world by students who are preparing for careers in everything from business to coaching and politics. Good advice, apparently, never loses its usefulness.

The virtues of wisdom, sincerity, benevolence, courage, and discipline espoused by Sun Tzu and his Asian contemporaries are still very much a part of modern training in the martial arts, as well as leadership training in general.

Photo by Raymond Screws.

> # Leadership Challenge
>
> Identify a leadership quote from Machiavelli, Sun Tzu, Confucius, the Koran, the Bhagavad Gītā, or some other source that inspires you to do all the things you want to do. What about that quote inspires you?

Niccolo Machiavelli, Italian diplomat and historian, warned sixteenth-century leaders in his treatise *The Prince* that "the populace is rather fickle; it is easy to persuade them of something, but difficult to confirm them in that persuasion" (1999, p. 25). He noted, however, that one "who builds his power on the people, one who can command and is a man of courage, who does not despair in diversity, who does not fail to take precautions, and who wins general allegiance by his personal qualities and the institutions he establishes, he will never be let down by the people . . ." (Machiavelli, 1999, p. 44). Machiavelli's writings, however, have been chastised by contemporary critics because he placed considerable importance on staying in power by almost any means, given good intent.

While we may now disagree with some of their basic premises about leadership and service, early writers on the subject played an important role in shaping the discipline. The fact that students at colleges and universities in classrooms around the world are still reading and debating the teachings of Sun Tzu and Machiavelli is a testament to the importance of their writings and teachings. They, and other previously mentioned early writers and philosophers on leadership, worked with others to lay the framework on which modern theories about leadership and service were constructed.

■ EVOLUTION OF MODERN LEADERSHIP STUDIES

Perhaps the most difficult problem with the history of modern leadership studies is where to begin—a methodological approach, a definitional approach, a review of the literature, or actual examples or case studies? A methodological approach to leadership is a comprehensive and heuristic one that attempts to explain the dynamics of leadership by paying attention to its most significant historical, social, political, psychological, and spiritual forces. A definitional approach selects a widely recognized definition of *leadership,* paying close attention to why this definition was historically chosen over others. A third approach might begin with a review of selected historical literature on leadership, such as an ancient text or an old, dust-covered doctoral dissertation. After this review, the researcher might analyze some aspect of leadership theory in historic perspective. A fourth option is to approach the question or "jump into" the research problem by simply choosing leaders most historians would agree were great leaders. The hope, in this instance, is that, some sort of general leadership theory might emerge as one examines lives, times, and challenges.

The first three are deductive approaches to the history of leadership, in that any methodological or definitional approach or review of the literature attends to the particulars first and from them draws some general theoretical leadership concepts. The fourth is inductive, in that it begins with obvious examples of leaders and, in the process of critical comparison, contrast, and historical reconstruction, attempts to draw particular conclusions about leadership. Although there is much merit in these starting points, the best place to begin on the subject of the history of leadership is at the intersection of two widely recognized sociological constructs: authority and legitimacy. From a theoretical perspective, leadership exists only when followers acknowledge and adhere to the leader's authority; otherwise, it is not leadership but something else. At the same time, the compelling force of leadership is highly relational between follower and leader. In other words, followers give authority to a leader, which legitimizes the leader to act for the followers. From a historical and sociological perspective, leadership can exist only in the midst of legitimacy and authority. Absent these two sociological constructs, leadership collapses and chaos ensues or someone else assumes the mantle of leadership.

■ LEADERSHIP, AUTHORITY, AND LEGITIMACY

If our perspective has any merit as a prolegomena on leadership theory generally, and as a means to discuss the history of leadership specifically, we actually begin on sociological and theoretical ground plowed before by Max Weber. In his book *The Theory of Social and Economic Organization* (1964), Weber wrote of the linkage among leadership, legitimacy, and authority. Although the focus of his work was leadership within a bureaucratic organization, we are persuaded that his insights on leadership can be generalized to most contexts in which leadership exists.

Authority

The term **authority** can be defined in several ways. First, it can refer to certain patterns in relationships where one person is expected to direct the behavior of others. An athletic coach is an example. He or she directs the behavior of players. Second, *authority* can refer to the right of someone to direct the behavior of others under certain circumstances. For instance, recently chapter co-author Robert Duffett was late for his daughter's volleyball game and was frantically driving through a neighborhood, looking for the school where the match was to be played. He was not mindful of how fast he was driving his car. Another car, with flashing red lights, pulled up behind him, summoning him to pull to the side of the road. An officer of the law, with badge and pistol in his holster, demanded, nicely, Robert's driving license and vehicle registration. Despite being late, being lost, and speeding, the flashing red lights and uniformed police officer compelled him to pull to the side of the road. If the officer had no badge or gun and drove a car with no flashing red lights or official markings, Robert would have ignored him. Authority is not limited, however, just to those who possess it in some formal, or titled, manner. It can be the quality of someone's action, as when it is said "She speaks with authority." Martin Luther King's sermons are an example of this way of understanding authority.

Finally, *authority* can refer to persons or groups themselves. Statements such as the following illustrate this type: "You should show respect for authority," and "He is an authority." Similar to the previous example, authority is given to certain people due to their role in society. Authority, at least in theory, should never be construed as brute force or power. Rather, it is approved power that is exercised according to norms established between persons and persons, persons and organizations, and persons and society. Weber defined authority as "the probability that a certain specific command (or most commands) from a given source will be obeyed by a given group of persons" (Weber, 1964, p. 324). We may be uncomfortable today with Weber's autocratic language, yet his point should not be missed. The link between leadership and authority is still about the likelihood of the leader influencing people's behavior.

Legitimacy

Historically, a key element in any treatment of the authority of leadership has been **legitimacy.** Legitimacy is the right of an individual to lead that is granted by followers, in both a social and a psychological sense. Weber argues that all leaders must cultivate belief in their legitimacy. Hence, legitimacy and authority are bound together in that leadership authority is grounded in legitimacy (Weber, 1964, p. 325). Most kings throughout human history proclaimed their divine right to rule as God's chosen representative of the people, and thus ensured their legitimacy.

It is on the basis of legitimacy that Weber argues that all leadership authority is derived from one of three types. Weber recognized that, in reality, these types are usually found in mixed, not pure, form. They explain, in part, why certain individuals become leaders and attract followers, while others do not. These types of authority, in a leadership setting, also say much about followers. Conversely, they also explain how leaders substantiate both their leadership and the devotion of their followers. These three typologies are rational authority, traditional authority, and charismatic authority (Weber, 1964, pp. 324–407).

Rational leadership authority rests on the belief in the "legality of patterns of normative rules and the right of those elevated to authority under such rules to issue commands" (Weber, 1964, p. 328). Obedience is owed to the legally established impersonal order. Rules and laws are the locus of authority. In its purest form, rational authority is exercised by multiple layers of persons in a bureaucratic organization. A person's authority derives from the office held, and obedience by subordinates is owed to the office—not the office holder. Relationships are impersonal and there is a clear distinction between the office holder and his or her personal life. The office is the sole, or primary, occupation of the incumbent. Technical rulers govern the workplace. The military and the US court system are examples of rational authority.

Traditional leadership authority rests "on established belief in the sanctity of immemorial tradition and the legitimacy of the status of those exercising authority under them" (Weber, 1964, p. 328). Obedience is owed not to enacted laws (rational authority) but, rather, to the person who occupies a position of authority by tradition. Obedience therefore is personal, not impersonal. The authority to lead in this type is broad and diffuse. Examples of this type vary from kings and fiefs, to chiefs of tribes, to certain religious leaders and professions, which are today sometimes outside the realm of rational authority.

Charismatic authority rests on certain individual personality qualities that seem to set the person apart from ordinary men and women. Obedience is therefore owed to the charismatically qualified leader by virtue of his or her perceived supernatural, superhuman, or at least exceptional powers or qualities. Charismatic authority is outside the realm of everyday routine. It is sharply opposed to rational and traditional authority. Charismatic power is thought by followers to come from a transcendent source. Weber borrowed the term itself, charismatic, from the vocabulary of primitive Christianity.

Charismatic authority is unstable. It remains only as long as leaders prove themselves by performance. Failure may be interpreted that God has forsaken them. For Weber, the basis of charismatic leadership is not administrative, legislative, or even rational. Rather, its source of power stands seemingly outside the historic nexus of cause and effect. Hence, when they die, the movement will collapse unless the charisma can be transmitted to successive leaders. Weber referred to this as the "routinization of charisma."

Weber points out a neglected aspect of contemporary leadership theory and a lens to evaluate leadership in historic perspective: Leaders draw their authority from followers and, in the process, establish their legitimacy to continue to lead. This Weberian "lens" can be applied to all arenas of leadership: political, educational, business, and religious.

As history attests, however, revolutions overthrow all types of leaders— traditional, rational, and charismatic. Rational and traditional types of leaders have been known to be both insensitive and oppressive to their followers. The instability of charismatic leadership is clearly demonstrated in the aftermath of the first Great Awakening in pre-Revolutionary America. This religious revival did more to disestablish the state church in the American colonies than anything Thomas Jefferson, David Hume, or Thomas Paine wrote, yet even the revivals of George Whitfield, William Tennant, and Jonathan Edwards that renewed the soul and tore down the Anglican Church in Virginia and Congregational Church in New England petered out. Edwards was even "fired" from his congregation. The charisma could not be routinized.

Weber's typology forces us to think again about not only the context that gave rise to leadership but also what it is about Martin Luther, John Wesley, John Calvin, and Jonathan Edwards or George Washington, John Adams, Alexander Hamilton, Thomas Jefferson, Abraham Lincoln, Theodore Roosevelt, and Martin Luther King that shook the world. What was it about these men and others that elicited loyalty from thousands? Why is it that we still read the writings and biographies that are yet being written about their lives and times? What did they do and say that gave them the authority to lead and why did so many follow? Although the Glorious Revolution during the seventeenth century assured the survival of the monarchy in Great Britain, it might be viewed as the forerunner of a shift that began a century later. With the American and French Revolutions during the second half of the eighteenth century, the world began to witness the decline of powerful monarchies. Even in Great Britain, where the monarchy remained influential during the nineteenth century, especially under Queen Victoria, the elected Parliament gained increasing authority and power. The newly formed United States broke from the shackles of the British monarchy and the French overthrew their king. In America a new form of democracy was fabricated, and in France the unstable situation led to the dictatorship of Napoleon Bonaparte.

Writing during the 1830s, Alexis de Tocqueville (2000, p. 117) observed "that the power of the president of the United States is exercised only in the sphere of a restricted sovereignty, whereas that of the king in France acts within the circle of a complete sovereignty." Although France ultimately became a democratic society after Napoleon's defeat in 1815, Napoleon's reign heralded the next stage in the evolution of leadership style that became so prevalent during the early twentieth century. In the United States, the emergence of a democratically elected leadership served as the catalyst for a revolutionary inclusive and collaborative democratic tide that swept much of the globe during the second half of the twentieth century.

■ LEADERSHIP IN THE NEW AMERICAN DEMOCRACY

One new twist to leadership that was introduced by democracy allowed for the replacement of unpopular leadership in a bloodless and civil manner. In other words, the option and the opportunity for a change of leadership are built into the system. However, the question of term limits for elected officials is debated to this day because some citizens still want to further limit the power of their leaders.

With American independence, with the formation of a democracy, and especially after the creation of the Constitution, the upper echelon of leadership in the United States was not given the same iconic standing by the populace as that previously held by royalty. However, America's first president, George Washington, was viewed with reverence by Americans. Historian Joseph J. Ellis (2004) titled his book about the first president *His Excellency George Washington,* which indicated that Washington was looked upon as American royalty by the citizens of the young country. Washington seemed like the ultimate leader—almost above reproach—and he still does. Ellis wrote that "Washington poses what we might call the Patriarchal Problem in its most virulent form: on Mount Rushmore, the Mall, the dollar bill and the quarter, but always an icon—distant, cold, intimidating" (Ellis, 2004, p. xi). Although to a certain extent all the well-known founding fathers of the United States are looked upon in an iconic sense, especially Jefferson, it is not to the same degree as Washington. Ellis also explained: "Looking back over two hundred years of the American presidency, it seems safe to say that no one entered the office with more personal prestige than Washington, and only two presidents—Abraham Lincoln and Franklin Roosevelt—faced comparable crises" (Ellis, 2004, p. 188). Unlike Lincoln, however, who faced the Civil War, and Roosevelt, who took on the Great Depression and World War II, Washington tackled the uncertainty of America's survival as a new country with a more passive, some might say laissez-faire, leadership style. But Washington was smart enough to include great minds in his Cabinet, such as Jefferson and Alexander Hamilton, although these two men often disagreed and were political rivals. Tensions mounted between Jefferson and Hamilton, but most of the time Washington was able to remain above the fray. In one regard, it could be said that Washington helped secure America's future through personal dignity. Although there were presidential elections every four years, Washington chose to relinquish his position voluntarily and not run for a third term, which set a precedent until Franklin Roosevelt during the 1940s. The world was not accustomed to seeing leaders replaced without violence or bloodshed. In this one decision, Washington almost guaranteed that a president would not act as a king and the presidency would not rise above democracy. Today, a constitutional amendment limits a president to two terms.

Although well respected and a founding father, the United States' second president, John Adams, did not carry the same national status as George Washington. He was the first president to be victimized by the new, evolving two-party system, which cost Adams the 1800 election when he lost to Jefferson. Adams, Jefferson, and those who followed were more proactive in their presidential leadership than Washington. With the two-party system, they could not lead passively, or they risked not being reelected. Very gradually, then, and especially into the twentieth century, political leaders at all levels began to make campaign promises, whether they kept them or not, and to become involved in popularity contests to win elections. The result was widespread political corruption, although most politicians were honest. As for Adams, Jefferson, and the other early American presidents, they most assuredly led with the understanding of the importance of establishing a legacy for the new United States: They understood the historical significance of their leadership. David McCullough reasoned that Adams "felt he had lived in the greatest of times, that the eighteenth century, as he also told Jefferson, was for all its errors and vices 'the most honorable' to human nature" (McCullough, 2001, p. 650). This kind of attitude helped John Adams understand the importance of early American leadership for the future of the United States.

■ THE RISE OF THE SOCIAL REFORMERS

Not all was perfect in early American history. During most of our history, most of those who held formally recognized positions of leadership were wealthy and all were men. Rich white men, whose wealth was measured by land holdings and property, were the only Americans with the financial means to afford a formal education. Women were rarely allowed an education, and for the poor an education was out of reach. Slaves, male and female, seldom received any education and, like most Americans of the times, were illiterate. Therefore, rich white men were the educated of society, they became the leaders, and they wrote the laws. In addition, in the young United States, propertied white men were the only Americans allowed to vote. Consequently, during the early republic period, America was run by elites and the country was not the democracy we recognize today.

Ironically, some argue that the concept of service has also been historically limited to those who held considerable wealth and status. After all, to be able to give of one's time and money implies that one has resources, in the form of time and money, to give away in service to others. Working single mothers with five children and two jobs, for example, do not typically have the ability to perform regular acts of service because they must concentrate all of their efforts on their own families' survival. Let's think for a moment about public servants. Do average Americans have the resources to leave their job for two years and run for the presidency? No, of course they do not, which begs the question "Just how democratic are we, really, if only one of great wealth can be the ultimate public servant in our country?"

Leaders and servants have not always let themselves be limited by societal constraints. Many who assumed the mantle of leader and service have also emanated from outside the political realm in America. During the nineteenth century, especially in the United States, new leaders were borne out of a reaction to social ills in the form of abolitionism and the fight for women's suffrage. These new social leaders included both men and women. Before the nineteenth century, it was rare to see women as leaders in any capacity. One exception was Anne Hutchinson of seventeenth-century Puritan Massachusetts, but she was banished to Rhode Island for heresy. Social leaders such as Sojourner Truth, Fredrick Douglass, Susan B. Anthony, and the Grimké sisters also became prominent. But social leaders faced risks. As historian Alan Trachtenberg argued, abolitionists and other reformers challenged the state, which placed them "outside the nation, to declare themselves antagonists to the corporate entity of America itself" (Trachtenberg, 2007). While this may have been true for whites, African American reformers already endured "outside the nation," and they already faced innumerable and dangerous obstacles. In some cases, these reform-minded leaders and true public servants put their lives on the line for social change.

The very nature of a social good or servant-leadership often means going against the grain of the social norm. Abolitionist Sojourner Truth was not only a former slave and an African American but also a woman. These three facts placed her about as far outside the mainstream of formally recognized leadership and service as possible. But Truth overcame these social obstacles. Although having been born into slavery and raised speaking Dutch, she was freed from bondage when New York abolished slavery, and she learned English, changed her name to Sojourner Truth, and became a remarkable and invaluable servant to others as an anti-slavery leader.

Two more unlikely servant-leaders were Sarah and Angelina Grimké, who fought against accepted norms to become leading abolitionists. Not only did the sisters embark on careers in which women were not respected, but their father was a South Carolina slave owner. During the 1830s, the Grimké sisters challenged the social system by becoming leading abolitionists and public speakers against slavery, at a time when most women were forbidden to speak in public.

Some of the most interesting leaders were those who led rebellions. From leaders of colonial slave revolts to the leaders of the American Revolution, all risked their lives and many lost them. One of the most compelling and successful of the rebellious leaders was Toussaint L'Ouverture. L'Ouverture was born into slavery on the French-held Caribbean island of Saint-Dominique, now Haiti, during the 1740s. He was intelligent and, unlike most slaves, had learned to read and write. In 1800, he led a force of ex-slaves against the French and won. He became the leader of the new independent Saint-Dominique but established a dictatorship, which he thought was best for the new country. Ironically, he was unable to conceive that the style of leadership, and some might argue public service, he had fought so hard to defeat would be his own downfall. Rubin Blackburn wrote that "Toussaint's style of rule echoed that of an autocratic and independent-minded colonial Governor—with the difference that he had no Intendant or metropolitan minister to dispute his authority" (Blackburn, 1988, p. 242)—in other words, a dictator. The fact that an ex-slave became the leader of a nation, regardless of leadership style, was extraordinary and destroyed many myths long held about race and leadership. Slavery was abolished in Haiti and L'Ouverture was considered a hero, especially among the leaders of other slave revolts throughout the Americas, but none ever came close to being as successful as L'Ouverture.

■ SOCIALIST MOVEMENTS, CAPITALISM, AND NEW APPROACHES TO LEADERSHIP

Out of the ashes of the 1848 revolution, a new form of ideological leadership emerged in Europe. Led by young German philosopher Karl Marx, this new ideology called for revolutionary uprising from the working class of industrial societies. In 1848 Marx and Frederick Engels wrote a pamphlet, known as the *Communist Manifesto,*

German philosopher Karl Marx rejected the notion that religious beliefs should influence government and the organization of society.

Library of Congress.

that was one of the most influential statements of the nineteenth century, as well as human history. Unlike the American Revolution, and the early US government, in which leadership emanated from the elite, Marx's form of socialism was a revolution of the masses against capitalism. In addition, socialism, and what later became known as Marxism, was purely secular. Marx rejected religion's influence on all matters related to government and the organization of society in general. Historian William A. Green (1998, p. 55) theorized that "Marx disdained concepts of divine intervention, insisting that human action has always been driven by material forces." Socialism, or Marxism, was the final nail in the coffin of faith-driven states in Europe and the leaders who claimed God had divinely selected them by right of birth to lead others. During the second half of the nineteenth century, socialism became popular in Europe, and during the twentieth century its influence spread across Asia.

Although socialist ideology spread rapidly in Europe, it never gained a strong foothold in the United States, in part because democracy was already so entrenched. However, during the late nineteenth century, America experienced an industrial revolution and an explosion of immigrants, both of which helped create a massive poor working class. In response, a working-class movement matured in the form of labor unions. Instead of being socialists, although some had those leanings, the working-class representatives emerged as leaders of labor organizations. Labor unions represented the needs of those exploited by industrialists. After the Civil War, unions were resisted by industrial leaders and violence was common. Labor leaders, such as Uriah Stephens and Terence V. Powderly of the Knights of Labor, led in secrecy as a result, which handcuffed them because it caused distrust and created difficulties when attempting to gain concessions for workers. During the 1880s, the Knights dropped their secrecy, led several successful strikes, and added thousands of members. However, Powderly despised strikes. By 1890, the Knights had lost considerable strength, in part because the organization had grown too fast and had become too large and difficult to lead.

Unlike the Knights of Labor, which included skilled and unskilled laborers, the American Federation of Labor (AFL), led by Samuel Gompers, consisted of smaller trade unions of skilled workers. The AFL was known as a labor organization that philosophically opposed political involvement. However, historian Julie Greene argued that this simply is not accurate. Greene explained that Gompers and the AFL rejected partisan politics but not political involvement by the organization. However, by 1908, Gompers had begun to change his opinion. Greene (1998, p. 225) wrote that, under the leadership of Gompers, the AFL "focused its effort on the elite world of lobbying and high-level contacts with Democratic Party leaders." Regardless of philosophy, American labor leaders during the late nineteenth century, as did the earliest leaders of the earliest human societies, represented the most basic needs and the safety of the people they served.

Of course, the rise of labor unions after the Civil War was a reaction to exploding industrialization. Powerful industrial leaders controlled money, people, and often politicians. These leaders were the men who had built modern America, or some would say the men who employed the people who had built America. Known as captains of industry, these men were the most wealthy and powerful leaders in the United States. However, they were also called Robber Barons because they robbed society for wealth and power. They were not the first businessmen to become wealthy. John Jacob Astor, the first millionaire, earned his wealth in the fur trade during the first half of the nineteenth century. But, during the Gilded Age, American businessmen took wealth and the power that followed to new levels. Men such as John D. Rockefeller, who monopolized the oil industry, and Andrew Carnegie, who was a force in steel, destroyed their competition and exploited the workforce. These men were industrial capitalists, meaning the companies they owned produced products and they answered only to themselves. By the turn of the twentieth century, industry had become controlled by powerful financers. Investment bankers, such as J. Pierpont Morgan and August Belmont, although not involved in production, became the leaders in the business world, and they worked to make profits for stockholders and themselves. They loathed labor unions and demonstrated little concern for society. Some of these business leaders, nonetheless, participated in philanthropic and service-related activities—for example, Carnegie gave millions of dollars for public libraries across the United States—but they did very little to supply stable incomes, to provide healthcare, or to feed or clothe those they exploited while amassing their exorbitant wealth.

Many late-nineteenth-century businessmen justified their ruthless actions through a new philosophy called **Social Darwinism.** This theory claimed that it was natural for some people to become leaders and for others to be followers. It was natural selection, Social Darwinists said, that a few people rose to the top of society. In what has become a famous statement, John D. Rockefeller told his Sunday school class that "the growth of large business is merely a survival of the fittest. . . . This is not an evil tendency in business. It is merely the working out of the law of nature and the law of God" (Corning, 2005, p. 388). Andrew Carnegie (1889, p. 6) explained that, while "the law may be sometimes hard for the individual, it is best for the race, because it insures the survival of the fittest. . . ." These men justified control and exploitation of the poor in a manner not so different from the tyrant kings of ancient times.

However, not everyone believed in keeping down the masses and controlling the less fortunate. In the 1850s, in response to the Know-Nothing Party, which was against Catholics and immigrants, Abraham Lincoln wrote to a friend: "As a nation, we began by declaring that '*all men are created equal.*' We now practically read it 'all men are created equal, *except negroes.*'" He continued: "When the Know-Nothings get control, it will read 'all men are created equal, except negroes, and *foreigners and Catholics.*' When it comes to this I should prefer emigrating to some country where they make no pretence of loving liberty" (Lincoln, 1855, p. 323).

Between Lincoln, whose presidency ended with his assassination 1865, and Theodore Roosevelt, who assumed office in 1901, when William McKinley was assassinated, no American president rose above party politics. Instead of being dominated by strong, independent-minded presidents, the American political system was led by political and financial bosses during these three and a half decades. The American two-party system bred corruption and fraud during the Gilded Age. Political bosses gave favors to rich political and business friends in exchange for their support, a practice known as the spoils system. These political bosses followed the straight party line and often set party policy. Other political bosses ran cities, such as the infamous William Magear Tweed, better known as "Boss Tweed," who ran New York City through the Democratic Tammany Hall. A virtual machine politician, he controlled the city, and the Tweed Ring was wrought with corruption. Tweed was also in bed with big business, such as the Erie Railroad. Corruption helped take Tweed to the top and helped him maintain his power. However, it also proved to be his downfall. Boss Tweed and his ring were exposed in 1872 for taking kickbacks and robbing the city's treasury—his political career and graft were over. Despite all the corruption, Tweed's leadership also benefited the city. "William Tweed had left enormous footprints on his city," wrote Kenneth D. Ackerman (2005, p. 7), "he had built as grandly as he'd stolen." Many political bosses combined a positive side with all the dishonesty.

Although political bosses, political machines, and graft did not disappear in the first half of the twentieth century, the United States witnessed a series of strong presidential leaders, such as Theodore Roosevelt, Woodrow Wilson, and Franklin D. Roosevelt, as well as Lyndon B. Johnson later in the century. As you will learn in chapter seven, women brought new life to the political process as active participants in the system, and with them came the notion that government should serve the people, all people. Theodore Roosevelt attacked the monopolies of the elite, Wilson created the idea of a global community through the League of Nations to protect the world's citizens, and Franklin D. Roosevelt called for the government to create safety nets for those who were unable to find employment, disabled, too old, or too young to provide for themselves. Johnson sent federal troops into southern states in an attempt to force integration and end segregation.

The democratization of America and much of the world, which began with the American Revolution, eventually allowed the poor, women, and minorities the privileges previously limited to an elite few. We find it difficult to believe today, for example, that less than 100 years ago women were finally given the constitutional right to vote. And don't forget that African Americans, for example, were not allowed to vote or go to school with whites in some southern states until the early 1970s. Of course, women and minorities had played vital leadership roles throughout human history, but their importance had not always been recognized by the male-dominated power structure, the same one that wrote America's history. Democratization, as a result, had a dramatic effect on society's view of those chosen to lead. If men and women were not born with the innate ability to lead, or placed in a position of power by birth as a result of the "will of God," then what made one a leader? These were questions twentieth-century scholars would begin to ponder at length.

■ LEADERSHIP, A NEW ACADEMIC DISCIPLINE

The realization that the difference between the success and failure of an organization can hinge on the behavior of an organization's leaders while interacting with followers led to an increased interest in the field of leadership research. Unlike some other academic fields, the study of leadership is truly interdisciplinary. As the research evolved during the 1900s, scholars in management, organizational behavior, psychology, history, political science, communication, education, and many other disciplines tried to discover the key to leadership success.

Early research in the field of leadership often focused on what characteristics made someone a great leader. The goal was to try to identify specific characteristics that all great leaders possess. Ralph Stogdill and Bernard Bass condensed the enormous volume of research and data and provided an overview of the findings during the 1940s. Their initial results pointed to a series of traits that allow leaders to experience success. Intelligence, persistence, and sociability are some of the most dominant traits they found in leaders. Physical traits are also said to contribute to one's ability to lead (Northouse, 2007). Later studies tried to isolate individual characteristics and behavioral patterns found in successful leaders. Known as "traits studies," these researchers were unable to produce conclusive results.

Most Americans in positions of prominence in universities at the end of the nineteenth century were veterans of the American Civil War. They had experienced the horrors of poor leadership first hand, not only on the field of battle but also in the emerging factories of the rapidly industrializing economies of the world. They were convinced that the battlefield was not the only place one could learn the art of war. They were also convinced that the development of human capital, in the form of leadership, would produce the nation's greatest weapon, educated and prepared leaders.

Jack Shulimson (1993), in his book *The Marine Corps' Search for a Mission, 1880–1898,* noted that the changing political, economic, and technological environment forced the American armed services to institutionalize and standardize education and training programs to meet the challenges created by emerging technology. The Marine Corps, according to Shulimson, was engaged in the "basic search for structure that characterized much of American life during the last decades of the nineteenth century." American business and community leaders of the day, along with military leaders, engaged in a struggle to develop leaders who would meet the needs of an emerging economic and military superpower. The new multinational corporations with thousands of employees, and the large, well-equipped armies of the twentieth century, created previously unimagined challenges.

Military historian and visiting professor at the United States Military Academy Carol Reardon (1990), argues that US military institutions during the late nineteenth and early twentieth centuries began placing greater emphasis on leadership—specifically, the role of "intangibles," such as those lessons learned by historical awareness that might reduce the "likelihood of gross misjudgement in battle." Ironically, the American Historical Association, according to Reardon, was critical of the army's disregard for accepted scholarly standards (Reardon, 1990). The conflict described by Reardon would be the first of many between competing disciplines over the emerging field of leadership studies.

In American factories at the beginning of the twentieth century, changes were also beginning to revolutionize leadership in the workplace. The most important early work in the field of management was done by Frederic Winslow Taylor (1997), who attempted to analyze human behavior systematically in the workplace. His model of management was one of a factory machine with interchangeable human parts (workers), each of which performs one specific function. Each action by all parts of the machine is independently evaluated in order to ensure efficiency. His goal was to improve productivity by removing human variability. While Taylor's approach to management did improve the overall bottom line for corporate America, there was a backlash among workers who resented the dehumanizing effects of the new management system. Workers resented daily production targets and managers hovering over them, watching their every move.

Pioneers of organizational behavior conducted studies in the 1920s in an attempt to determine whether the work environment had an impact on productivity, a novel approach at the time. The best known of these were the Hawthorne Studies, conducted at Western Electric in Cicero, Illinois. The results revealed that organizations are social systems. The workplace environment was one of many variables studied. How people are treated by their bosses, studies revealed, has a tremendous impact on productivity and organizational success. People want to be consulted and feel like part of a team (Weber, 2002). Later research determined that, if properly motivated by the right leadership, employees can be very creative and self-motivated. These obvious conclusions may sound strange to us today, but for most of human history it was believed that workers could not be trusted, were inherently lazy, and could be motivated only by coercion.

James MacGregor Burns, an interdisciplinary social scientist with a Ph.D. in government from Harvard University, forever changed the discussion on leadership when he published what would soon become a standard in the field. His magnum opus, simply titled *Leadership,* was a groundbreaking work. Burns argued that, in order to understand how leaders succeed, researchers must recognize the importance of "collective" motivation (Burns, 1978, pp. 452–53). In short, Burns placed equal importance on the role of both the followers and the leader in organizational success. He approached the study of leadership from a "transformational" perspective. Good leadership, he noted, does not just achieve organizational success; it transforms people's lives. It is a process that motivates all involved and gives them purpose.

In the late 1980s and early 1990s, researchers were engaged in a more holistic approach to leadership study. Leadership studies, quite simply, had evolved into preparing individuals to make the right choices when called upon to do so. And it was now understood that an individual may be the right individual to lead under one set of circumstances, but not necessarily in all circumstances. The concept of the servant-leader, while by no means a contemporary idea, was also embraced by most leadership scholars after the release of Robert Greenleaf's seminal work, *Servant Leadership,* in 1977. Today, many college courses include a **service learning** component designed specifically to incorporate hands-on community service as part of the curriculum (refer to Service Learning side bar on page 21 in chapter one).

The study of leadership is an ever-evolving and expanding field. The works of Burns and Greenleaf, while now considered classics in the field of leadership studies, only accelerated the interest in the field of leadership studies. Burns and Greenleaf opened the floodgates for the new theories and paradigms that would continue to emerge well into the new millennium. Since 1980, the study of leadership has become one of the fastest-growing disciplines in the academy. More than 900 universities in the United States now offer a major, minor, certificate, or graduate degree program in leadership studies (Sorenson, 2000). Several universities now offer leadership programs specifically tailored for women and minorities.

■ LEADERSHAPE

Jenell Barnard, Contributing Author

LeaderShape family clusters, like this one hosted by CMU, foster a sense of family within the group through self-disclosure, team-building activities, and reflection coordinated by a facilitator.

Photo courtesy of Daniel M. Gaken.

One of the most widely recognized leadership development programs for young adults, LeaderShape has been committed to helping men and women lead with integrity for over twenty years. Initially conceived in the 1980s by a group of fraternity men at the University of Illinois Urbana–Champaign, as a way to help their fraternity chapter create a vision of the future and an action plan to make their vision a reality, the program was so successful that soon students from across the university were clamoring to attend. Realizing the potential impact of the program, the creators wisely decided to establish a non-profit organization to manage the LeaderShape Institute.

A session of the LeaderShape Institute is comprised of about sixty young adults, a faculty member, and two lead facilitators. Each day of the Leader-Shape session is intense and demanding. However, though twelve-hour days may seem intimidating, each is packed with interactive and engaging activities. While much of the instruction occurs with the entire group in the "learning community," the most intense portions of the program take place within "family clusters." Cluster Facilitators lead and help foster a sense of family within the group through self-disclosure, team-building activities, and reflection. Their most crucial role is to serve as a vision coach as the students examine their passions and values to develop bold and compelling vision statements of the world as they would like to see it.

The end product is powerful and the work of LeaderShape graduates can be seen around the world. Ashley Radawski, a graduate of the Central Michigan University LeaderShape Institute, had a vision to help eradicate the dangerous land mines still remaining in Vietnam. As part of her action plan, Ashley focused on individuals who were significantly affected by the late war for support and inspiration. Through a number of fundraising initiatives, Ashley and nine other CMU students participated in a service outreach program in Vietnam. Her commitment led to the reclamation of lands previously riddled with dangerous mines. While in Vietnam, she also helped build playgrounds on lands purchased and made safe by her efforts. This is just one of many such examples of how LeaderShape has changed our world for the better.

LeaderShape's success continues, with students traveling annually from colleges and universities across the nation to the Allerton Conference Center in Illinois. The first campus-based LeaderShape program was held at the University of Michigan in the early 1990s. Since that first session in Ann Arbor, campuses all across the United States have also hosted sessions. In 2007, the first international program was launched in Qatar, followed by sessions in both Mexico and Canada. For more information about the LeaderShape Institute, visit www.leadershape.org.

The International Leadership Association **(ILA),** whose membership consists of scholars, students, researchers, and others who have an interest in the field, was established in 1999. The first ILA conference was held in Atlanta, followed by the 2000 conference in Toronto, Canada, which was attended by 300 participants from across the globe. Within a year of its founding, the organization had hired a two-person staff, an executive director, and a program director (Cherrey & Wilsey, 2007). The organization now hosts meetings and conferences around the world for individuals interested in exchanging ideas and research related to the field of leadership studies.

Leadership Quarterly *(LQ)* and *Leadership Review,* two peer-reviewed academic journals dedicated to the study of leadership, were first published in 1990 and 2001, respectively, in response to increased demand from the academic community. A third publication, the quarterly *Journal of Leadership Studies,* is also a helpful resource for the emergent leader. *LQ* is affiliated with the International Leadership Association and regularly solicits articles from presenters at ILA conferences. ILA members are also eligible for discounted subscriptions to *LQ. Leadership Review,* an on-line journal available at www.leadershipreview.org, is published quarterly by the Kravis Leadership Institute of Claremont McKenna College.

The first hands-on programs designed to prepare individuals for leadership roles, however, were not developed in universities. Most early leadership training programs, as we have already discussed, were developed by industry or the military.

Ironically, one of America's most recognized and successful leadership programs for youth did not have an institutional foundation at all. Inspired by 1952 Nobel Peace Prize recipient Albert Schweitzer, Hugh O'Brian saw a need and wanted to make a difference. The Hugh O'Brian Youth **(HOBY)** Leadership Program, founded in 1958 by O'Brian, who portrayed lawman Wyatt Earp on broadcast television, is perhaps the most respected youth leadership program in the world. Limited initially to young high school males from the Los Angeles area, women joined in 1972, and since 1982 HOBY has offered annual high school leadership seminars for young men and women in all fifty states and in many foreign countries. Seminars hosted by HOBY strive to follow the motto of the organization, which is to teach students "how to think, not what to think." Boasting an alumni base of more than 355,000, HOBY is arguably the largest leadership program in the United States, if not the entire world (*The History of HOBY,* 2007). Similar youth programs, not affiliated with HOBY, have since developed in many states. Young adults ages seventeen through twenty-five can develop their leadership skills through programs such as the LeaderShape. LeaderShape Institutes are intensive educational programs designed to encourage and educate young adults who desire to become extraordinary leaders (refer to the LeaderShape sidebar on page 70).

Actor Hugh O'Brian, founder of The Hugh O'Brian Youth (HOBY) Leadership Program, addresses students at a recent HOBY event.

Photo courtesy HOBY.

Your study of leadership should not end with your college career. Leadership training is a lifelong endeavor. As you move through your life and career, you will probably want to revisit your beliefs and thoughts on leadership. There are thousands of leadership programs available to individuals who want to succeed in the academic, business, or non-profit world. Many cities, for example, offer leadership programs for business and community leaders. Now, more than ever before in human history, the importance of leadership preparation and training is considered a vital part of personal and organizational growth and success.

■ KEY TERMS

Authority—The right of someone to direct the behavior of others by right of position held within a social structure or hierarchy.

HOBY—Hugh O'Brian Youth Leadership Program, which is one of the oldest and largest leadership programs in the world.

ILA—International Leadership Association, whose membership consists of scholars, students, researchers, and others who have an interest in the field leadership studies.

Leadership Quarterly—An academic journal dedicated to the study and research of leadership. *LQ* is affiliated with the ILA.

Legitimacy—The right of an individual to lead that, in both a social and psychological sense, is granted by followers.

Niccolo Machiavelli—The sixteenth-century Italian diplomat who authored *The Prince* and other texts designed to help monarchs be more successful.

Service Learning—Educational experience in which students participate in organized community service–related activities for course credit.

Social Darwinism—The social theory promoting the belief that nature and natural selection determine who will be leaders and followers.

Sun Tzu—The Chinese general and philosopher who authored the *Art of War*.

■ SUGGESTED READINGS

Machiavelli, N. 1999. *The Prince.* George Bull (trans.). New York: Penguin Books.

McCullough, D. 2001. *John Adams.* New York: Simon & Schuster.

Tzu, S. 2003. *The Art of War.* Dallas Galvin (ed.). Lionel Giles (trans.). New York: Barnes & Noble Classics.

Weber, M. 1964. *The Theory of Social and Economic Organization.* New York: Free Press.

■ REFERENCES

Ackerman, K. D. 2005. *Boss Tweed: The Rise and Fall of the Corrupt Pol Who Conceived the Soul of Modern New York*. New York: Carroll & Graf.

Blackburn, R. 1988. *The Overthrow of Colonial Slavery, 1776–1848*. London: Verso.

Burns, J. M. 1998. *Leadership*. New York: Harper & Row.

Carnegie, A. 1889. "Wealth." In *An American Primer*, D. J. Boorstin (ed). Chicago: The University of Chicago Press, 1966.

Cherrey, C. & Wilsey, S. 2007. *A Brief History of the International Leadership Association*. http://www.ila-net.org/About/history.htm.

Corning, P. A. 2005. *Holistic Darwinism: Synergy, Cybernetics, and the Bioeconomics of Evolution*. Chicago: University of Chicago Press.

Ellis, J. J. 2004. *His Excellency George Washington*. New York: Alfred A. Knopf.

Green, W. A. 1998. "Periodizing World History." In *World History: Ideologies, Structures, and Identities*, P. Pomper, R. H. Elphick, & R. T. Vann (eds). Malden, MA: Blackwell.

Greene, J. 1998. *Pure and Simple Politics: The American Federation of Labor and Political Activism, 1881–1917*. New York: Cambridge University Press.

History of HOBY (The). 2007. www.hoby.org/about/history/html.

Holy Bible. 1994. Grand Rapids, MI: Zondervan.

Lincoln, Abraham letter to Joshua Speed dated 24 August 1855. 1953. *The Collected Works of Abraham Lincoln*, Vol. II, R. P. Basler (ed). New Brunswick, NJ: Rutgers University Press.

Machiavelli, N. 1999. *The Prince*. George Bull (trans.). New York: Penguin Books.

Marx, K. 1893. *Communist Manifesto*. New York: Labor News.

McCullough, D. 2001. *John Adams*. New York: Simon & Schuster.

Northouse, P. G. 2007. *Leadership: Theory and Practice*. London: Sage (4th Edition).

Reardon, C. 1990. *Soldiers and Scholars: The US Army and the Uses of Military History, 1865–1920*. Lawrence: University of Kansas Press.

Shulimson, J. 1993. *The Marine Corps' Search for a Mission, 1880–1898*. Lawrence: University of Kansas Press.

Sorenson, G. 2000. *An Intellectual History of Leadership Studies*. Paper presented at the annual meeting of the American Political Science Association, Washington, DC, August 31–September 3.

Taylor, F. W. 1997. *The Principles of Scientific Management*. Mineola, NY: Dover.

Tocqueville, A. de. 2000. *Democracy in America*, H. C. Mansfield & D. Winthrop (eds.). Chicago: The University Chicago Press.

Trachtenberg, A. 2007. *The Incorporation of America: Culture and Society in the Gilded Age*, New York: Hill & Wang.

Tzu, S. 2003. *The Art of War*. Dallas Galvin (ed.). Lionel Giles (trans.). New York: Barnes & Noble Classics.

Weber, A. 2002. "The Hawthorne Works." *Assembly Magazine*, August 1.

Weber, M. 1964. *The Theory of Social and Economic Organization*. New York: Free Press.

CHAPTER THREE REVIEW QUESTIONS

1. How do early writings on leadership differ in focus from more recent texts on the subject? What was their primary objective?

_____

_____

_____

2. Critics often dismiss Machiavelli because he places considerable importance on staying in power by almost any means if one has good intentions. Do you agree with his philosophy that the "end justifies the means"? Why or why not? Explain.

_____

_____

_____

3. The findings of Stogdill and Bass pointed to specific traits that allow leaders to experience success. What are two of them? Do you agree that they are important leadership traits? Why or why not? Explain.

_____

_____

_____

4. Shulimson seems to argue that American business and the US military were driven by economic and political forces to develop leaders that would meet the needs of an emerging economic and military superpower. Do you agree or disagree with his assessment of what has driven modern leadership development? In your opinion, how is his approach different from what drove people such as Hammurabi or Machiavelli to pontificate about leadership development? Explain.

_____

_____

_____

5. In your opinion, how democratic are we as a society? Do you agree with the assessment of the authors that only the elite, and not the average American, can run for the presidency? Why or why not?

_____

_____

_____

CHAPTER THREE SELF-TEST

1. For the earliest of nomadic peoples, identifying qualities of those who might be best suited to lead was of vital importance because failure might mean _____ and _____.

2. In his book *The Theory of Social and Economic Organization,* Max Weber wrote of the linkage among leadership, _____, and _____.

3. _____ is the academic journal affiliated with the International Leadership Association that is dedicated to the study and research of leadership.

4. _____was the final nail in the coffin of faith-driven states in Europe and their leaders who claimed God had divinely selected them by right of birth to lead others.

5. The model of management developed by _____was one of a factory machine with interchangeable human parts (workers), each of which performs one specific function.

6. More than _____universities in the United States now offer a major, minor, certificate, or graduate degree program in leadership studies.

7. _____, an on-line journal, is published quarterly by the Kravis Leadership Institute of Claremont McKenna College.

8. Military historian Carol Reardon argues that US military institutions during the late nineteenth century began placing greater emphasis on the role of _____.

9. The Grimké sisters challenged the social system at a time when most women were forbidden to _____ in public.

10. _____ is one of the most respected youth leadership programs in the world.

Servant-Leadership

John A.
Kline

■ SEEKING TO SERVE OTHERS

Servant-leaders lead because it is the best way for them to serve others. Their desire to serve causes them to seek leadership opportunities. Robert Greenleaf, who popularized the term **servant-leader** and is credited with starting the current emphasis on servant-leadership, said, "It begins with the natural feeling that one wants to serve, to serve first. Then conscious choice brings one to aspire to lead. This is sharply different from the person who is leader first, perhaps because of the need to assuage an unusual power drive or to acquire material possessions." (Greenleaf, 1970, p. 7)

The term *servant-leadership* brings to mind public servants, clergypersons, and others in the helping professions, yet more and more individuals in today's corporate world strive to be servant-leaders because it is the right thing to do and because it yields greater personal satisfaction. But there is also a utilitarian reason for being a servant-leader; servant-leadership promotes follower and employee satisfaction—and satisfied people are productive people. Simply stated, people accomplish more under servant-leadership.

■ WHO WAS ROBERT GREENLEAF?

Robert Greenleaf was born in Terre Haute, Indiana, in 1904. After graduating from Carleton College in Minnesota, Greenleaf went to work for AT&T. In 1964, after thirty-eight years with the company, he retired; his final position was director of management and research. During his last years at AT&T, Greenleaf, known as a "seeker" (influenced to be one by his Quaker background) and a person with revolutionary ideas, lectured at the Massachusetts Institute of Technology's Sloan School of Management and the Harvard School of Business, as well as holding teaching positions at both Dartmouth College and the University of Virginia.

On his retirement, Greenleaf founded the Center for Applied Ethics. It was the first step in what would become his twenty-five-year second career of writing, speaking, and consulting to universities, corporations, foundations, churches, and not-for-profit organizations. During his early years at the center, Greenleaf wondered why so many young people were rebelling against the nation's institutions during the 1960s. He concluded that institutions were doing a poor job of leading because they were doing a poor job of serving. Greenleaf's conclusion was influenced by his religious beliefs, his long experience in attempting to shape institutions, and finally by the effect of having read Hermann Hesse's short novel *Journey to the East*—an account of a mythical journey by a group of people on a spiritual quest. Greenleaf concluded the story's central meaning was that a great leader must first of all be a servant. True leadership emerges from the desire to help others.

Thus, in 1970, Greenleaf published a powerful essay titled "The Servant as Leader," which said true leaders seek first to serve. Two years later, he published another essay, "The Institution as Servant," contending that institutions can also be servants. As he became more aware of the effect of trustees on companies, he wrote "Trustees as Servants." These foundational essays, along with others that relate servant-leadership to businesses, churches, education, foundations, and society, appear in *Servant Leadership: A Journey into the Nature of Legitimate Power and Greatness* (Greenleaf, 2002). Throughout all his writings and lectures, Greenleaf's main premise was that those who lead best are those who seek to serve.

By the time of his death in 1990, Greenleaf had forever left his mark on the discipline of leadership studies though his lectures, consulting, and written works; however, as a practicing servant-leader, he had also influenced others by his life—a life devoted to improving the people and institutions around him. Soon after his death, his private writings were published; those recently discovered writings, along with those previously published, have had a strong impact on the study of leadership. Two collections of Greenleaf's private writings, *On Becoming a Servant Leader* and *Seeker and Servant: Reflections on Religious Leadership,* give insight into the man who is responsible for the emphasis today on servant-leadership (Frick & Spears, 1996). In 1984, Greenleaf's Center for Applied Ethics was renamed the Robert K. Greenleaf Center for Servant Leadership. Today, the mission of this not-for-profit institution is "to fundamentally improve the caring and quality of all institutions through a new approach to leadership, structure, and decision making." The center's website features an on-line catalogue, information, resources, membership information, and more. Visit http://www.greenleaf.org to see the resources offered by the Greenleaf Center and the number of leading writers and practitioners of leadership who have written about and endorsed servant-leadership.

Although Greenleaf popularized the term *servant-leader,* and many others encourage individuals to be servant-leaders, the concept has been around for thousands of years. In the East, Kautilya, a fourth-century thinker from India, said a king or leader should consider as good not what pleases self but what pleases the subjects or followers (Shamasastry, 1923). In the West, Jesus influenced Christian thought by his claim that he came not to be served but to serve, and he reminded his followers in Mark 10:43 that "whoever wants to become great among you must be your servant" (Committee on Bible Translation, 1978). In a period of human history when autocratic power and status were paramount, these radical ideas of submission and service to others were perceived as a threat to the status quo. The Romans executed people for saying such things. One of the most influential writers and teachers of our time, Ken Blanchard, co-authored a book showing how the servant-leadership principles taught by Jesus can be used effectively by leaders of today in any area of life (Blanchard & Hodges, 2003).

Jesus, according to author Ken Blanchard, taught servant-leadership principles that can be used effectively by leaders today.

Library of Congress.

■ BECOMING A SERVANT-LEADER

It takes more than just wanting to be an effective servant-leader to be one. Desire is not enough—although it is a good start. You need two other things—character and competency. **Character** is who you are. **Competency** is what you can do. To be effective, servant-leaders must have a desire to lead because they believe it is the best way for them to serve; they must have the competency or leadership skills and abilities to lead; and, finally, they must possess strong character—the moral, ethical, and spiritual values necessary to lead. These three attributes are needed, no matter what leadership style you use.

Your Leadership Style

In chapter one, you were introduced briefly to some basic styles of leadership. Servant-leadership is often discussed as a "style," or class, of leadership in the same way some discuss authoritative or participative leadership styles. But servant-leadership is more than a style of leading—it is a way of living. Perhaps

Leadership Challenge

Identify five of your areas of competency. What three competencies do you value that you do not personally possess? What can you do to achieve competency in those areas?

this can be understood best by taking a much more in-depth look at the major styles of leadership. Although some writers list as many as a dozen different styles of leadership, most who study the discipline have focused on three major styles: autocratic, or authoritarian; participative, or democratic; and delegative, sometimes associated with free-reign or laizze-faire styles of leadership (Department of the Army, 1973).

Authoritarian Leadership

In authoritarian leadership in its purest form, the leader tells what to do and how to do it. At times, this style is both necessary and effective. When leaders know what needs to be done, when they have all the information or resources needed to do it, and when time is short and followers are well motivated, authoritarian leadership works well. Authoritarian leadership is ineffective if others don't recognize and respect leaders' authority, competency, and character. Authoritarian leadership should not be confused with "bossing people around." This is not the authoritarian style; rather, it is abusive, it is demeaning to followers, and it should have no place in the servant-leader's repertoire. While the authoritarian style should not be overused by servant-leaders, there are times when it is appropriate and effective.

Military commanders, corporate managers, classroom teachers, clergypersons, and parents must at times be authoritarian. Imagine a commander in the heat of battle taking time to ask soldiers if they think it is a good idea to take a hill, to retreat, or to follow a given course of action; or think what would happen if an experienced teacher were to let her high school students decide what to study and whether they should take tests. Finally, what responsible parent would let a three-year-old decide whether to play in the street or drink cleaning fluids? The fact is, all servant leaders must at times be authoritarian.

Participative Leadership

Participative leadership, also often referred to as democratic leadership, motivates and encourages followers by involving them in decision making. Followers' involvement in the process yields a high level of happiness and satisfaction with the task, with themselves, and with others around them; it builds their feeling of self-worth and makes them feel a part of the organization and what is going on. But there is another benefit: Involvement helps individuals develop their skills. Furthermore, they feel more in control of their own destiny (such as getting the promotion they desire), and they are motivated to work hard for more than just financial award or recognition.

While the authoritative style may yield faster results, the extra time needed for the participative style often compensates by yielding better decisions and is particularly effective if the leader has only part of the information and followers have other information or can get access to it. Leaders aren't expected to have all the information; that's why they want expert and knowledgeable people on their teams. Participation in decision making may involve a large group of people—perhaps even the entire membership of the group, company, or organization—but one fact remains: The leader always retains final responsibility for the group's decisions and actions.

Delegative Leadership

Delegative, or laissez-faire, leadership demonstrates trust in followers by giving them specific responsibilities. Delegation demonstrates a leader's confidence in the competency and character of the one to whom tasks or responsibilities have been delegated. The leader expects good decisions and actions from the delegate. As Jesus reminded in Luke 12:48, "From everyone who has been given much, much will be demanded" (Committee on Bible Translation, 1978). As with the other two styles of leadership, the leader retains final responsibility for the decisions and actions of the group. Since servant-leaders want to do what is best for the group—institution, organization, team, and so on—they should delegate carefully. More specifically, they must select the right person to delegate something to, communicate clearly what they expect, assign the necessary authority and support for getting the job done, give honest feedback, and be available, so that delegates can communicate with them when guidance is needed (Kline, 2006).

Effective servant-leaders will use all three leadership styles as appropriate, but with each style the leader must assume responsibility for the decisions and actions of the group. With that thought in mind, true servant-leaders give credit to others when things go well and take the blame when things go poorly. Leaders who give credit and take blame build strong relationships with group members and demonstrate concern not only for getting the job done but also for the people doing it.

Your Leadership Focus

Every servant-leader faces the challenge of getting the job done while caring for the needs and concerns of followers. For years, theorists and writers have asked whether leaders should focus on the **task** (the mission, the job to be done) or on the **people** (the group of followers, the organization, or the team). *They should do both.* In order to understand better the necessity of focusing on both the task and the people, consider situations in which a leader puts focus on either one or the other.

Task Focus

Task-focused leaders generally consider the task or job to be done as more important than the individuals doing it. Furthermore, this type of leader may believe individuals lack a desire to achieve, are unwilling to assume responsibility, and are incapable of directing their own behavior. Therefore, individuals must be told what to do and how to do it. Furthermore, this type of leader often believes individuals are indifferent to group goals. Task-focused leaders may communicate their distrust or lack of confidence in followers by withholding information, giving orders, controlling upward and lateral communication in the group, and actually discouraging open communication. Followers often respond by trying to discover "company secrets;" they resist taking on responsibility, start rumors (since the truth is withheld from them), and demonstrate the very indifference to group goals the leader expected. They simply fulfill the leader's expectations.

The task for these emerging servant-leaders is building a house for a needy family.

Photo courtesy of Dave and Cindy Baar.

People Focus

People-focused leaders often believe human relations are so important that conflicts and tensions must be reduced at all cost. They believe individuals are intrinsically motivated to work and assume responsibility and that participative decision making is always best. They communicate this focus by attempting to satisfy the needs and desires of individuals even at the expense of deemphasizing the mission of the group or organization—that is, at the expense of getting the job done. This type of leader often lets individual concerns override task accomplishment. Followers often respond by creating an appearance of harmony while relieving conflicts elsewhere—at home, with friends, or in other social groups and settings. Furthermore, if and when individuals do receive directives from leaders and those in authority over them, they often react with dissatisfaction, displeasure, and even rebellion. Consider when children who have spent a week with doting and indulgent grandparents return home to parents who wish to exert more authority over them; they often rebel against the parents' tighter rein.

Dual Focus

Dual-focused leaders focus appropriately on both the task and the people. They understand the importance of being flexible, sometimes focusing more on the task and at other times on people concerns. They are what Hersey and Blanchard refer to as situational leaders (Hersey & Blanchard, 2000). Dual-focused leaders know that followers are not usually resistant to group needs; in fact, they realize that individual and group needs are often consistent. If the group, team, organization, or company thrives, so do group members, team members, or employees. If the group fails, individuals will suffer. Dual-focused leaders demonstrate a willingness to adjust and adapt to individual needs when possible. But they also expect a certain return from individuals, for the job must be done. Individuals with this type of leader respond by showing increased esteem for themselves and others in the group. They communicate more openly among themselves and with those in leadership positions. Productivity increases and individual behavior falls in line with group or organization objectives. Servant-leaders must maintain a balance between their concern for the task and their concern for the people. This fact is true irrespective of the style of leadership—authoritarian, participative, or delegative—the leader is using at the time.

■ CHARACTERISTICS OF SERVANT-LEADERS

Although leaders are unique individuals influenced by their backgrounds and experiences, five characteristics are found in successful servant-leaders. They communicate a strategic vision, listen to understand, implement change, motivate others, and mentor future leaders.

Servant-Leaders Communicate a Strategic Vision

Leaders must be able to communicate a strategic vision. A **vision** is a mental portrait that guides the group's behavior toward a goal. Many leaders have a vision, but in order to achieve success the vision must be strategic. It must not only tell people which way to go but also must provide a strategy, or plan, for getting there. Proverbs 29:18 says, "Where there is no vision the people perish." (Schofield Reference Edition, 2000) Effective servant-leaders know the requirements of a strategic vision, how to develop the vision, and how to communicate it to others.

Knowing the Requirements
Knowing the requirements for strategic visioning will help you develop and communicate the vision. Here are five requirements for strategic visioning:

- *It must be group-specific.* Although you can learn much from studying the vision statements of other groups, their vision will seldom be your vision. Your vision will spring from the group, its individuals, and where it needs to go or what it should do. The vision must fit the group.
- *It must be attractive.* The vision must attract followers. It must be something they want to do or something of which they want to be a part. To be attractive, the vision must be meaningful and worthwhile. Individuals participate in, invest time in, expend energy toward, and commit financial resources to things that are attractive and meaningful to them.

- *It must be challenging.* A vision must challenge people. Over several years, many people at my school, Troy University in Alabama, willingly participated in helping implement a vision and strategic plan to combine four major campuses, an e-campus, and dozens of worldwide sites to implement shared policies and procedures, remove barriers to academic transfer, and promote a worldwide brand identity for "students who wish to excel in a globally competitive world." The challenge to make positive changes motivated Troy University personnel to work together on a difficult task.

- *It must be realistic.* While a certain amount of idealism may be appropriate and even motivating, the vision should be achievable. For a leader of a small group with few resources and no significant financial backing to have a vision to start a new brick-and-mortar institution, such as Troy University, would be unrealistic, unachievable, and demotivating. The vision and the goal it points toward must be attainable. People must possess hope to accomplish the vision. Dr. Jack Hawkins, Jr., chancellor of Troy University says, "True leadership is the management of hope" (Hawkins, 2008).

- *It must be strategic.* A vision is where the group, organization, company, or team plans to be at a given point in the future. Simply stating where you want to be is not enough. You must have a plan to get there. The adage "If you fail to plan, you plan to fail" is true. The vision must be accompanied by a strategic plan that gives specific steps and milestones for how to achieve the goal. The total vision bridges now to the future and provides people with the hope of achieving it. But how do leaders develop a strategic vision?

Developing the Vision

Formulating a vision is a crucial task for leaders. You may be afraid you don't possess enough natural visionary ability to develop a strategic vision. Take heart! Strategic visions are not developed by a single person in isolation. The following five things will ensure you have a good strategic vision.

- *Learn all you can about the group or organization.* Remember, the vision must be group-specific; it must fit the group. There is no substitute for a thorough understanding of the organization to provide a foundation for the strategic vision.

- *Bring others into the visioning process.* Don't try to do it alone. Involve other officers, the next level of supervisors, people at the lowest level of the organization, and other interested parties, including those with whom you interact or do business.

- *Keep an open mind.* Leaders should not solicit input with no intention of listening or being open to ideas. First, this action limits the amount of information that goes into developing the strategic vision. Second, people see through this type of leadership, lose respect for leaders, and are reluctant to support the vision and work to make it a reality.

- *Write a vision statement.* This statement will guide development of the strategic plan. Avoid being too terse or too long-winded. A vision must be more than a slogan or a "bumper sticker." The US Postal Service slogan "We deliver for you" is a good marketing tool, but it doesn't capture all the essential elements of a vision. On the other hand, a statement telling the organization's philosophy and strategic plan is too complex to be the vision statement. The key is to strike a balance.

■ *Develop the strategic plan.* The strategic plan tells the strategy, or ways decisions will be made; how the necessary changes will occur; and the way capital and human resources will be allocated to pursue the strategy. The plan answers three questions—usually in some detail. What do we do? For whom do we do it? How well do we do it? For businesses or competitive teams, the last question becomes "How do we beat the competition?"

Communicating the Vision

Sharing the vision is the key to success. Many efforts to institute a strategic vision fail due to poor communication. Here are five important elements to consider when communicating the vision.

■ *Be sure of your credibility.* Earlier, we said leaders need to possess strong character and competency. These are two major determinants of credibility. If others believe you have these qualities, along with a desire to serve and put the needs of the group and the people ahead of your own, you will be considered credible. Servant-leaders strive for credibility.

■ *Don't try to do it alone.* Engage the help of others in the organization to communicate the strategic vision. This is important for three reasons. Involving others in communicating the vision gets "buy-in," or commitment, from them. Second, individuals need to hear the strategic vision communicated to them from those they work for and with on a day-to-day basis—both to receive information from them and to have someone nearby to field their questions. Third, more people talking about the vision will generate more excitement and enthusiasm.

■ *Inform all constituencies.* Everyone affected by the vision—those inside the group or organization and those without—must be fully informed. Failure to communicate the vision and answer questions is most often the reason leaders are unable to accomplish goals and achieve group or organizational success.

■ *Help them see their role.* The biggest resistance to a new strategic vision is fear of change or failure to see positive effects on those affected by the vision. If people realize the positive effects of implementing the new vision, see how they can make necessary changes, and know the role they will play once the vision has been realized, they will be more supportive and will work to make it happen. Later, we will discuss how leaders help people adjust to change.

■ *Ensure communication goes both ways.* Effective communication goes two ways. It is not just one person doing all the communicating. When communicating anything—especially a vision that requires change—make certain to allow more time for listening than for speaking. Larry Spears, who was CEO of the Greenleaf Center for Servant-Leadership for nearly two decades, believes listening is the chief characteristic of servant-leaders (Spears, 2000).

Servant-Leaders Listen to Understand

Servant-leaders listen. They listen to find out what is going on and they listen to understand and show positive regard for those around them. Leaders won't be effective and may not stay long in their position if they don't listen well. Chief executive officers and senior managers almost universally agree poor listening is the number one problem in organizations. They are equally convinced that good listening is a major determinant of success (Kline, 2003, p. 6). Servant-leaders must be able to listen empathically, listen critically, and listen to gain information.

Empathic Listening

Empathic listening is the hallmark of servant-leadership. Empathic listening is crucial for servant-leaders who focus on serving others and the needs of society. Don't confuse empathy with sympathy. Sympathy is a feeling of compassion for another. Empathy is feeling and thinking *with* another person. The true empathic listener is able to get into the world of another—to see, hear, feel, and understand as that person does. Empathic listening builds trust and respect and communicates to others that you care about them and care what they are saying. How can you be a better empathic listener?

- *Want to listen.* True servant-leaders listen not only with their ears but also with their nonverbal behavior. Once when a colleague came into my office to talk, my eyes began to wander over the pile of work on my desk. I shifted uncomfortably in my chair. My colleague read my body language and excused himself, saying he would return when I had more time. I protested I was really listening to him, but my body language told a different story. Good empathic listeners communicate with their whole being that they want to listen.
- *Encourage others to share.* Noncommittal acknowledging responses—such as "uh-huh," "I see," or "Tell me more"—encourage others to keep talking. Nonverbal acknowledgments, such as head nodding, facial expressions, and a relaxed body expression, demonstrate interest in what the person is saying. Maintaining appropriate eye contact with others—not staring, not looking around the room, but looking into their eyes while maintaining an "understanding" look on your face—communicates you care about what the person is saying.
- *Don't interrupt.* Think about somebody that has a habit of interrupting others. It's difficult to share with such a person. Often, when individuals decide to share something with a leader, they have thought through what they want to say. Interruptions hinder the flow of information and, even worse, may intimidate the person doing the talking. Furthermore, interruptions often communicate rudeness, certainly not what a servant-leader wishes to communicate to others. Take note how many times you interrupt others. The results may startle and embarrass you, but they may start you on the path to reducing or even eliminating such behavior.
- *Avoid being judgmental.* One of the surest ways to prevent individuals from sharing openly and honestly is to pass judgment on them for things they tell you. Remember to judge what they say and not to judge them for telling you something. The less judgmental you are, the more people will tell you, for they won't fear judgment or retribution.

- *Avoid defensiveness.* About fifteen years ago, when I was a senior executive leader of a large organization, I realized I needed to be careful not to insulate myself from true feedback. One of my most valued subordinates would regularly ask if he could speak with me. He was very respectful and would often begin, "Sir, you may fire me for what I am about to say, but here is the way I see it . . ." I was careful not to interrupt him or become defensive. He was the last person I wanted to fire; he told me what I needed to know. Hans Christian Anderson told of a leader—an emperor who bought a suit of clothes from a couple of swindlers who told him stupid people or those not fit to be emperor would be unable to see the suit. The emperor allowed himself to be dressed in the suit and parade through town. Neither the townspeople nor the emperor wanted to admit they could not see the suit of clothes, for they didn't want others to think they were stupid. Everyone wildly praised the magnificent clothes—all but one small child, who said, "But he has nothing on!" Servant-leaders need people who will speak the truth. Avoiding defensiveness increases the chances of that happening.
- *Reflect back on what the person said.* Instead of responding immediately to what people say, focus on their words to show you understand. Instead of asking a lot of questions, giving advice, or taking issue with what others tell you, summarize the essence of what they have just said. This practice demonstrates you were listening, causes you to think again about what they have just said, and gives speakers a chance to clarify what they have said if your summary shows you don't understand. Furthermore, the practice keeps you focused on what others say, rather than on what you want to say.

Critical Listening

Critical listening is necessary for leaders who must make important decisions and lead others in making decisions that affect the well-being of the group, the individuals in the group, and those outside the group. How can you be a better critical listener?

- *Know yourself.* Know your strengths and your weaknesses. Know your good times and bad times; for instance, some people should never make critical decisions first thing in the morning or after they have just paid bills or had an argument with a friend. Know yourself, so that you can assess things that may affect your judgment. Servant-leaders must know themselves before they can lead others.
- *Take responsibility.* You are responsible for yourself, your actions, and your decisions. Many people rationalize to provide themselves and others what they consider to be justifiable reasons for their actions; they explain or blame things on their environment, other people, or the way they were raised. Unless you know yourself, admit your mistakes, and take responsibility for yourself, you will not be an effective servant-leader. To know yourself, first understand how your knowledge, beliefs, attitudes, experiences, and feelings have affected your life; second, explore repetitive behavior patterns and the origins and consequences of your behaviors; and third, make conscious decisions to change things that need changing.

- *Keep an open mind.* Making up your mind before getting all the facts or hearing other points of view greatly limits your effectiveness as a leader. Confident leaders welcome new information because it gives them more data to make a decision or lead a group in making decisions. Don't be like the leader who said, "Don't confuse me with facts; my mind is already made up."

- *Consider the source.* Information is no better than its source. Ask yourself whether the person providing the information has a hidden agenda or stands to gain from your acting favorably on it. Apply both the competency test and the trustworthiness test to sources of information. For example, a salesperson for a certain brand of computer hardware might be an expert in computers, but, because she wants to sell her brand, I might question whether or not she is unbiased. She would be a competent source of information, but perhaps not a trustworthy source of information on what brand I should purchase. My good friend who knows nothing about computers would be trustworthy, but he lacks the competency to help me decide what brand to buy. Make certain the source is both competent and trustworthy.

- *Delay the decision if you're not sure.* Many leaders believe indecision shows weakness. This is not always true. Making *poor decisions* demonstrates weakness in listening and thinking critically. It also demonstrates ineptitude. If you don't have enough information or are unsure, take extra time to study the issue. I made far more mistakes as a leader by acting hastily than I ever did by delaying until I could listen to more information.

Informative Listening

Informative listening, or listening to gain information, is important for everyone, but it is especially important to leaders who need to process large amounts of information to stay informed. Here are four things you can do to be a better informed listener:

- *Be ready to listen.* Business briefings and reports waste no time in getting to the heart of the matter. If you are not ready to listen from the time the speaker opens his or her mouth, you may be spending the rest of the time trying to catch up. And often if you miss the first few words, the rest of the message makes little sense. When others begin to talk, be ready to listen. Effective listeners are in the spring-loaded position. They are ready to listen.

- *Adjust to the situation.* Many things affect how well we do or don't hear—our emotional or physical health; environmental factors, such as room temperature or outside noise; and stress factors, such as weariness or things weighing on our mind. Skilled listeners work hard to offset or minimize such things. If you must listen carefully early in the afternoon, consider eating a light lunch, so that you will be less apt to get sleepy. If you must listen to challenging material, do background reading on the subject to help you understand what you will hear. Skilled listeners take the steps necessary to adjust to the listening situation.

- *Focus on the key ideas.* Skilled public speakers present their main points very clearly, so that the audience will focus on them. In the same way, skilled listeners look for the key ideas or main points and keep focused on them, rather than letting their mind drift off to less important things. Decide what information is most important and what information is simply nice to know, or extraneous; then focus on the important information.

■ *Relate what you hear to what you already know.* Effective listeners don't see new information as discrete pieces of knowledge; instead, they fit it to what they already know. Students often commit facts to rote memory when studying for a test on a subject unfamiliar to them, and they forget them as quickly as they memorized them. On the other hand, studying for a test on a familiar subject is easier; facts make sense because they fit with what is already known. Strive to fit everything you hear with what you already know. It makes listening and learning easier.

Servant-Leaders Implement Positive Change

As discussed earlier, leaders must carefully communicate a strategic vision to others in order to get buy-in. Much of the challenge comes because people resist change. They resist because they fear that the new way might not be better, they might lose control, or they might be unable to function effectively in the new situation. With the accelerating rate of change in most organizations, people and things must keep pace. Servant-leaders know that, rather than forcing change, the way to keep organizations and their people healthy is to involve them in the process. After both leading change and being an observer of change, I discovered seven steps to implementing positive change (Kline, 2007, pp. 35–38).

Seven Steps to Implementing Positive Change

■ *Assess and address human concerns.* Servant-leaders serve others and the organization. Most organizations claim to put people first because people are their greatest asset; servant-leaders actually do it. They invest time and effort into listening and understanding human concerns, put themselves in the place of those affected, and then practice the Golden Rule; that is, they treat others the way they want to be treated.

■ *Demonstrate strong leadership throughout the organization.* The change at Troy University mentioned earlier in this chapter would not have happened without strong leadership from the chancellor and his leadership team, but just as important were hundreds of other people in the organization who demonstrated strong leadership. They were committed to change and made it happen. Servant-leadership cannot be the domain of only one person—it must reach down into organizations. This is especially true when change must occur.

■ *Build trust in the leadership.* **Trust** is the belief you won't be harmed when vulnerable. Persons feel especially vulnerable in times of change. They may fear loss of status, control, and power. They may become unsure of their role in the changed group or organization. They may fear the loss of their job or place on the team. Jobs, self-esteem, community standing, and economic stability may hang in the balance. Servant-leaders must display absolute integrity, reliability, openness, and fairness. They must behave in socially ethical and responsible ways. Servant-leaders must communicate they care about both the people and the organization. These characteristics are foundational to trust. Once lost, trust is difficult—and often impossible—to regain.

■ *Clearly articulate the process to all.* Not only must people understand the strategic vision—that is, where they are going and how they are going to get there—but they must also understand how they as individuals and parts of the organization or group will make the transition. Change expert William Bridges outlines the following four steps to help people with the transitioning process (Bridges, 1991).

  • *Purpose.* People need to understand the reason for the change. Be ready to answer these questions: What is the problem? Who said so? What happens if we don't change?

  • *Picture.* People need to be able to visualize how things will look after change occurs and especially how the change will affect them. Don't expect people to be willing to make changes too quickly. People need time to let go of the past.

  • *Plan.* Most people need a detailed implementation plan for how the transition will occur. This isn't the strategic plan that outlines the actual changes, details, or dates new systems will be in place; rather, it's a plan for how they as individuals will make the transition. Change is about the organization; transition is about people. They need to know what will be done to help them adjust, how and when necessary training will be provided. It tells Fred, Demetrius, and Dorothy when and how their worlds will change. It takes people step by step through the process and helps facilitate the transition process.

  • *Part.* People need to know the part they are to play. First, they need to know how they will fit into the changed organization. Second, they need to know how they will interact with others. Third, they need to know their part in implementing the change. People who are involved in implementing change will be committed to making the change a reality.

■ *Create an enabling environment.* Servant-leaders ensure the environment will enable success. They identify potential barriers—the driving and the restraining forces that may affect implementation. Mandates from higher headquarters or senior administrative officials and pressure from the competition might be forces driving change. Apathy, hostility, and lack of knowledge may be restraining forces affecting implementation. Leaders identify and address forces that can cause barriers or obstacles and forces that can overcome them. Leaders break the old structural silos—people may want to do things a new way, but organizational structure, old loyalties, and fragmented resources keep them from doing so. They ensure people get the needed training and resources to do things the new way. It is folly to put people into new settings and not give them the training or resources to do the job right. Servant-leaders ensure everyone has the opportunity to be heard and express their concerns and frustrations, from the time the strategic vision is presented until after implementation is complete. Finally, servant-leaders remain positive about both individuals and the organization in order to create an enabling environment.

■ *Celebrate success.* Celebrating success on the road to implementation recognizes accomplishment, motivates people, and sends a positive message. Celebrate milestones and short-term wins. Examples of short-term wins are improved performance and positive feedback that has resulted from early changes. Celebrate those things that are visible to others and clearly related to the change effort.

■ *Institutionalize the change within the culture.* Leaders cannot easily change the culture—the norms and shared values of the organization or group—especially if it has existed for some time. Change that depends on a cultural transformation won't last. Look for ways to graft change into the existing culture.

To Institutionalize Change

To succeed, change must become part of the organization; otherwise, people will slip back into old ways of doing things. Therefore, leaders should do the following:

■ *Communicate.* Communicate openly and often about what is happening during the transition period. Especially communicate strong, documented evidence linking performance improvement to the change. This behavior motivates workers to continue doing things the new way.

■ *Praise.* Deserved praise is a motivator, so praise the organization for making change possible. Show compatibility between the culture and the change; in other words, communicate how the culture—the organization at this place and time—has embraced change.

■ *Mentor.* Mentor and coach others in the organization on the value of change, especially the change that has just been accomplished.

Servant-Leaders Motivate Others

Every servant-leader faces the challenge of how to motivate others. One web search engine produces a list of over 10 million sites from the entry "leadership, motivation." Leaders must motivate themselves before they can motivate others.

How to Motivate Yourself

Consider these things as you seek to motivate yourself:

■ *Desire.* Servant-leaders desire to achieve things that will help others.

■ *Determine.* Servant-leaders evaluate themselves often—and ask for honest feedback from others—to determine their own strengths and their weaknesses. And then they capitalize on their strengths and take steps to shore up their weaknesses.

■ *Decide.* Servant-leaders consciously decide to take action—learn a skill, gain new information, listen to others—so that they can lead successfully.

■ *Discipline.* Servant-leaders are disciplined. They are willing to delay gratification and take the road less traveled rather than go with the crowd.

■ *Direct.* Servant-leaders direct their energies for the common good—for the benefit of the organization and others.

Ten Guidelines for Motivating Others

Consider these things as you seek to motivate others:

1. *Display confidence.* Others are more easily motivated when leaders look, act, and feel confident. Furthermore, leaders must confidently deal with adversity and handle setbacks. Nothing inspires or motivates others more than a person who triumphs over adversity—one who doesn't quit but perseveres until the task is finished and people are secure.

2. *Demonstrate enthusiasm.* If you are not enthusiastic, don't expect others to be. Effective leaders not only have a vision for the group but also have a personal vision for their lives, which includes the desire to serve others. A passion for their vision and the group vision spills over, so that others see genuine enthusiasm. A leader's passion is contagious, causing others to rally behind him or her.

3. *Ask **What's in It for Others (WIIFO)?*** Know what motivates others. Effective leaders ask group members what they hope to achieve. Armed with this information, they design tasks to be self-rewarding; that is, they develop and assign tasks to hold the attention of others and provide a sense of accomplishment, fulfillment, and reward. Furthermore, effective leaders find out what kinds of reward appeal to followers. Some want more pay; others want time off; some are most concerned about getting recognition. Don't assume the same rewards appeal to all people. Leadership would be a simple task if we were all motivated by the same things and all people thought alike. Finally, for maximum motivational effect, recognize good work as soon as possible.

4. *Delegate responsibly.* Delegation is often necessary. Leadership, by definition, implies one works well with and delegates responsibilities to others. Effective servant-leaders don't delegate recklessly; they select the right person for the task, make the objective clear, agree on the standards of performance, and help the person feel responsibility for the task while remaining available and accessible to them. And then, they recognize the good work, remembering the old saying "Criticize in private; praise in public."

5. *Help people learn from their mistakes.* Some leaders don't want to point out the mistakes of subordinates, but a mistake must not go unnoticed—especially if there is a chance it could happen again. Let people know it's all right to make honest mistakes and that you will not get angry or punish them; otherwise, people will not try new things for fear of failing. When people make mistakes, ask them what they could have done differently or how they will do it next time. Affirm them for their efforts; let them know you appreciate them. Treat them the way you would like to be treated.

6. *Listen effectively.* Listening demonstrates interest in others and what they have to say. People are more motivated by those who they think are interested in them and they hold these listening leaders in higher esteem. In addition, by really listening, leaders can sense the joys, concerns, fears, emotions, and things people hold dear, thereby allowing them to motivate others more effectively.

7. *Communicate clearly.* Clear communication portrays a positive image, causes others to see us as more honest and trustworthy, demonstrates positive regard toward others, and enables others to understand us. Often, people in groups

or organizations don't lack motivation; they simply don't understand what leaders want them to do. Communication allows you to connect with others and thereby motivate them to perform well.

8. *Give helpful feedback.* Good people fight for **feedback;** that is, they want to know how others evaluate their performance. Unfortunately, some leaders fail to give good constructive feedback. Feedback should be specific and under-standable and it should be of value to the receiver and not just a release for the leader. Also, it should be given at appropriate times and on time. Give feedback as close as possible to the time the behavior occurred. On the other hand, giving feedback when people are tired, hurried, or in the wrong frame of mind may be counterproductive.

9. *Lead the way.* People are motivated by those who actually show the way rather than just tell it. Although leaders shouldn't get in the way of those doing the task, they must be available and accessible, and they must set the example. Nothing motivates followers more than one who leads by example. Actions do speak louder than words. The great American poet Edgar Guest said it this way: "I'd rather see a sermon than hear one any day; . . . It is not the one who tells them, but the one who shows the way" (Guest, 1976, p. 599).

10. *Encourage others.* The most important thing leaders can do to motivate others is encourage them. An author admiring photographs taken by a professional photographer commented, "You must have a great camera," to which the pho-tographer replied, "You must have a great typewriter." The author was, no doubt, trying to encourage the photographer, but his choice of words was not encouraging. The prefix "en" means "in." We literally put courage in others when we encourage them. We take courage away when we discourage them. Someone said for every discouraging word we hear we need ten encouraging ones to offset it. But even then, people most likely remember the discouraging one. Be an encouraging servant-leader.

Servant Leaders Mentor Emerging Leaders

The biggest failing of most organizations and their leaders is failure to **mentor,** to train and develop more leaders. Reading books, attending courses or seminars, and studying the leadership styles and techniques of successful leaders train emerging leaders and help them grow, but true leadership development requires mentoring. Simply put, nothing takes the place of the mentoring future leaders get from current ones. While many leaders don't want to be troubled with mentoring, true servant-leaders—those who put service first—mentor future leaders.

Failure to Mentor Future Leaders

There are several reasons many fail to mentor future leaders. First, it takes time and effort. A leader's time is limited and time spent helping future leaders is time that can't be spent on current tasks of leadership. Second, some leaders are afraid to men-tor others for fear those being mentored might take their job. Third, most leaders have not considered how many people along the way have mentored them and how they might pass on their acquired knowledge and skills to others; they may be both

Students at universities and colleges are often unknowingly and informally mentored by faculty members, both in and outside the classroom.

Photo courtesy of Diana Goldammer.

ignorant and apathetic about mentoring. Fourth, most leaders don't place a high priority on mentoring. Finally, many leaders give little thought to succession planning—that is, how to prepare those who may assume leadership when they leave.

Mentoring Future Leaders Is a Priority

Servant-leaders know mentoring is important for at least the following five reasons:

- *Future orientation.* Successful servant-leaders attach importance to the future; they invest in the future by mentoring. Mentoring shows commitment to the future success of the organization by preparing those who will be its future leaders.
- *Knowledge transmission.* It takes time to learn. But the time can be reduced by learning from the successes and failures of others. You can touch a stove and get burned, or you can learn not to do it from somebody who has already "been there and done that."
- *Organizational growth.* Mentoring keeps organizations strong by preparing those who will become its leaders. But it also promotes organizational health and personal growth by establishing and strengthening networking and communication. Emerging leaders benefit from networking and the opening of more channels of communication to them.
- *Needs of leaders to help others.* Most people have an inner need to help others and be instrumental in promoting their growth. Seeing the long-term positive effects of mentoring fulfills this need and enhances a servant-leader's self-worth.
- *Responsibility to give back.* Servant-leaders want to repay an organization that has provided opportunity to them. One of the best ways to do that is mentoring future leaders who can ensure the long-term success of the organization.

Servant-Leaders Structure the Mentoring Process

While informal and casual mentoring by leaders helps emerging leaders, structuring the mentoring experience ensures that the process happens regularly and accomplishes its purpose. This is an important point: Individuals on the servant-leadership chain—those at the top—and those in lower leadership positions should both be mentored and mentor others. Here are some suggestions and general guidelines you might want to consider as you enlist the help of a mentor or as you mentor others:

- *Write a contract.* Consider writing a contract spelling out what both the mentor and the one being mentored will do—perhaps including frequency and times for meetings and deliverables or preparation needed by each of them. Although not always necessary for informal mentoring, a contract specifies the expectations of each party and reduces the chance of misunderstanding.
- *Set meeting times.* Set times, such as every other Thursday at 10:00 A.M., knowing the time can change if either party has a conflict. If a meeting has to be cancelled, reschedule it. Regularity helps mentoring. Missed meetings tend to lead to more missed meetings and deterioration of the mentoring relationship.
- *Maintain symmetry.* Often, the mentor is senior in position, rank, and age; therefore, proper respect must be shown. But as in any relationship, mutual respect and balance are necessary. Without symmetry, the mentoring relationship will not last.
- *Ensure dual input.* Both must have a say about what is discussed. While the mentor will have more knowledge, the one being mentored will have specific questions and concerns. As in any balanced relationship, both should have input about what is to be accomplished.
- *Stress candor and openness.* Honesty and trust are crucial. There must be no hidden agendas and no falsifying of information. The effectiveness of mentoring depends on both parties being candid and open. Mentors must be honest in their assessments and the mentored must be honest in their questions, discussion, and information presented.

Characteristics of Effective Mentors

The characteristics of effective mentors fit the definition of servant-leaders given in the first paragraph of this chapter; servant-leaders lead because it is the best way to serve others. Effective mentors do the following:

- *Invest time and effort.* Mentoring takes time. When time is short, mentoring often falls by the wayside if the leader is not a servant. This is unfair to individuals who need mentoring and to the organization that needs people to be mentored. Regular, ongoing mentoring is important.
- *Coach and develop.* The terms *mentoring* and *coaching* are often used together. Mentor-coaches provide on-the-job training—a way for the person being mentored to learn by doing. Effective mentors stand on the sidelines, offering words of positive criticism and encouragement.
- *Enlist help from others.* When mentors don't have the necessary expertise, they willingly connect the person to someone who can help. Effective mentors realize the importance of using their contacts to help the person being mentored.

- *Challenge and stretch.* Effective mentors don't allow those being mentored to do less than their best. Mentors challenge others to think creatively, try new things, and act in new ways. Mentors encourage others to stretch beyond the boundaries of their previous accomplishments.
- *Identify knowledge, skill, and ability* **(KSA)** *deficiencies.* Everyone has KSA deficiencies. Mentors can observe the deficiencies and arrange for the person being mentored to take tests and inventories to identify KSA shortfalls, so that he or she can take action to correct them.
- *Provide a positive role model.* The most effective thing a mentor can do is to be a positive role model. Again quoting from Edgar Guest, "I soon can learn to do it if you let me see it done; I can watch your hands in action but your tongue too fast may run . . . And the lecture you deliver may be very wise and true, But I'd rather get my lessons by observing what you do" (Guest, 1976, p. 599). Never underestimate the value of modeling.

■ CONCLUSION

We began by saying servant-leaders lead because it is the best way for them to serve others. Their desire to serve causes them to seek leadership opportunities. To be an effective servant-leader, you must develop your competencies and guard your character, focus dually on the task to be done and the people doing it, use the style—authoritative, participative, or delegative—that fits the situation, and develop the characteristic qualities of servant-leadership. In summary, you must communicate a strategic vision, listen to understand, implement change, motivate others, and mentor future leaders. Pay attention to these things, for the world and individuals around you need qualified servant-leaders.

■ KEY TERMS

Character—Who an individual is as a person—specifically, the qualities that distinguish him or her from others.

Competency—What an individual is capable of doing using his or her knowledge, skills, and abilities.

Dual-Focused Leaders—Leaders who focus appropriately on the task and the people involved.

Empathic Listening—Listening to see, hear, feel, and understand from the perspective of others.

Feedback—Evaluation of performance by others.

KSA—Knowledge, skills, and abilities.

Mentor—To train and develop future leaders.

People—Individuals, the organization or the team that follows a leader.

People-Focused Leaders—Leaders who tend to let individual concerns override accomplishing the task.

Servant-Leader—A leader or an organization that seeks first to serve others.

Task—The job or mission to be completed.

Task-Focused Leaders—Leaders who consider the task or job more important than the people doing it.

Trust—The belief that one will not be harmed by another when vulnerable.

Vision—A mental portrait that guides group behavior toward a goal.

What's in It for Others? (WIIFO)—A question good leaders always ask themselves.

■ SUGGESTED READINGS

Greenleaf, R. K. 1970. "The Servant as Leader," Indianapolis, IN: Robert K. Greenleaf Center for Servant-Leadership.

Greenleaf Center for Servant-Leadership website, http://www.greenleaf.org.

Kline, J. A. 2003. *Listening Effectively: Achieving High Standards in Communication.* Columbus, OH: Pearson-Prentice Hall.

■ REFERENCES

Blanchard, K. & Hodges, P. 2003. *The Servant Leader: Transforming Your Heart, Head, Hands & Habit.* Nashville, TN: Thomas Nelson.

Bridges, W. 1991. *Managing Transitions: Making the Most of Change.* Reading, MA: Addison-Wesley.

Committee on Bible Translation. 1978. *The Holy Bible: New International Version.* Grand Rapids, MI: Zondervan Bible Publishers.

Department of the Army. 1973. *US Army Handbook of Military Leadership.* Washington, DC: US Government Printing Office.

Frick, D. F. & Spears, L. C. eds. 1996. *On Becoming a Servant Leader.* San Francisco: Jossey-Bass.

Frick, D. F. & Spears, L. C. eds. 1996. *Seeker and Servant: Reflections on Religious Leadership.* San Francisco: Jossey-Bass.

Greenleaf, R. K. 1970. *The Servant as Leader.* Indianapolis, IN: Robert K. Greenleaf Center for Servant-Leadership.

Greenleaf, R. K. 1996. *On Becoming a Servant Leader.* San Francisco: Jossey-Bass.

Greenleaf, R. K. 2002. *Servant Leadership: A Journey into the Nature of Legitimate Power and Greatness.* Mahwah, NJ: Paulist Press.

Guest, E. A. 1976. *Collected Verse of Edgar A. Guest.* New York: Buccaneer Books.

Hawkins, J. January 29, 2008. Troy University Capstone Leadership Lecture. Troy, AL.

Hersey, P. & Blanchard, K. H. 2000. *Management of Organizational Behavior: Leading Human Resources* (8th ed.). Upper Saddle River, NJ: Prentice Hall.

Hunter, J. C. 1998. *The Servant: A Simple Story About the True Essence of Leadership.* Rocklin, CA: Prima.

Kline, J. A. 2003. *Listening Effectively: Achieving High Standards in Communication.* Upper Saddle River, NJ: Pearson-Prentice Hall.

Kline, J. A. 2006. "Motivating Others: Delegating Responsibility." www.Klinespeak.com (September).

Kline, J. A. 2007. "How to Implement Change in Your Organization," *Armed Forces Comptroller, 52,* 1, pp. 35–38.

Kolp, A. & Rea, P. 2006. *Leading with Integrity: Character-Based Leadership.* Cincinnati, OH: Atomic Dog.

Maxwell, J. C. 1995. *Developing the Leaders Around You: How to Help Others Reach Their Full Potential.* Nashville, TN: Thomas Nelson.

Nabers, D., Jr. 2006. *The Case for Character: Looking at Character from a Biblical Perspective.* Cleveland, OH: Cedar Hill Press.

Schofield Reference Edition, 2000. *The Holy Bible: Authorized King James Version.* New York: Oxford University Press.

Shamasastry, R., trans. 1923. *Kautilya's Arthashastra.* Mysore, India: Wesleyan Mission Press.

Spears, L. C., ed. 1998. *Insights on Leadership: Service, Stewardship, Spirit, and Servant-Leadership.* Hoboken, NJ: John C. Wiley and Sons.

Spears, L. C. 2000. Presentation at the Greenleaf Centre Australia–New Zealand Conference. Melbourne, Australia.

CHAPTER FOUR REVIEW QUESTIONS

1. Explain the following statement: While Robert Greenleaf is credited with intro-
ducing the emphasis on servant-leadership, the concept is an ancient one.

_____

_____

_____

2. Leaders constantly face the challenge of accomplishing the mission (task concerns) while responding to the needs of group members (people concerns).
What suggestions would you offer to leaders who want to show concern for
both the task and the people? Why should servant-leaders focus on both task
and people concerns?

_____

_____

_____

3. Some writers claim servant-leaders should always use the participative style of
leadership and avoid using the authoritarian style. Either agree or disagree
with this claim and explain your position. Include discussion of the delegative
style in your answer.

_____

_____

_____

4. The chief executive officer of the Greenleaf Center for Servant-Leadership
believes listening is the chief characteristic of servant-leaders. Tell why you do
or do not agree with him. Is listening more important for servant-leaders than
for those who are not servant-leaders? Explain your answer.

_____

_____

_____

5. The chapter discusses five characteristics of servant-leadership; they communicate a strategic vision, listen to understand, implement change, motivate others, and mentor future leaders. List and discuss other characteristics you might
add to the list.

_____

_____

_____

CHAPTER FOUR SELF-TEST

1. _____ was the person who is credited with having popularized the term *servant-leader.*

2. _____ was the fourth-century thinker from India who said a leader should consider good not what pleases self but what pleases subjects.

3. _____ co-authored a book showing how servant-leadership principles taught by Jesus can be used effectively by leaders in any area of life.

4. _____leaders are those who focus appropriately on both the task and people.

5. _____ is a mental portrait that guides a group's behavior toward a goal.

6. Larry Spears, former director of the Greenleaf Center for Servant Leadership, believes _____ is the chief characteristic of servant-leaders.

7. Information is no better than its _____.

8. List five things you can do to become a better listener.

9. What is the biggest failing of most organizations?

10. List the five characteristics or qualities of servant-leaders.

Leadership and Service in Theory and Practice

PART 2

Theories of Leadership

5

■ INTRODUCTION

Theories are, in short, proposed but unproven explanations that are debated and tested by experts in a field of study. For many of you, this may be your first introduction to leadership theories. This chapter provides a short discussion of how a theory is developed and how it may be used in the classroom and in practice. It will allow you to consider practical uses for particular theories, as well as provide a framework that will allow you to compare and evaluate the various theories presented.

In short, this chapter is a "toolbox" that will provide you with instruments that will help you describe or categorize leadership theories; it also presents an inventory of major leadership theories and ways of describing leadership, and it introduces the major theoretical definitions and indicators of sources of power. These theories and constructs, when applied, should allow you to examine a wide variety of leaders and leadership situations and gain a greater understanding of them.

Gregory E.
Christy

Daniel M.
Gaken

Amy
Radford-Popp

■ WHAT IS LEADERSHIP THEORY?

Theory is essential for further understanding, explaining, and predicting any phenomena, although disciplines often express the nature of theory from very contrasting perspectives. For example, social scientists and humanists approach the use of theory differently. A political scientist, Richard Couto, noted that social scientists emphasize that theories are created to explain and predict (Goethals & Sorenson, 2006, p. 6), while philosopher Joanne B. Ciulla's understanding of theory was less restrictive and adopted a more inclusive approach (Ciulla, 2004, p. 7). She advocated for approaching theory from a systems perspective. She believed that a systems approach to theory allowed for the ability to make connections and inferences, while focusing on the process to understanding phenomena rather than on the product that they produced.

In leadership education literature, many scholars have tried to explain the leadership process (Northouse, 2007; Hughes, Ginnett, & and Curphy, 2006). Stogdill (1974, p. 7) noted that there are almost as many different definitions of leadership as there are people who have tried to define it. Northouse (2007, p. 2) noted that, over a sixty-year period, as many as sixty-five different classification systems were developed to define the dimensions of leadership. Pulitzer Prize–winning scholar James MacGregor Burns also engaged in this exercise, in an attempt to legitimize a field of study that some skeptics still dismiss as being without academic rigor and ill-defined (Goethals & Sorenson, 2006, p. 2). Burns undertook the challenge to identify a general theory of leadership; as a result, he is universally recognized as one of the leading experts in the relatively new but rapidly growing academic discipline.

In 2001, Burns assembled an interdisciplinary group of leadership scholars at the Jepson School of Leadership Studies at the University of Richmond in Virginia. Although representing various backgrounds and disciplines, they set out to identify a general theory of leadership (Goethals & Sorenson, 2006). Burns believed that the identification of a general theory of leadership would help those studying and practicing leadership to build a set of guiding principles that would be universal and could be adapted to different situations (Mangan, 2002, p. 1).

As the team attempted to address the creation of a general theory of leadership, they did a metatheoretical review of leadership theory. A metatheoretical approach focuses on the explanations for the explanations that are used to describe how one understands, expresses, predicts, or prescribes the world. Another way to think of it, in describing a phenomenon, is to think in terms of metaphors (Goethals & Sorenson, 2006, p. 67). The scholars identified a variety of metaphors to portray various leadership theories, including service, the market, and perception (p. 68).

Many theories of leadership—for example, servant-, citizenship, and transformational leadership—focus on service to, or a sense of acting for or on behalf of, others. The metaphor of the market refers to transactional leadership that addresses a reward or exchange process between leaders and followers. The paternal, another of the metaphors, represents behavior-focused, sometimes referenced as "Great Man" theories. In these theories, the focus is on the leader, not on the relationship between leaders and followers. Cognitive leadership theory, for example, emphasizes the metaphor of perception and how diverse viewpoints, individual- or group-based, are valued.

As described previously, the multitude of approaches to leadership challenge both theorists and educators to define, first and foremost, what leadership means. Various themes that are central to the expression of leadership include (1) leadership as a process; (2) leadership as influence; (3) leadership as it occurs in a group context; and (4) leadership that involves goal achievement (Northouse, 2007, p. 3). In viewing leadership as a process, it is important to focus on the experience that one has in the presence of leadership and the interactions that occur between leaders and followers. Leadership is not based on one's formal title or position but instead on the ability to influence. For example, one may also be characterized as a charismatic leader, which is based on the perceptions of one's followers. Leadership occurs in a group context and among individuals that have a shared purpose. It can be exercised among a small group, a community, or an entire association. And finally, it involves goal achievement. Leaders, by definition, work with and direct others toward the completion of a task or an end goal.

As we evaluate the leadership process, it is important to remember that both leaders and followers play a significant role. There is a reciprocal relationship between leaders and followers; one needs the other (Burns, 1978; Heller & Van Til, 1983; Hollander, 1992; Jago, 1982). Leaders and followers exist in relation to each other (Hollander, 1992). Without followers, there can be no leaders. One depends on the other to accomplish the goal or task. In an organizational setting, leaders may be assigned, elected, or appointed to a formal position or role. This is typically referred to as **assigned,** or positional, **leadership.** In a leader/follower relationship, the assigned leader may not always, in reality, be the real/perceived leader of the followers. In situations where others perceive that or act in a manner such that an untitled individual is the most influential member of a group, that person is an **emergent leader** (Northouse, 2007, p. 5).

Emergent leaders acquire their status through other people's belief, trust, and support of their leadership, influence, and guidance within the organization. Emergent leadership tends to occur over a period of time as a result of many factors. Researchers have found that certain personality traits are also related to leadership emergence tendencies (Smith & Foti, 1998). Individuals who are more dominant, confident, and intelligent about their own performance are more likely to be identified as leaders by other members of their group (Northouse, 2007, p. 6).

The concepts of **power** and leadership are often viewed as like terms by laypersons because, when one has the trappings of power, many incorrectly assume the ability to influence others. Typically, in organizations there are two types of power: positional and personal power (p. 7). As in the case of assigned leadership, positional power comes from a particular rank, or position, within an organization. Influence capacity in such cases, one might naturally assume, is derived from having a higher status than followers or subordinates within the organization. Personal power, on the other hand, highlights the influence capacity a person exemplifies from being viewed by followers as likable, respectable, knowledgeable, and competent. In this type of dynamic, power is based on how individuals are seen in their relationships with others. Burns (1978) and scholars who followed his lead emphasize the power of relationships. For them, power is not something that leaders hold over others to achieve desired ends; instead, it must happen in a relational context, one in which leaders and followers interact to achieve shared goals. The best and most effective leaders are those who choose very carefully when and how they use power, especially their positional power. They make a conscious effort never to abuse it.

▪ LEADERSHIP AND POWER

When James MacGregor Burns wrote his seminal work *Leadership* in 1978, he helped establish the truly interdisciplinary field of leadership studies. In this work, Burns argues that leadership is not simply the will of great people but, rather, their ability to exert that will through influence. The measure of their ability to move others to action is the measure of their leadership. Leadership, then, is the measure of true power.

The relationship between leadership and power is complex. While the two are certainly not interchangeable, they are interdependent. If leadership, as discussed in chapter one, is the capacity of an individual to influence others to action, then power is a critical component of leadership. If a leader does not have the power to create action, then he or she will be ineffective as a leader.

▪ SOURCES OF POWER

If power is indispensable to a leader, understanding its source is a tool of great importance to an aspiring leader. John French and Bertram Raven researched the bases of power and isolated five primary sources from which leaders generate power. While they believe that each individual is predisposed to a particular source, an understanding of the five sources allows emerging leaders to both understand (and maximize) their principal base of power and possibly add to their repertoire (Hackman & Johnson, 2004, p. 130).

Legitimate Power

When a leader's power comes from the position he or she holds rather than from him- or herself, that power is known as legitimate power. Legitimate power is held by teachers, law enforcement officials, elected officials, and managers or supervisors. As a society, we have collectively given legitimate power to individuals who meet the qualifications of their position. College professors have the power to construct assignments, administer exams, and assign grades because they were given that authority by their respective institution. When you see a police car's lights in your rearview mirror, you know that the officer driving has the power to enforce the speed limit. In most instances, the first days on a new job are dominated by learning the chain of command and who is whose boss. We are all quite familiar with examples of legitimate power.

Expert Power

Unlike those with legitimate power, those who use or exercise expert power are using power that they have accumulated through past performance, prior experience, or formal education. In many instances, we see leaders who exert power because they are experts. Today, a prominent example of this is the debate concerning carbon emissions and the dangers posed by global warming. Scientists who have the appropriate academic credentials and experience with climate-related issues wield a great deal of power in dealing with these issues. Likewise, talent can be construed to be expert power, particularly in athletic leadership. Very often, we see captains of athletic teams, at both the professional and collegiate levels, who exhibit very few of the traditional qualities that we associate with leadership. However, coaches, teammates, and even the fans on the sidelines may look to them as leaders based solely on their athletic power and ability.

Referent Power

Referent power is the power of respect or admiration. Often, leaders who gain power through this avenue are said to be those who lead by example or who are role models. When an individual is liked, respected, or admired, we often transfer power to that individual. In Native American societies, for example, tribes place great value, and subsequently referent power, on tribal elders. Great value is placed on the experience of the elders in the tribe, and their wisdom is often sought by tribal members. Referent power, because it is rooted in relationships, takes time to develop. If referent power is abused or overused, the leader will have to work particularly hard to reestablish the referent source of power.

Reward Power

A leader's ability to confer something of value onto followers or potential followers gives the leader the power of reward. The impact of the reward, and thus the degree of power, is directly related to the follower's perception of the value of the reward. The reward can be material, such as a pay raise or a gift, but it also can be something that is not tangible but equally valuable in the eyes of the follower, such as praise, approval, or support.

To maximize the power of the leader, the reward must be deemed significant. The more attractive the reward, the more power it gives the leader. For example, if the president of a student group wants to entice the membership to participate actively in recruiting new members for the organization, he or she can offer something that is desirable to the members, such as a semester's worth of textbooks. This reward is likely to motivate people to act, as it is significant, while a gift with a perceived lesser value (say, a free meal in the student union) may not be as effective. While reward power certainly can be effective, it is limited by the leader's resources and ability to understand what the followers see as valuable.

Coercive Power

A leader's ability to give negative reinforcement bestows coercive power. If it is likely that the leader will punish the followers, and as a result, the followers comply to prevent receiving a punishment, this power is known as coercion. Research has shown that the most effective use of coercive power occurs when the leader's expectations are clear and well known, and when the penalty for failing to meet these expectations is well publicized. For employers, the most obvious punishment is termination. However, if threats or punishments are not carried through on a regular basis, this practice will promote negative behaviors among the followers and decrease the power of the leader (Hackman & Johnson, 2004, p. 131).

French and Raven indicate that, while a leader usually has a preference or tendency to utilize a single source of power, it is quite common for successful leaders to combine sources to maximize their effectiveness. Consider the professor who exerts legitimate power. While he or she certainly has positional power granted by the university, he or she also can obtain power from his or her ability to reward students (high grades and letters of recommendation are certainly coveted rewards for college students) or from negative reinforcement (deduction of points or penalties for missing class, academic dishonesty, etc.). The ability to ascertain which sources of power will be most effective in your position will enable you to be a more effective leader.

■ EARLY LEADERSHIP THEORIES

Leadership has been one of the eternal fascinations of human beings. As long as there have been humans, there have been leaders. And for as long as there have been leaders, people have tried to understand how they attained the position.

In its infancy, the study of leadership was an informal process. People with leadership aspirations looked to leaders they viewed as successful and attempted to ascertain what distinguished them from others. This manner of thought became more and more prevalent, until society's collective schema of leadership emerged as the first theories of leadership. Early research and writings on the subject focused primarily on the abilities possessed by leaders.

■ GREAT MAN AND TRAIT THEORIES

Historian Thomas Carlyle wrote, "The history of the world is but the biography of great men" (1869, p. 17). Indeed, this characterized the popular view of leadership throughout most of human history. While today the general public is now somewhat reluctant to accept anyone as a "born leader," early theories of leadership decreed that this was the process by which one became a leader. Kings reigned, it was believed, because they were born to lead. Leadership was a compilation of characteristics innate to the leader. These traits differentiated the leaders from their followers in some manner. These "great man" theories (appropriately named, as one assumed characteristic was that of being a man) were readily accepted because they provided affirmation for commonly held societal beliefs. Great man theories were especially appealing and confirmed the notion that leaders are somehow special, gifted, or sent by God, which was a comfort to many.

By the early 1900s, researchers had begun an attempt to provide support for their long-held assumptions about leadership. A variety of political scientists, historians, and other academicians sought to identify and describe those unique and intrinsic traits possessed by leaders that allowed them to lead. Experts identified exemplary leaders in the social sectors, successful politicians, and great military leaders. For each study, there was a seemingly new set of characteristics and **traits** that were "necessary" to lead.

Ralph Stogdill and Bernard Bass sought to condense this enormous volume of data and provide a synthesized overview of the findings from years of trait research. Their initial report was published in 1948, and it indicated that the data from nearly a half century of research pointed out a series of traits that allowed leaders to experience success. Namely, a leader had to be born with intelligence, persistence, sociability, and a host of other traits. There was some degree of evidence that supported the concept that physical traits also lead to leadership capacity (Northouse, 2007, p. 19).

While these theories may initially have resonated with those who believed they captured what they observed to be true, many trait theories failed to hold up to the scrutiny of critics. While at the time there was no clear replacement for the trait approach, the scholarly community largely abandoned it when it became apparent that no amount of research could produce a definitive set of characteristics or traits that would equate to successful leadership in every situation.

"On the charge of identity theft, how do
you plead?"

© Mike Baldwin www.cartoonstock.com

■ SKILLS AND BEHAVIORAL APPROACHES

The 1950s and 1960s saw leadership scholarship shift away from traits that were innate and toward behaviors or **skills** that could be learned. Robert Katz (1955) reviewed the skills necessary to be an effective manager and leader; his findings showed three basic skills sets as being paramount. According to the Katz three-skill approach, the appropriate ability to use technical skills, human skills, and conceptual skills will allow for effective leadership and management.

Technical skills are those tasks or concepts that are specifically related to a job. In an auto assembly plant, for example, technical skills include the ability to operate the equipment used in the production process, the aptitude to correctly identify which materials are suitable for use, and an understanding of the sequence of production. Katz asserts that these skills are most necessary at the lower and middle levels of management (Northouse, 2007, p. 41).

Human skills are related to the leader's ability to work with people. The process of managing projects, assigning tasks within an organization, understanding how to motivate team members, and encouraging community buy-in of the project are all human skills. Human skills are essential at all levels of management, according to the three-skills approach.

At the middle and upper management levels, Katz places considerable emphasis on conceptual skills. Those skills are the ability to conceive and frame ideas. Leaders who excel at conceptual skills are often referred to as "big picture" leaders. Big picture leaders understand how the individual components of an organization complement the mission and objectives of the organization as a whole, can work with abstract ideas, and still plan for the future. Using the same example, the auto company that manages the assembly plant would require conceptual skills to forecast the demands of the auto industry in future years, develop vehicles that appeal to an ever-changing market, and implement a strategic plan that incorporates all levels of the company, such as the procurement of supplies for fabrication of the products and the development of a marketing plan (Northouse, 2007, p. 42).

While leaders at all levels use each skill, the importance of specific skills depends on where the leader resides within the organizational hierarchy. Later attempts at formalizing a skills approach to leadership—namely, the work done by Mumford, Zaccaro, Connelly & Marks (2000, p. 155) and others, suggested that outcomes are the result of the leader's ability to master problem-solving skills, make judgments, and utilize knowledge or experience. Skills approaches to leadership, in general, have been an effective means of describing leadership by cataloguing behaviors that are consistent with effective leadership. For many, however, the skills approach is too trait-driven to be effective, as many of the skills that have been identified as essential cannot be differentiated from innate abilities or traits. The skills approach, like the trait theory, has also failed to establish a set of skills that universally predicts the success of a leader.

■ STYLE THEORY AND THE SITUATIONAL ERA

Although the **great man theory** and behavior theory still have prominent proponents, the scholarship of leadership has progressed toward the view of leadership as a relationship between leader and follower. By viewing leadership as a relationship, not something limited to the leader, theorists have expanded the realm of theory to include not only the individual in a leadership position but also the context in which he or she leads.

The style approach is unique in that it identifies two general categories into which all leadership behaviors are placed: task behaviors and relationship behaviors. **Task behaviors** are those items that define structure, outline roles, or otherwise directly facilitate the accomplishment of group goals. **Relationship behaviors** contribute to the overall harmony and morale of the organization. From the mid-1960s through the 1980s, much research was conducted in an attempt to validate this approach; most notable were the studies at the University of Michigan and Ohio State University, as well as work done by Blake and Mouton (1964).

The studies at Ohio State University sought to describe how individuals act when leading a group. What was unique about this research was the instrument used. Participants completed a 150-item questionnaire in which they evaluated supervisors based on how often they engaged in specific behaviors. Two main behavior patterns emerged from the data: initiating (task-related behaviors) and consideration (relationship-orientated behaviors) structures.

Almost simultaneously, researchers at the University of Michigan were conducting a similar study. From their work, two types of leadership behaviors were identified: employee orientation and production orientation, which align with relationship- and task-orientated behaviors.

The two studies differed in their perception of the interdependence or independence of the two types of behaviors. The Ohio State studies treated the two as independent variables on two independent spectrums (therefore, a leader could exhibit a high number of both task and relationship behaviors). Conversely, researchers at Michigan placed both types of behaviors on one continuum, making the behaviors mutually exclusive (a leader may be task-oriented *or* relationship-oriented) (Northouse, 2007, p. 72).

In 1964, Blake and Mouton put forth their interpretation of this two-factor approach in what has famously become the managerial grid (subsequently renamed the leadership grid). This descriptive tool places "concern for results" on the x-axis and "concern for people" on the y-axis of a grid. Each axis measures its respective behaviors in nine segments. For each pair of coordinates, Blake and Mouton named the corresponding leadership style and used their survey data to provide a description for that style. The grid is still used widely in leadership development programs and managerial training, and it is often paired with leadership assessment tools to measure leadership behaviors.

■ SITUATIONAL LEADERSHIP

The concept of leadership style had expanded considerably by 1969, when Hersey and Blanchard introduced their situational leadership model. While earlier research in leadership style provided evidence that leadership can be described in terms of relationship and task behaviors, Hersey and Blanchard's model went to the next level in asserting that each of the two dimensions must be applied appropriately to match the leadership context (Hersey, 1984, p. 13).

Although the situational leader model is leader-focused in its discussion of leadership behaviors, it necessitates that the leader consider followers and their developmental level as a major component of the situation. The model requires that leaders assess their followers' competence and commitment (Hersey, 1984, p. 45). Through applying varying degrees of directive behaviors and supporting behaviors, the leader is able to adjust his or her style to fit the situation and achieve desired results.

The situational leader model places these two behavioral patterns on their own axis, creating a model with four quadrants, each one representing a leadership style. The style must be appropriate for the task and team, and followers are placed on a developmental continuum (see figure on next page).

The lower-right quadrant represents leadership that is highly focused on task-orientated behaviors but less focused on supportive behaviors. Hersey and Blanchard have named this style the directing style (previously the telling style), and it is appropriate for followers who exhibit a fair amount of ability and competence but who lack commitment. For these types of followers, Hersey and Blanchard argue, excessive support may lead to followers believing their leader is willing to reward them for any performance and, as a result, they do not need to excel (Hersey, 1984, p. 62).

Situational Leadership II The Model

From the *Situational Leader* by Dr. Paul Hersey, The Center for Leadership Studies.

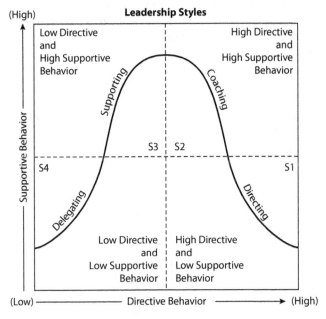

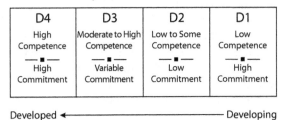

Moving up the grid, the second quadrant describes leaders who are both supportive and task-orientated. The leader provides both direction and guidance but is also concerned with the followers' attitudes toward the project. This leadership style is characterized by a leader who communicates the importance of goal achievement while also soliciting input from subordinates. Followers who respond well to this type of leadership are both competent and motivated (Hersey, 1984, p. 62).

In the supportive, or participatory, style, found on the upper-left corner of the grid, the leader does not focus solely on the achievement of goals or tasks but, rather, uses supportive behaviors to develop employees while accomplishing tasks. A supportive leader is typified by a willingness to give subordinates ownership of tasks through delegation while remaining accessible, should a problem arise. Followers with a high commitment, but perhaps not enough competence or experience, respond well to this leadership style (Hersey, 1984, p. 63).

When followers are not competent or committed to the task, or when the leader seeks to increase the subordinates' confidence in their ability and understanding of the task, the leader may adopt a delegating style. This style is distinguishable by low levels of support and low levels of task-oriented behaviors.

The situational leader model has enjoyed success in leadership development programs because it refutes the notion that leadership is elitist. Within this framework, a leader has the ability to adopt the appropriate style. If the leader has an understanding of the task structure, and the developmental level of the followers, the situational leader model prescribes a specific set of behaviors that should allow the leader to be successful in that endeavor.

■ CONTINGENCY THEORY

Another prominent leadership theory, contingency theory, was developed by Fred Fiedler and introduced in 1976 in his book *Improving Leadership Effectiveness: The Leader Match Concept*. The contingency theory attempts to match leadership and situations. Fiedler does this by assessing and evaluating the leader, given a series of situational variables (Northouse, 2007, p. 113).

The core of the theory is the assessment of the leader's style. According to the theory, all leaders have a natural style, or way in which they typically behave. Again, the styles are centered on whether the leader is concerned primarily with task-related issues or behavior issues (this is done using the least preferred coworker instrument). Fielder's theory then characterizes each situation using three variables: leader/member relations, task structure, and positional power. Leader/member relations seek to evaluate the group's cohesiveness and the degree to which the group respects and admires the leader. Task structure measures how clearly the tasks are defined, while positional power is a description of the authority the leader has.

Using these variables, and comparing them to the leader's style, contingency theory predicts whether a leader will be successful in a given situation. While it does provide comfort and a sense of realism, by asserting that not all leadership will be successful in every situation, it fails to specify what can be done if a leader is in a situation that does not match his or her style.

■ CONTEMPORARY LEADERSHIP THEORIES

Recently, there has been a revival of interest among scholars in trait theory. Although, early trait theories were referred to as the "great man" theories, more recent scholarship references relationships between people in a social situation. As we look at historical leaders, we tend to identify with the values and ethics that guided their decisions and leadership. We now recognize that the leadership exhibited by those historically admired and revered leaders happened within an interactive context between followers and leaders (Komives, Lucas, & McMahon, 2007). It is now understood that, rather than focusing solely on the individual traits of a single leader, it is essential to understand leadership from a relational context and that an understanding of follower traits is equally important. Wheatley (1992, p. 144) states, "Leadership is always dependent on the context, but the context is established by the relationships . . ." The following section will describe some contemporary relational leadership theories, including the leader-member exchange theory, the team leadership model, transformational leadership theory, and the social change model.

Leader-Member Exchange Theory

The leader-member exchange (LMX) theory was first identified in 1975 by Dansereau, Graen, and Haga. Prior to LMX theory, scholars approached leadership as leader-, follower-, or situation-driven. The LMX theory challenged all to view leadership as a process that focused on the interactions between leaders and followers, and it recognized that those interactions may be different between each leader and follower within an organization (Northouse, 2007).

A significant research area of LMX theory addresses how it applies to organizational effectiveness. The literature shows that the practice of LMX theory is related to positive organizational outcomes. Some outcome examples might be performance, job climate, empowerment, distributive justice, and innovation (Graen & Uhl-Bien, 1995). LMX theory emphasizes the interactions between leaders and members in an organization and it is therefore essential to recognize that most organizations have an in-group and an out-group. The in-group tends to be those individuals who take on expanded roles that are beyond the formal job description. On the other hand, the out-group represents those members who have more defined roles based on what is expected of them in their roles. In an organizational environment, personality characteristics can influence how individuals are perceived to be a part of the in- or out-group (Dansereau, Graen, & Haga, 1975). A member's designation is often based on how well he or she works with, or is respected by, the leader and, reciprocally, how well the leader works with him or her.

Considering the in-group and the out-group frames of reference, it is inevitable that power issues will play a role in relationships with the leader. Those members in the in-group tend to have the eye and ear of the leader in the group and therefore yield more power through access to more information, opportunities, and influence. On the contrary, the out-group is more inclined to not be as involved in the organization or connected to the leader. In most cases, out-group members are not very invested in the future of the organization; instead, they just do their job and go home (Dansereau, Graen, & Haga, 1975).

The LMX theory encompasses a variety of strengths and challenges related to leadership in organizational settings. First, it is perceived as a descriptive theory that describes the dynamics that occur in a work setting. As most know, there are those in an organizational setting who contribute more to the progress and well-being of the group, as well as those who sit back, disengaged, and look for the easy way out to do the bare minimum. The LMX theory is the only leadership approach that focuses on the interactions between leaders and members, collectively and individually. Due to the focus on the relationship and interactions between leaders and members, LMX highlights the essential need for communication. Communication exchanges between leaders and followers should be honest,

In order to avoid conflict, it is critical that leaders promote fairness in the work setting.

Photo courtesy of Diana Goldammer.

respectful, and trust-forming. Finally, the LMX theory's approach serves as a warning for leaders not to consciously or unconsciously allow their personal biases to influence who is part of the in-group—specifically, biases related to race, sex, age, ethnicity, or religion (Northouse, 2007, p. 159).

There are a few challenges that leaders should recognize when engaging in leadership based on the LMX theory in their organization (Northouse, 2007, p. 160). The very existence of an in-group and an out-group breeds an environment of privilege and the potential for discrimination against the out-group. Therefore, it is critical that leaders promote fairness in the work setting. Since the in-group typically gets extra attention from the leader, the out-group members often feel left out of the loop. Hence, it is essential for the leader to create an environment that is fluid and allows for out-group members to join the in-group from time to time, if they so choose. Another challenge is the level of commitment members have to the company or organization. The promotion of an in-group sometimes creates the perception that the in crowd "brown noses" the leader; as a result, some may question their true commitment to the organization.

Many critics of LMX theory argue that it is not fully developed. A research review of over 147 studies of LMX theory indicated that an improved understanding about LMX may be needed (Schriesheim, Castro, & Cogliser, 1999). In particular, questions have been raised about the measurement of leader-member exchanges. No empirical studies have used dyadic measures to analyze the LMX process. Also, many leader-member exchanges have been measured with different versions of exchange scales, hence exhibiting noncomparable results (Northouse, 2007, p. 161). These concerns reflect the need for further study of LMX theory.

Team Leadership Model

A historical review of group or team research suggests a long, extensive study of human group relations (McGrath, Arrow, & Berdahl, 2000; Porter & Beyerlein, 2000). In the 1920s and 1930s, the study of groups started with an emphasis on human relations, specifically related to collaborative initiatives in the work environment. During the 1940s, the study of group dynamics and the development of social science theory led the way for group and team research. The 1950s followed with an emphasis on sensitivity training and training groups (referred to by McGrath as T-groups) as they related to leadership theory development.

By the 1960s and 1970s, organizational development that promoted teamwork and leadership effectiveness through ongoing work teams was in vogue. The 1980s introduced quality teams, benchmarking, and continuous quality improvement, as a counter to the competitive market threat to American business from Japan and other Asian countries. Hence, by the 1990s, the focus on organizational teams adjusted to a more global perspective that prioritized organizational strategies and encouraged a competitive advantage. Recently, team research shows that studies have become more complex, emphasizing more team variables and no longer exclusively focusing on team performance issues. Currently, investigations are underway regarding the role of affective, behavioral, and cognitive processes in team leadership success (Northouse, 2007, pp. 207–208).

In the team leadership model, the leader takes on additional responsibility for making sure that the team is successful. Leadership behavior focuses on team-based problem solving. The leader assesses the team goals and how internal and external environment concerns may influence the team's ability to accomplish them. One key concept of the model includes the leader's mental model, which encompasses the characteristics of the problem encountered, as well as the environment and organizational influences that direct team actions. An effective leader is one who is behaviorally flexible and has a continuum of responses and skills to anticipate the diverse needs of the team (Barge, 1996).

Leaders often use the team leadership model to make decisions about the current status of a team and to decipher what actions need to be taken in order to improve or maintain the team's ability to progress. As a leader assesses a challenge, problems can be framed as internal relationship problems, internal task problems, or external environmental problems (Northouse, 2007, p. 223). In cases of group dynamics or personality issues between members, some teams may have members who strive for control or power of the group. The lack of cohesiveness in a group, through the need for one or more members to yield power or the inability to work together for the common good, exemplifies internal relationship problems. Internal task problems signal a possible lack of clear expectations of individual roles or a blurred understanding of the structure of the team. External environmental problems are influenced by factors from outside the purview of the individual team. It may include a lack of clarity regarding the understanding of autonomy that the team has within the overall organization.

It must be assumed that, in order to be effective, the team leadership model must emphasize a philosophy of continuous analysis and improvement (Northouse, 2007, p. 224). There are similarities to a coaching model in this form of team leadership. Just as a coach continues to help his or her players to grow, develop, strategize, and improve, so should the leader in a team leadership model.

The strength of the team leadership model is its focus on real-life commonplace work within the context of the organization, industry, or society; the cognitive guide within a complex process; and the changing role of leaders and followers (Northouse, 2007). This model is one of the only leadership theories that take into account the leader's ability to diagnose and correct problems as they occur, regardless of their origin. As any leader approaches problem solving in an organization, the team leadership model leader recognizes that leadership and group development are complex processes. He or she focuses on viewing an organizational problem from multiple perspectives and at varied levels of the organization. Team leadership models view the roles of leader and follower as interchangeable. Hence, it does not frame leadership from a positional, or titled, approach. Instead, leadership is shared among the team members, with each person able to assess group effectiveness and suggest changes when appropriate.

Critics of the team leadership model have noted that it is rather complex and does not readily provide answers to common organizational problems, nor does it diagnose them. To date, little research has been completed on the team leadership model (Northouse, 2007, pp. 225–226). The practical focus on real-life organizational workgroups and team effectiveness is a somewhat new approach to the research (p. 225). The complex nature of the model, although viewed as strength, also serves as fertile ground for critics. Obviously, due to the ever-increasing shared leadership that occurs in modern organizations, multiple leaders increase the necessity for diverse approaches to problem solving within team settings. The model's very complex nature does not facilitate easy or automatic answers to organizational problems. Leaders must also take into account the situation that they are presented with and how different personalities or cultural norms may influence how one seeks to resolve a problem. Last, generally speaking, there has historically been a lack of a team diagnosis within organizations. Encouraging a team diagnosis philosophy would allow for all members of an organization, regardless of their level of responsibility, to feel more empowered to take on leadership roles.

Transformational Leadership Theory

Since the early 1980s, much attention has been paid to the transformational leadership approach. Bass and Riggio (2006) believed that the popularity of transformational leadership theory could be due to its emphasis on intrinsic motivation and follower development (Northouse, 2007, p. 175). In the simplest terms, transformational leadership is a process that changes and transforms individuals (Northouse, 2007, p. 176). In other words, transformational leadership is the ability to get people to want to change, to improve, and to be led. It involves assessing others' motives, satisfying needs, and valuing them (Northouse, 2007, p. 178). Therefore, a transformational leader can, in this manner, achieve organizational success.

The transformational leader serves as an agent of change and creates an environment for a shared vision for the future of the organization. The vision serves as a reference point for all decisions/activities and gives meaning to the role of every member through the creation of shared goals (Case, 2003). In addition, the organization's level of consciousness is heightened in a transformational environment (Hoover, 1991) through symbolism and meaning-making activities. Leaders need to communicate the vision to both internal and external stakeholders. A significant element of this form of leadership encompasses the leader-follower relationship.

Burns (1978) identified the emergence of transformational characteristics as a contrast to those of transactional leadership, in which leadership and followership roles incorporated motives, as well as issues of ethics/values. Burns suggests Mahatma Gandhi as a classic example of a transformational leader. Gandhi mobilized and inspired millions while acknowledging his own growth and development process. Leaders serve as role models for the community or group members in relation to the behaviors that lead to change. Since change tends to be a slow process, the transformational leader must have passion (Peters, 1992) regarding the ability to make a difference, to achieve goals, or to improve the current state of affairs.

House (1976) established a theory of charismatic leadership that, in research, has become synonymous with the transformational approach. He found that charismatic leaders act in unique ways. Being dominant and having a strong desire to influence others, self-confidence, and strong sense of one's own moral values (Case, 2003) are examples of the qualities of charismatic leaders. There are various potential results of this type of leadership, including follower trust in the leader, allegiance and obedience, emotional attachment to the leader's goals, and confidence in goal achievement. Max Weber (1947) constructed the most widely used definition of charisma: "as a special personality characteristic that gives a person exceptional powers, is reserved for a few, and results in person treated as a leader." Adolph Hitler, for example, definitely possessed charisma, but obviously good leadership involves more than just charisma and the ability to convince others to follow you. Although Weber emphasized charisma to be a personality quality, he also acknowledged the important role of followers regarding the validation of their leaders (Northouse, 1997), as well as the dangers of charisma absent other important qualities.

Bernard Bass (1985) built on the transformational leadership scholarship of Burns (1978) and House (1976) by paying more attention to follower rather than leader needs, as well as emphasizing emotional elements and the origins of charisma. Bass' model argues that transactional and transformational leadership can be viewed in a single continuum that highlights the seven leadership factors (Northouse, 1997): *idealized influence, inspirational motivation, intellectual stimulation, individualized consideration, contingent reward, management by exception, and laissez-faire style.* Research seems to indicate that individuals exhibiting transformational leadership tend to have a strong set of internal values and are effective at motivating followers in ways that support the greater good, rather than one's self-interest (Kuhnert, 1994).

The seven factors can be broken down in the continuum of leadership to areas that reflect three characteristics: transactional leadership, transformational leadership, or nonleadership. In transformational leadership, there are multiple factors: idealized influence, inspirational motivation, intellectual stimulation, and individualized consideration. From a transactional leadership perspective, the issues of contingent reward and management by exception would be typical. The final factor is laissez-faire leadership behavior (Northouse, 1997, 2007).

The *idealized influence* factor, also referred to as charisma, incorporates leaders who act as strong role models for followers, typically have high standards of moral and ethical behavior, and work to provide a vision and mission for members. *Inspirational motivation* describes individuals who work to communicate high standards to their members, therefore inspiring them to become more involved in and a part of the shared vision of the organization. Team spirit is enhanced through this type of leadership.

The third tenet, *intellectual stimulation,* invites followers to be creative and innovative while challenging their own beliefs and values, as well as those of the leader and organization in order to make the group function at a higher level. The last of the transformational factors entails *individualized consideration,* in which leaders work to create a supportive environment and listen to the individual needs of followers, often acting as coaches and mentors. Delegation strategies may be used to challenge members to grow in their own abilities and confidence levels. Overall, transformational leadership promotes greater effects than transactional leadership. The research suggests that transactional leadership is more outcome-focused, while transformational leadership incorporates the individual and organizational learning process.

A final concern related to transformational leadership is that it has great potential to be abused when in the hands of the wrong leader. Since a major premise of transformational leadership is changing an organization or individuals' values, leaders could manipulate the environment to focus on their own needs. On the other hand, who determines if the new direction or vision is good or what is needed for the organization? The qualities of charisma exemplify this concern in which a leader can be motivating, exciting, and very enthusiastic, causing folks to jump on the bandwagon before knowing what they truly have signed up to do. History is littered with tales of good people who were led to their destruction by leaders who transformed.

Social Change Model

As the need and desire for promoting inclusive leadership and socially responsible environments became obvious, the social change model (SCM) of leadership emerged as one that incorporates the characteristics of socially responsible leadership. The SCM has two essential goals: (1) enhance student learning and development through greater self-knowledge and leadership competence and (2) facilitate positive social change in organizations and communities (Astin, Astin, Boatsman, Bonous-Hammarth, Chambers, Goldberg, Johnson, Komives, Langdon, Leland, Lucas, Pope, Roberts, & Shellogg, 1996; Tyree, 1998).

In 1993, Alexander and Helen Astin applied to the Dwight D. Eisenhower Leadership Development Programs of the US Department of Education for funding a leadership program. They worked with a team of leadership educators across the country (known as the "Working Ensemble") to conceptualize a model of leadership development that would "prepare a new generation of leaders who understand that they can act as leaders to effect change without necessarily being in traditional leadership positions of power and authority" (Astin et al., 1996, p. 12). In 1996, the Working Ensemble established the social change model (SCM) of leadership development, which supports the notion that "leadership is ultimately about change, and that effective leaders are those who are able to effect positive change on behalf of others and society" (Astin et al., 1996, p. 10).

This model of leadership development highlights the concept that leadership is not based on one's position or title but, instead, focuses on how the leader, irrelevant of position within the organizational hierarchy, encourages others during the process. The SCM of leadership development promotes the values of equity, social justice, self-knowledge, empowerment, collaboration, citizenship, and service (Astin et al., 1996; Outcalt, Faris, McMahon, Tahtakran, Noll, 2001). In addition, the SCM reflects an inclusive approach because it was designed to enhance and develop qualities in all participants. These values connected to similar characteristics found in Nemerowicz and Rosi's (1997) definitions of social responsibility and inclusive leadership, consisting of diverse people uniting in the search to define and act on common goals, specifically promoting the collective well-being, the values of justice and equality, and an appreciation of the role of service, ethics, values, and diversity (p. 15).

The SCM consists of seven principles, known as the seven C's, that can be organized into three domains (individual, group, and community). The seven C's of the SCM consist of the following constructs:

Individual: *consciousness of self, congruence, commitment*

Group: *collaboration, common purpose, controversy with civility*

Community: *citizenship*

The objectives of this domain (consciousness of self, congruence, and commitment) encouraged self-knowledge through reflection and active participation. The next level introduced group values that focus on collaboration, common purpose, and controversy with civility. This area strived to increase leadership competency that is defined as the capacity to mobilize others to serve and work collaboratively. In general, the goal of the SCM of leadership development was to bring about change for the betterment of society (Outcalt et al., 2001).

■ MOTIVATIONAL THEORY AS A LEADERSHIP TOOL

In the leader's toolbox, one skill is paramount above all others. A leader who is a skilled motivator will find success in his or her endeavors to create change. There exists a paradox in contemporary American culture. We indoctrinate our youth with the idea that hard work and perseverance will equate to success (the definition of which we assume to be socioeconomic status). However, social norms cast a stigma on anyone who seeks personal gain. Humility forbids us from publicly asking the question "What's in it for me?"

In early American politics, humility and accepted social norms discouraged people such as Thomas Jefferson from actively seeking public office by campaigning because it would appear too self-serving. Instead, politicians "stood" for public office while supporters publically advocated on their behalf.

Library of Congress.

It is our contention that it is only natural that all individuals weigh, even if at a subconscious level, each decision they make through the use of this fundamental question. An understanding of how one's followers perceive this question, and an ability to provide its answer, can be of great use to a leader. In essence, effective leadership can be achieved by providing a desirable answer to the follower's question of "What's in it for me?" Discerning what motivates people can be essential to effective leadership. Before a leader can analyze the motives of followers, he or she must first understand the nature of motivation.

Motivation's origins lie in the Latin word *movere,* which means to move. When we consider this in the context of our working definition of leadership, the process whereby an individual influences a group of individuals to achieve a common goal, we can see clearly the relationship between leadership and motivation. A leader is charged with moving a group to action. Each follower must decide if he or she is going to follow the leader. An individual's motivation is the collective processes that stimulate behavior. A leader who attempts to influence these processes to initiate behaviors that benefit the organization as a whole is effectively manipulating motivation.

Motivation itself can be conceptualized as the sum of three components: effort, persistence, and direction. Effort is the magnitude and intensity of the behavior the leader desires. Persistence is effort sustained over time. The quality of the effort—that is, behaviors that constitute an invested and sustained effort over time, which result in progress toward the goal—is the direction of the motivation. To understand the nature of motivation, psychologists have created two fields of motivational theory. Content theories seek to understand what energizes human behavior. Process theories are concerned with how motivation occurs. To utilize motivation as a leader, an understanding of both fields is helpful.

Content Theories

Maslow's Hierarchy of Needs

Perhaps the most straightforward approach for the application of motivational theory to a leadership function is the hierarchy of needs proposed by Abraham Maslow in 1954. Maslow reviewed a generation of social science research and synthesized it into eight needs (see figure below). To ascribe to these beliefs is to declare that the core of motivation is meeting the needs of the follower.

At the base of Maslow's hierarchy are physiological and safety needs. These consist of basic bodily needs, such as needs for food, sleep, and a sense of safety. Human nature dictates an aversion to personal harm. For a leader, the implication of physiological needs is obvious: If you cannot meet your follower's basic needs, they will not be able to move beyond the desire to satisfy these needs to consider the welfare of the organization.

Maslow's Hierachy of Needs

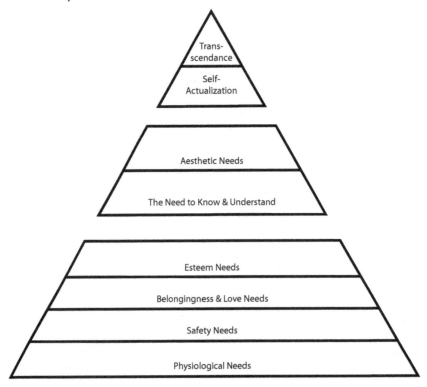

As a follower develops according to the hierarchy, the complexity of the needs grows progressively. Gradually, the need to be celebrated as an individual (esteem needs), the need for change, and the need for freedom consume the follower. The ability of leaders to meet these needs is directly proportional to their ability to understand their followers. Through understanding and nurturing, a leader can see that the organization can meet all followers' needs. When this has been accomplished, the followers will transcend to the final stages of development.

The third tier of Maslow's hierarchy is not achieved by all organizational members. However, those who do reach the stages of self-actualization and transcendence become the members on whom the leader can rely. Self-actualized individuals are characterized by their need to achieve their potential and whose actions transcend themselves and are done for a cause they believe to be bigger than themselves. The organizational benefits of having members who achieve this level of development within the context of the organization are self-evident.

To employ Maslow's synthesis of human needs as a leader, one must successfully facilitate followers' development through the stages prescribed. To ensure that the physiological needs of the followers are met, the leader has to consider the experience of the followers. In the context of employment, this equates to compensation. Does the company pay employees enough to provide a comfortable standard of living? Are employees confident that they will have food on the tables for their family? Clearly, when one does not have this need met, one cannot focus on one's duties and will not serve the organization well. Belonging and individual needs can be met by the environment created by the leader. An organization that celebrates individuals will allow them to feel a sense of belonging necessary for them to care about the organization. It is in this arena that leaders' abilities to know their followers pay dividends. The organizational member who is ensured of his or her safety, who feels important as an individual, and whose need for change is met by being incorporated into the decision-making process has the potential to become self-actualized. This occurs when the member internalizes the values, mission, and goals of the organization and they become the primary focus.

Motivation-Hygiene and ERG Theories

Another popular content theory is the motivation-hygiene theory. Known as the two-factor theory, this view reduces Maslow's eight needs into two major categories: hygiene factors and motivators. Leaders who employ this view attempt to balance these two factors. Hygiene factors relate to the needs on the lower portion of Maslow's hierarchy. While they must be met, meeting those needs does not necessarily equate to satisfaction. Motivators correspond to the higher needs of Maslow's hierarchy. These provide satisfaction, and this satisfaction drives behaviors that allow people to achieve beyond minimum performance.

Another variation on Maslow's theory is the ERG theory. This view has categorized the hierarchy of needs into three main areas: existence needs, relatedness needs, and growth needs. The letters that begin each category lend themselves to the acronym that has become the theory's name. Existence needs correspond to the physiological needs. Relatedness needs are a broad category that encompasses the vast array of interpersonal and social needs of an individual. Growth needs are those driving forces that require that each individual grow, develop, and realize his or her potential.

Equity Theory

Perhaps one of the most basic tenets of motivational theory is equity theory. This theory simply states that people must believe that the output of their efforts is equal to or greater than their input. For most, this rationalization is accepted prima fascia. Few individuals are willing to lend their time or talents for an effort if they do not feel that the worth of the end result will not be greater than or equal to the worth of their time.

■ CONCLUSION

The study of leadership is one of the most difficult endeavors you will ever undertake. When you hear someone talk about leaders or leadership, intuitively you know what leadership is; we all have an understanding of what constitutes a leader. But can you respond to the question "What is leadership?"

This chapter presented a wide variety of ways in which leadership is described and conceptualized. Which one(s) resonate with you? Which do you believe is an accurate assessment of the complex relationship among leaders, followers, and the context in which they operate? With a command of these theories, models, and methods for approaching leadership, we hope that you will have the necessary understanding to evaluate leaders, both contemporary and historical, and understand the reasons for their success or failure.

Even more important, we hope that these tools will allow you to reflect on your own leadership style and, where possible, help you become a more effective leader. Theories, however, are of little use to emerging leaders unless they are applied. Three of the most important things aspiring leaders can do to grow in leadership are:

- Lead something, whether it is a club or an organization on campus or a team.
- Read about learning how to lead others; find out everything you can about the subject and study the writings and teachings of successful leaders.
- Find a mentor who will help you grow as a leader; observe and emulate leadership skills.

Now that you are somewhat familiar with the major theoretical concepts and practices of leadership studies, we hope that you will add them to your personal leadership toolbox and refer to them often as you continue your life's work as an emerging leader.

■ KEY TERMS

Assigned Leadership—A leader whose power is derived from title, office, or other legitimate position.

Emergent Leadership—A leader who has acquired influence and status through the beliefs, trust, and support of his or her ideas and guidance.

Great Man Theory—Early views of leadership were often called great man theories, as they attempted to describe leadership in terms of the men who embodied it.

Power—One's ability to cause another to take action.

Relationship Behavior—An act by a member of a team that contributes to the overall group harmony of the organization.

Skills—Abilities or behaviors that contribute to one's ability to lead. Unlike a trait, a skill can be practiced or learned.

Task Behavior—An act by a member of a team that contributes to the completion of a project or the attainment of a goal.

Traits—Innate qualities that allow one to lead. The assumption that leaders possess traits that allow them to lead suggests that the ability to lead is something one has from birth.

■ SUGGESTED READINGS

Hackman, M. J. & Johnson, C. E. 2004. *Leadership: A Communication Perspective.* Long Grove, IL: Waveland Press.

Reicher, S. D., Haslam, S. A., & Platow, M. J. 2007. "The New Psychology of Leadership." *Scientific American Mind,* Sept. 2007, 22–29.

■ REFERENCES

Astin, A. W., Astin, H. S., Boatsman, K. C., Bonous-Hammarth, M., Chambers, T., Goldberg, L. S., Johnson, C. S., Komives, S. R., Langdon, E. A., Leland, C., Lucas, N., Pope, R. L., Roberts, D., & Shellogg, K. M. 1996. *A Social Change Model of Leadership Development: Guidebook* (Version III). Los Angeles: University of California Los Angeles, Higher Education Research Institute.

Barge, J. K. 1996. "Leadership Skills and the Dialetics of Leadership in Group Decision Making." In R. Y. Hirokawa & M. S. Poole (eds.), *Communication and Group Decision Making* (2nd ed., pp. 301–342). Thousand Oaks, CA: Sage.

Bass, B. M. 1985. *Leadership and Performance Beyond Expectations.* New York: Free Press.

Bass, B. M., & Riggio, R. E. 2006. *Transformational Leadership* (2nd ed.). Mahwah, NJ: Lawrence Erlbaum.

Blake, R. R. & Mouton, J. S. 1964. *The Managerial Grid*. Houston, Tex.: Gulf.

Burns, J. M. 1978. *Leadership*. New York: Harper & Row.

Carlyle, T. 1869. *On Heroes, Hero-Worship and the Heroic in History*. London: Chapman & Hall.

Case, A. 2003. *Transformational Leadership: A Brief Review of the Literature*. Retrieved 17 April, http://wings.buffalo.edu/academic/department/edoap/case.html.

Ciulla, J. B. (ed.) 2004. *Ethics, the Heart of Leadership*. Westport, Conn.: Praeger.

Dansereau, F., Graen, G. B., & Haga, W. 1975. "A Vertical Dyad Linkage Approach to Leadership in Formal Organizations." *Organizational Behavior and Human Performance, 13*, 46–78.

Goethals, G. R., & Sorenson, G. L. J. (eds). 2006. *The Quest for a General Theory of Leadership*. Northampton, MA: Edward Elgar.

Graen, G. B., & Uhl-Bien, M. 1995. "Relationship-Based Approach to Leadership: Development of Leader-Member Exchange (LMX) Theory of Leadership over 25 Years: Applying a Multi-Level, Multi-Domain Perspective." *Leadership Quarterly, 6(2)*, 219–247.

Hackman, M. J. & Johnson, C. E. 2004. *Leadership: A Communication Perspective*. Long Grove, IL: Waveland Press.

Heller, T. & Van Til, J. 1983. "Leadership and Followership: Some Summary Propositions." *Journal of Applied Behavioral Science, 18*, 405–414.

Hersey, P. 1984. *The Situational Leader*. New York: Warner Books.

Hollander, E. P. 1992. "Leadership, Followership, Self, and Others." *Leadership Quarterly, 3(1)*, 43–54.

Hoover, N. R. 1991. *Transformational and Transactional Leadership: An Empirical Test of a Theory*. Paper presented at the annual meeting of the American Educational Research Association, Chicago. (ERIC Document Reproduction Service No. ED 331 177).

House, R. J. 1976. "A 1976 Theory of Charismatic Leadership." In J. G. Hunt & L. L. Larson (eds.), *Leadership: The Cutting Edge* (pp. 189–207). Carbondale, IL: Southern Illinois University Press.

Hughes, R. L., Ginnett, R. C., & Curphy, G. J. 2006. *Leadership: Enhancing the Lessons of Experience* (5th ed.). New York: McGraw-Hill.

Jago, A. G. 1982. "Leadership: Perspectives in Theory and Research." *Management Science, 28(3)*, 315–336.

Katz, R. 1955. "Skills of an Effective Administrator," *Harvard Business Review,* (Jan.–Feb.), 33–42.

Komives, S. R., Lucas, N., & McMahon, T. R. 2007. *Exploring Leadership: For College Students Who Want to Make a Difference*. San Francisco: Jossey-Bass.

Kuhnert, K. W. 1994. "Transforming Leadership: Developing People Through Delegation." In B. M. Bass & B. J. Avolio (eds.), *Improving Organizational Effectiveness Through Transformational Leadership* (pp. 10–25). Thousand Oaks, CA: Sage.

Mangan, K. 2002. "Leading the Way in Leadership: The Unending Quest of the Discipline's Founding Father, James MacGregor Burns." *Chronicle of Higher Education,* 31 May, vol. 48, no. 38, pp. A10–A12.

Maslow, A. H. 1987. *Motivation and Personality*. New York: Harper & Row.

Maslow, A. H. 1954. *Motivation and Personality*. New York: Harper.

McGrath, J. E., Arrow, H., & Berdahl, J. L. 2000. "The Study of Groups: Past, Present, and Future." *Personality and Social Psychology Review, 4(1),* 95–105.

Mumford, M. D., Zaccaro, S. J., Connelly, M. S., & Marks, M. A. 2000. "Leadership Skills: Conclusions and Future Directions." *Leadership Quarterly, 11(1),* 155–170.

Nemerowicz, G., & Rosi, E. 1997. *Education for Leadership and Social Responsibility*. Washington, DC: Falmer Press.

Northouse, P. G. 2007. *Leadership: Theory and Practice* (4th ed.). Thousand Oaks, CA: Sage.

Northouse, P. G. 1997. *Leadership: Theory and Practice*. Thousand Oaks, CA: Sage.

Outcalt, C. L., Faris, S. K., McMahon, K. N., Tahtakran, P. M., & Noll, C. B. 2001. "A Leadership Approach for the New Millennium: A Case Study of UCLA's Bruin Leaders Project." *NASPA Journal, 38(2),* 178–188.

Peters, T. 1992. *Liberation Management*. New York: Knopf.

Porter, G., & Beyerlein, M. 2000. "Historic Roots of Team Theory and Practice." In M. M. Beyerlein (ed.), *Work Teams: Past, Present, and Future* (pp. 3–24). Dordrecht, The Netherlands: Kluwer.

Schriesheim, C. A., Castro, S. L., & Cogliser, C. C. 1999. "Leader-Member Exchange (LMX) Research: A Comprehensive Review of Theory, Measurement, and Data-Analytic Practices." *Leadership Quarterly, 10,* 63–113.

Smith, J. A., & Foti, R. J. 1998. "A Pattern Approach to the Study of Leader Emergence." *Leadership Quarterly, 9(2),* 147–160.

Stogdill, R. M. 1974. *Handbook of Leadership: A Survey of Theory and Research*. New York: Free Press.

Stogdill, R. M. 1948. "Personal Factors Associated with Leadership: A Survey of the Literature." *Journal of Psychology, 25,* 35–71.

Tyree, T. 1998. *Social Change Model Assessment*. National Clearinghouse for Leadership Programs, http://www.inform.umd.edu/OCP/NCLP/.

Weber, M. 1947. *The Theory of Social and Economic Organizations*. (T. Parsons, Trans.). New York: Free Press.

Wheatley, M. J. 1992. *Leadership and the New Science: Learning About Organization from an Orderly Universe*. San Francisco: Berrett-Koehler.

CHAPTER FIVE REVIEW QUESTIONS

1. Describe experiences of social responsibility and socially responsible leader-ship on your campus. How do we model socially responsible leadership? Give positive and negative examples. What are challenges to being an SR leader?

   _____

   _____

   _____

2. How are the seven C's of the social change model of leadership development reflected in your own personal leadership development? In your organization's leadership development? Take an inventory of your strengths and weaknesses related to the seven constructs of the SCM of leadership development.

   _____

   _____

   _____

3. If you were to create a general theory of leadership, what would be your key principles? How do you define leadership personally? Organizationally?

   _____

   _____

   _____

4. You are leader of a group project for a class. The other group members seem insecure about whether they can complete the project, but it is apparent that they are competent enough to do a good job. In prior meetings, you have been coaching them on the project. Based on the situational leader model, which leadership style should you exhibit at the next meeting?

   _____

   _____

   _____

5. The three-skill approach to leadership requires high levels of technical, human, and conceptual managerial skills at which level(s) of management?

   _____

   _____

   _____

CHAPTER FIVE SELF-TEST
(Circle the correct answer.)

1. A manager at an automotive plant is an example of
   A. an emergent leader.
   B. a contextual leader.
   C. an assigned leader.
   D. a classic leader.

2. The source of power when Bill Gates and Paul Allen founded Microsoft is
   A. referent.
   B. legitimate.
   C. coercive.
   D. expert.

3. Elizabeth, a new intern in the campus office in which you work, has not been following through on her duties as of late. To help her, you specify what she must do to complete the tasks while incorporating her suggestions. According to the situational leadership model, you are utilizing what leadership style?
   A. directing
   B. coaching
   C. supporting
   D. delegating

4. The great man (trait) theory stresses traits that are learned.
   A. true
   B. false

5. According to contingency theory, no leader can be expected to perform well in every situation.
   A. true
   B. false

6. The contingency theory is a leader-match theory.
   A. true
   B. false

7. The situational leadership model contends that leaders exhibit both directive (task-oriented) and supportive behaviors.
   A. true
   B. false

8. By definition, a boss has *position power* over a subordinate.
   A. true
   B. false

Name: _____   Date: _____

SHORT ANSWER

1. Outline trends in the study of leadership over history. Begin with the great man theories and end with contemporary views of leadership.

2. Describe, in your own words, how an understanding of Maslow's hierarchy of needs might be useful for the emerging leader of a group or organization. Cite an example of how you, perhaps unknowingly, were influenced by one of your "eight needs" when making a decision about how to proceed in a leadership role.

How Leaders Communicate

6

Karla M.
Hunter

Bruce
Tucker

■ COMMUNICATION IS ONE OF THE MOST IMPORTANT SKILLS REQUIRED IN LEADERSHIP

You honestly believe that you could be a good leader. You are a good decision maker. You plan well. You have always finished your projects on time, and you have been goal-oriented and personally motivated. However, you cannot get people to follow you. Your colleagues often ignore you. You cannot even get your dog to obey. Chances are, it is not that you are lacking many important leadership skills; you may not have the glue that holds all the pieces together. You cannot sell a car unless you ask a person to buy it. You cannot have more fries unless you say "super-size it." You cannot marry the love of your life if you never propose, and you cannot effectively lead without communication skills.

■ LEADERS ARE JUDGED, AND COMMUNICATION SKILLS ARE ONE OF THE VISIBLE CRITERIA FOR JUDGMENT

You are the new leader. You were elected, hired, or chosen to be in this new position of respect, authority, and recognition. Until now, glass houses were just poetic metaphors, or homes of goldfish, guppies, and swordtails. At the present time, being on the pedestal simply means that you can see more easily over the crowd. It also means that the crowd can more easily see you. Even though everyone appears excited, sending you congratulatory emails, invitations to lunch, and tickets to football games, it is time for a reality check. Not everyone is delighted that you were chosen. A certain percentage wanted someone else in the position that you now hold. Some may think that they, themselves, should be receiving those congratulatory fruit baskets. Some of those tickets may, in reality, be a political strategy either to move up the food chain or to keep from being a course in it. There will be a certain percentage of people that will quietly sit by and wait until the honeymoon period is over. Some will try to hasten your demise.

An undeniable fact of leadership is that leaders are judged. They are judged concerning their philosophies and values. They are judged on their success rate in accomplishing tasks, though few will agree on which tasks or what qualifies for success. They will even judge you on your appearance—inappropriate, yes, but a fact of life. How much did your haircut cost? Few publicly will claim that they can judge your motives. In private everyone is a mind reader. However, there are some things that are obvious and open to criticism. Decision making is one example, but communication often sits at the top of the heap. A great communicator can absolve a number of leadership sins. A poor communicator will open a Pandora's Box of criticism regardless of his or her other skills. Whether one likes it or not, communication is an extremely important component of leadership.

▦ COMMUNICATION IS THE LEADERSHIP GLUE THAT HOLDS MOST OF THE QUALITIES AND SKILLS OF LEADERSHIP TOGETHER

There are a number of important qualities and skills that a leader should possess to be effective. Communication is the key factor in maximizing many of these indispensable qualities in leadership. While people initially think that leadership should be rather easy to define, it becomes a task of surprising difficulty. While we may have our favorite one-liner definitions taken from a mentor, a poster, or a Hallmark® card, the fact of the matter is that few agree exactly on what leadership is. People usually define leadership by listing qualities and skills that they find in people whom they look up to and respect, people they would classify as leaders. Unfortunately, because of differing cultures, backgrounds, experiences, personalities, and contexts, those lists of qualities and skills can vary significantly. People define leadership by whom they choose to follow, not by the charisma we, as leaders, claim to exude. While people may not agree on all the qualities and skills one must possess, and which ones are the most important, one thing we can agree on is that communication enhances most of them. The following are some examples of important leadership qualities and skills requiring communication to be successful.

Inspiring Vision

Preeminent in the pantheon of leadership qualities is vision. You cannot have a vacation without having a destination, you cannot teach rhetoric without having a dream, and you cannot discuss leadership without beginning with vision. Leaders are visionaries. However, if the leader is simply sitting and gazing off into the air in serene bliss, you are at best confused about what he or she is thinking about; at worst, you are tempted to put a quarter into his or her coffee cup. Unless leaders can communicate their vision to others, no one will have a unifying direction. Leaders are expected to inspire vision. Vagueness is not inspiring; it makes significant others wonder what you did last night.

Clarifying Expectations

Your three-month evaluation is coming up. If you pass your probationary period satisfactorily, it will be Outback® tonight. However, you are shaky and the fried onion is in jeopardy. Your supervisor never clarified his or her expectations. You were not sure of the goals or what specifically your purpose is. "Well, punk, do you feel lucky?" Leaders must clarify goals and purposes for people to have direction and motivation. There are two ways that can be done: Have your subordinates watch your example and see if they can play charades well or tell them directly. We recommend the direct approach, communication.

Motivating

No matter how hard you try, you cannot herd cats without fish. Likewise, you cannot motivate followers without communication. Intrinsic motivation is dependent on people understanding the "motive"—that is, the purpose for acting in accordance with the leader's wishes. Extrinsic motivation depends on a variety of actions and techniques. Motive is clarified through communication, and the actions effective in extrinsic motivation are based on both verbal and nonverbal communication skills.

Persuading

Not everyone will agree with what you want to do, or how you want to do it as a leader. Imagine that! To accomplish your goals and to gain support, you must be able to persuade others. We are not in Wonderland with Alice. We cannot garner support by threatening, "Off with your head!" We are more sophisticated in the new millennium; we just down-size. If you depend on down-sizing too much, your job may be outsourced. Leaders must have the ability to debate and persuade.

These students are preparing for a national forensics tournament. Joining your college debate team is a great way to enhance your ability to debate and persuade.

Photo courtesy of Karen Christensen.

Teaching

Those who can, do. Those who cannot, teach. Better stated, those who can do often forget who taught them how. Leaders cannot forget. To be a leader requires you to be a teacher. You are an instructor and a trainer. You do not make decisions unilaterally; you direct the decision-making process with a team. You do not dump assignments onto others; you delegate responsibilities with all the directions, expectations, and timetables required. You define the vision and purpose. You teach. Teachers make good leaders.

Establishing Morale

Morale is down in the company. Rumors are running rampant. The grapevine has crashed, and no one is in anyone's loop. These are all the results of poor communication. To dispel rumors, or at least limit their being the source of "official" information and leaks, an effective system of communication is foundational.

Resolving Conflict

Place five people together and you will have ten different opinions. If you have three new employees and only two offices, you will be drawing straws. Your department's budget gets cut 10 percent; the politicking begins. Too much champagne at the holiday party and the headaches will last weeks longer than the hangover. Conflict is inevitable. As a matter of fact, no conflict in a group may be an indication of two significant problems, apathy among the members and intimidation. Group members who really care about the purpose and values of the group will express and defend their views. This will inevitably lead to tension as the group works through these issues. If there is no conflict, it may indicate that the members lack conviction, which is unfortunate, or the leader has intimidated the members so that they fear challenging the leadership. This, too, is a negative situation. The ability to resolve them will require communication skills.

Promoting Teamwork

The philosophy of leadership has been transitioning from **X-styled leadership,** a hierarchical philosophy of top-down, task-oriented leadership, to relational, or **Y-styled leadership.** Teamwork is now the name of the game. Team-building retreats, ropes courses, and sharing of one's feelings are indispensable responsibilities of the human resources department. You cannot lead without teamwork. You cannot have teamwork without emphasizing relationships, and you cannot have relationships without communication.

■ COMMUNICATION IS A FUNDAMENTAL INGREDIENT OF ONE'S LEADERSHIP STYLE

A key principle of leadership is not so much what you do but how you do it. This is referring to one's leadership style. Style, in this case, is not a reference to wearing an Izod® gator on your shirt in the 1970s or driving a hybrid Toyota® now. People often respond favorably or unfavorably to leadership because of the way leaders lead.

Moreover, as qualities and skills are often the means by which people define one's leadership abilities, leadership style explains how people prefer to apply those qualities and skills. For example, in giving directions and training others, what is your personal preference—to tell people what you want or to show them what you mean? Some say that leaders should lead by example, demonstrate what they want, walk the walk. Others are firmly convinced that those are nice platitudes that fit well on motivational posters and T-shirts, but the major problems in groups and organizations are a lack of communication, a lack of clarity, vaguely defined expectations, and immense assumptions that people will actually catch your intent and vision by osmosis or intuition. Both of these style preferences, whether demonstrating or speaking, depend on communication, either verbal or nonverbal.

Each individual has a **leadership style,** a preference on how he or she relates to others in a leader/follower dynamic. We are all different, and as genetics, environment, experiences, and a whole variety of factors have molded us into valuing different qualities in our leaders, the same factors govern how we feel comfortable leading. People are different. Personalities are different. People respond differently to different things; as leaders, we all have a preference in how we feel most comfortable and successful relating to others. Many people often love or hate leaders because of the leaders' leadership styles more than their abilities or qualifications.

While a number of methods have been developed to define leadership styles, such as colors, letters, metaphors, and personality type indicators, leadership styles can be best assessed directly by four specific issues, which are the basis for all the aforementioned methods: priority, control, participation, and interaction.

Priority: Task Versus People

The most frequently discussed, and most important, issue is priority. What is the leader's priority? Is it getting a task accomplished on time, or is it taking care of the people? To those who emphasize the task, and see success measured by getting things done on time and see their tenure based on that success, there is no question that the task is the most important. If the leader must step on some toes or bruise some fragile egos, then so be it. How can it be leadership if you never accomplish your objectives?

On the other hand, those who prioritize relationships believe that the people are the priority. They feel that, if a leader wishes to accomplish more than one task, then that leader will have to garner the support and loyalty of the people. That means developing good relationships. Leadership effectiveness is measured by more than just achieving the final project or goal; it is also reflected in the process of getting that project completed and that goal met. Both preferences must employ distinct communication skills to be effective, either firm, direct instructions or relational, interpersonal interaction.

Control: Unilateral Versus Consensus

Bruce and his female husky, Hershey, are in a constant battle over who is in control of his house. When Hershey cannot use a direct approach to have her own way, she finds a more subtle way. She sleeps on the couch only because she chooses to. Bruce, on the other hand, must please his wife, so he "chooses" not to. It seems that one of the most crucial issues in human relationships is the issue of control: who gets his or her way and how he or she gets it. Those who pursue unilateral control believe that they are the leader because they are the most qualified or the most experienced, they deserve it, or at least they were appointed the title. If they are going to be held accountable for the decisions and the results, then they feel that they should make the final decisions.

On the other hand, some believe that, even though they may be the ones held accountable, the chances of success increase when the knowledge, experiences, and skills of a team of people can reach true consensus. Shared authority not only produces better decisions but also more motivation and ownership among the group. It also provides a bigger list of people to blame when things do not turn out as planned. Directing a consensus-oriented process requires significant interpersonal communication skills, while unilateral control requires persuasion and justification.

Participation: Active Versus Passive

Some are committed to the principle that followers appreciate and respect leaders who roll up their sleeves, get down in the dirt with their followers, and slug it out as one of the group. People follow leaders who lead by example, who are not too proud to work alongside them and experience all that their followers do.

However, many disagree with this approach. Too often, such a leader is simply micromanaging and making sure things are done his or her way. Excellent leaders find qualified individuals, delegate responsibilities to them, and then get out of the way, so that they can get their work done. Leaders who spend all of their time pouring punch at the office party are not always showing servant humility but trying to stay so busy that no one can criticize them for dodging the bigger responsibilities and decisions of leadership that may require vulnerability and too large of a risk. Active participation demands one set of communication skills, while passive leadership involvement demands another.

Interaction: Verbal Versus Listening

The leader is a cheerleader. A major problem in groups is poor communication, even if that group is a group of two, a husband and wife. If there is a breakdown in morale, it probably is due to a lack of understanding. If rumors are running rampant then conflicts can occur and people can become insecure. If no one is sure what is supposed to be done, and expectations are as clear as an IRS tax form (not very clear at all), then productivity can suffer. Followers want to know what is going on and what their leaders expect from them. Without clear instructions, mistakes are often made. You may want to lead by example, but if no one knows what you are being an example of, what does it matter?

However, it makes no sense to talk the talk if you can't walk the walk. We don't need carnival hawkers, though a laudable profession; we need people who are role models and examples. Some leaders talk too much. It seems that they call meetings only to hear themselves speak. Leaders should show people what they want, not just tell them. Talk is cheap. Vision is caught, not taught. If we listened better, we wouldn't have to talk so much later, trying to correct our mistakes and misunderstandings.

**"A good leader is also a good listener.
I could listen to myself all day!"**

Copyright Randy Glasbergen, www.glasbergen.com

The important point is that everyone has a style, and effectiveness in applying that style depends on effective communication skills being adapted and developed for each situation and preference.

■ THE COMMUNICATION SKILLS REQUIRED FOR EFFECTIVE LEADERSHIP

How Bruce gives commands to his dog and to his cat requires different techniques. Bruce simply speaks to his dog, who actually appears to be listening—the tail is a dead giveaway—and she usually responds. Holding a dog biscuit at the time of his command is a motivational technique that Bruce has discovered produces better results. On the other hand, with his cat, Pan, communication borders on begging, and treats are irrelevant because Pan sees the entire issue as one of principle. She will not be bribed, nor will she do anything that gives the appearance of submission.

Leaders, likewise, must use different sets of communication principles in differing forums and contexts. Leaders must develop communication skills when speaking before larger groups; before smaller groups, such as a board or committee; or individually in a one-on-one context.

The Communication Skills Required for Effective Leadership Have Changed Over Time

Now the plot has thickened even more. With ever-present media watching every move a leader makes, seeking an appropriate quotation for the evening news has been raised to an art form. A single careless, spontaneous or emotional sentence will be recorded, archived, and used in the most inopportune times or, worse, for time immemorial on YouTube! One learns to fear camera phones, much less video cameras. In the "old days," a speech could develop a theme and reach a climax. Today, sound bites are the modus operandi of both policymakers and media practitioners; and contextual information is often cut to fit a sixty-second news spot. Sometimes it is not merely what we say but how we say it that can make or break us as a leader.

In the 1984 presidential debates, incumbent President Ronald Reagan's PR team were concerned about his image—that Americans would think that a seventy-three-year-old man was too old to be president. Reagan, also known as the "great communicator," chose to use humor to defuse this age concern, rather than addressing it directly. Thanks to his crack team of political debate consultants, the president was armed and ready with the now-famous political quip "I will not make age an issue in this campaign. I refuse to exploit for political purposes the youth and inexperience of my opponent."[1] His stance disarmed the "age factor" criticism and played a major role in leading Reagan to beat Mondale by "the largest electoral landslide in history."

---

1. For additional information about President Reagan, refer to the following website: http://www.pbs.org/wgbh/amex/presidents/40_reagan/reagan_politics.html.

By contrast, President Richard Nixon gives us an example of communication that harmed a politician's image. During the now-famous 1960 Kennedy-Nixon televised presidential debates, for instance, Nixon wore a white shirt, making him look pale. He was sweating profusely, making him look guilty—guilty of what we did not yet know. Nevertheless, his appearance hurt his image.

Having discussed many philosophies of the effective leader-communicator, as well as several principles of the verbal content that good leaders habituate, this chapter now turns to a discussion of research findings regarding the actions of leadership communication. As a wise man once said, "Your actions speak so loudly, I can't hear a word you're saying." To be an effective leader, one must understand nonverbal communication and how it impacts the success and failure of leadership.

▪ NONVERBAL COMMUNICATION IMPACTS LEADERSHIP SUCCESS

A vital tenet of the communication discipline states that "one cannot not communicate [in the presence of another human being]" (Watzlawick, Beavin, & Jackson, 1967). In other words, everything we say or do and, sometimes equally as important, what we do not say or do, sends a message, whether intended or not. Clothing, movements, office decor, even whether a message is delivered face-to-face versus via email—the effective leader knows it all matters. Have you ever met a brilliant professor whose desk was hopelessly cluttered with stacks of papers and heaven knows what, or one who was repeatedly late to class? Would your comfort in following such a leader translate far beyond the classroom?

According to classic nonverbal communication scholarship by Mehrabian and Wiener (1967) or Birdwhistell (1955), verbal communication might account for only 7 to 40 percent of all communication in any given interaction. Birdwhistell and Mehrabian differ greatly regarding the exact percentage of meaning their studies found to be derived from *nonverbal* communication. Birdwhistell reports that it is certainly above 60 percent, but Mehrabian's work found a whopping 93 percent!

Nonverbal communication is vital to leadership for two reasons: (1) The nonverbal behaviors of our followers may not always support their verbal communication and (2) we need to ensure that our own nonverbal behaviors fortify our credibility through supporting our verbal messages and exuding a balance of strength with warmth, integrity with receptivity.

Riggio (1986) studies "social skill"—the ability to encode nonverbal messages, the ability to decode them when they are delivered by others, and one's success at controlling nonverbal expressions appropriately. An effective leader must be able to do all three. When communicating with someone whose verbal and nonverbal messages fail to match, which do you think most people tend to rely on? They attend to the nonverbal, of course. As a leader, do you trust that your followers are truly "fine" when they say that they are, even if they frown, slump, or look away from you as they say it? What about when they say they support your position on something but use a lackluster tone of voice and give a slight headshake and a "dead fish" handshake as they say so? Have you ever met someone who smiled upside-down? There's a facial expression to decipher. Perhaps the person knows that smiling would be an appropriate response to the context but feels an internal animosity toward the situation or individuals involved.

If these examples spark your interest or lead you to question your own nonverbal communication, consider the challenge of undergoing an inventory of your own nonverbal communication, by taking stock of your own patterns in several key nonverbal areas laid out in the remainder of this chapter: vocalics, kinesics, proxemics and territory, haptics, olfactics and chronemics, artifacts, and channel effects.

Vocalics

Vocalics are a special form of nonverbal, also known as paralanguage (or "beyond language," in the same way as paranormal is "beyond normal." This form of communication includes rate, pitch, volume, tone of voice, modulation or vocal variety, and even silence. Silence communicates, sometimes more strongly than words can. In fact, to reiterate the idea that we "cannot not communicate," consider what it communicates when you fail to respond to an email (or when your significant other suddenly stops calling, emailing, or text messaging).

Most effective leaders know that the modulation of all the other characteristics is what can make them sound charismatic, when necessary, and low-key when that mood is more apropos. It is probably not hard for you to envision your instructor saying, "You did a great job on the exam," yet how many meanings might this simple sentence take on when stated using different vocalic patterns? Even if the vocal channel is the only one present, as on the telephone or on an audio recording, a congratulatory meaning or a sarcastic meaning might be derived. Attempt to deliver that sentence as if you are contrasting the exam performance with the entire body of that student's work. Then attempt to deliver it in a way that singles you, that student, out from the rest of the class.

Imagine your employer coming to you and saying, "Great job." If she is being sarcastic and you cannot tell, it may be due to her lack of skill, or your own, but the end result is the same—you continue working in the same way you have been working and continue achieving results she finds unsatisfactory. If you miss the point, her leadership has been derailed.

Leadership Challenge

Try your hand at creative vocalics. Say the following statements to a friend or classmate using various levels of pitch, volume, tone, and vocal variety to deliver different meanings: (1) "I was truly inspired by what you said."
(2) "Sure, I believe you." (3) "You look really nice in that outfit."

Nonverbal/Nonvocal Communication

Studies show that about 70 percent of communication is nonverbal and nonvocal (Mehrabian and Weiner, 1967), and this type of communication can occur in several distinct categories. The limited space of this chapter allows for only a brief discussion of each of these categories, but literally volumes of information exist on each of these topics for the interested scholar who wishes for further insights (see the "Suggested Readings" list at the end of this chapter).

Kinesics

The largest message-type category of nonverbal communication is known as **kinesics.** If you have ever heard the term *telekinesis,* you likely know that it refers to one's ability to move objects without touching them. Leaders do not need to possess that skill. Not literally, anyway. Good leaders do, however, know how to move their own bodies in the ways that enhance their credibility via others' perceptions of their skill, integrity, or kindness (in so doing, perhaps they motivate others to move the objects they want moved for them, which may be nearly as impressive as any form of extrasensory perception).

Good leaders know how to move their own bodies in ways that enhance their credibility with others.

Photo courtesy of Richard R. Boyd.

Kinesics is what is commonly referred to as "body language," and it includes hand gestures and bodily movement, facial expressions, and eye behavior. The credible leader knows that one's behaviors in each of these areas necessarily differ, dependent on context.

Gestures

While speaking in front of a large crowd, for instance, one might gesture more largely than when having an intimate discussion with an individual conversational partner. Imagine, however, standing a mere foot away when someone talking with you begins large hand gestures! Would you be a bit frightened? Might you believe the person is angry, or at least acting inappropriately? Would you be afraid of negative attention being drawn to the conversation, perhaps even reflecting negatively on you? Would it inspire you to follow that person, or to slowly back away?

Another vital consideration for those who aspire to greater leadership opportunities is the risk of "overgesturing." Make and watch a video recording of yourself speaking (or simply ask someone to watch you) and answer the following question: Are your gestures always meaningful, or might they tend to distract your audience? If every statement deserves a gesture, then none does. Many charismatic leaders have to work to balance and discipline gestures and movement, in order to avoid distracting the audience, or appearing "flighty." Enthusiasm and charisma are tremendous assets for leaders and prospective leaders, but credibility is a constant tension between these characteristics and their counterparts, competence and trustworthiness. Too much display of enthusiasm may lead some to believe that one is "slippery," or "all talk and no action."

Facial Expression

Another important area of kinesics is that of facial expression. Literally hundreds of facial expressions have been coded and categorized by nonverbal scholars (Burgoon, Buller, & Woodall, 1995). An effective leader must memorize every one of them. Just kidding; he or she must, however, optimize his or her ability, as Riggio's (1986) theory of social skill suggests, to encode and control his or her own facial expressions appropriately and to decode the expressions of others accurately.

Child development researchers Metzloff and Moore (1983) theorize that humans, as infants, actually learn which faces "fit" with which emotions through a process known as **intermodal matching.** In this process, a baby observes the facial expressions of parents and other caregivers and then practices the facial expressions, observing how the expressions make him or her feel in order to "catalogue" his or her own understanding of the proper use of expression for future use. The theory says people make the face first and the feeling follows, rather than the other way around. Biologists claim that smiling actually releases feel-good hormones.

Allowing ourselves to commit fully to a facial expression gives it a great deal more power, especially when the expression is such an important one at enhancing others' evaluations of our credibility and warmth. Perhaps if the biologists are right, our own enhanced positive feelings might also contribute to our effectiveness as well.

In cinematic computer graphics technology, the morphing of a human face begins with an initial or "default" face. Real humans each have their own "default face," as well. It is the face each person makes when feeling no particular emotion—it might also be referred to as a "reset" or "resting face." It is a rare person, indeed, who is truly even aware that the default face exists, much less what his or hers looks like. Also of interest are unfortunate individuals who have an angry-looking **default face.** It is quite a challenge to accurately decode the facial expression of someone who always looks angry. How might this misencoded facial expression and people's standard interpretation of a frown harm one's effectiveness at obtaining and performing leadership roles?

Eye Contact

Like vocalic communication, eye behavior necessarily varies from context to context as well. A public speaker is wise to avoid the traditional advice of looking over audience members' heads. For one reason, people can tell when you actually look them in the eye, and it attracts their eyes to meet naturally with yours, enhancing not only your credibility but also your interactional ability and therefore your enjoyment of your speaking experience. While not all good leaders adore public speaking, many of them have a healthy respect for and understanding of the principles necessary to deliver a successful speech. One of the greatest is to be engaging, and this cannot occur without eye contact. For that reason, scripted speech delivery is of limited value to the truly excellent leader *unless* he or she has developed the amazingly difficult skill of reading from a script while sounding truly natural. Watch the news. One key distinction between a good anchor and a great anchor is that, despite the fact that they are all reading from teleprompters, the seasoned pro neither looks nor sounds as if he or she is being literally spoon-fed every word, yet he or she is. Other professionals, politicians or the CEOs of major corporations, have an added challenge—nearly every word they utter is recorded and public. One slipup or poor wording choice can equate to political suicide, or at least to decreased political efficacy. For the rest of us, however, speaking from extremely limited notes is generally recommended. Prepare. Practice. Then you are free to look at your audience and engage them fully.

Effective leaders also know and respect the reality that eye contact expectations, as with all forms of nonverbal communication, differ from one culture to another. According to the classic intercultural communication text *Communicating with Strangers: An Approach to Intercultural Communication,* by William Gudykunst and Young Yun Kim (1984), most people are unaware that communication patterns are unique to the culture in which they were raised. Different cultures (and subcultures) have different rules and norms. Effective leaders are able to adapt not only their own behavior but also their expectations of others' behavior based on this knowledge. An excellent reference for knowledge of the communication in other cultures is the text *Kiss, Bow, or Shake Hands: The Bestselling Guide to How to Do Business in More than 60 Countries* (Morrison & Conaway, 2006). Nonverbal scholarship finds that Western societies, such as the United States and most European countries, uphold the person who gives and receives a large amount of eye contact as a respected and credible individual. Eastern (e.g., Asian) and Native American cultures, however, interpret too much eye contact as a signal of disrespect for a person of authority or as a sign of a failure to listen—if the eyes are used extensively, how can the ears be expected to work to their full potential? Even among non-native North Americans, a difference exists between the eye contact usage of those of European and those of African descent. Communication research has shown that, similar to Asian peoples, African Americans show respect more often by avoiding eye contact, while Caucasians tend to show respect by giving it. "Look at me when I talk to you!" If this sounds familiar, you might consider the ethnic background of the person saying it and the person to whom it was said. Also consider, was it a line delivered by an African American on a television show that may have been written by a white screenwriter?

A humorous examination of eye contact and gender was portrayed on the popular television series *The Simpsons* when Homer Simpson was holding a conversation with a Simpsonized cartoon version of sexy television icon Carmen Electra, who said, "Homer, my face is up here." Homer, unmoving, replies, "I've made my choice." This example can be instructive interpersonally as well. If a new significant other—or a longtime spouse, for that matter—suddenly starts to avoid eye contact to look at the view, keep an eye on how he or she communicates with others before you make any plans for your happily-ever-after.

An excellent leader can apply what the Drucker Foundation text *The Leader of the Future* (Hesselbein, Goldsmith and Beckhard, 1996) calls "self-leadership," something Homer's actions in the above example fail to convey. Some would call it discipline, but it is a vital component in leadership communication, including that via eye contact. One of the simplest (although not always easiest) ways for a leader to be treated with respect is to act respectably.

Eye contact is, indeed, a discipline. It takes practice, even for the confident leader. An excellent piece of advice far superior to the "look over their heads" (and not nearly as frightening as the "picture them naked") advice is to look your audience members in the eye. Talk to them as you would to a friend over coffee. If you are in close proximity to your conversational partner, you may feel as though you are shifty, looking first in one eye then the next. Try this simple exercise and see whether the following advice helps you. Stand approximately 2 feet from, and facing, another person. Look the person in one eye. Ask the person if he or she can tell where you are looking. Now try looking at the spot in the center of the triangle formed between the person's eyes and nose. Ask the person again. These two approaches are generally undetectable, and vastly more comfortable than the feel of shifting from one eye to the other.

Eye contact is one way many scholars claim they can identify deception, making it a hot topic for self-help books and magazines. Of course, there is some truth to this notion. Interpersonal scholars who study deception, such as H. Dan O'Hair at the University of Oklahoma, state that most scholars believe that someone who looks up and to the right is likely being truthful because it is as if the person were looking in a mental filing cabinet to access information that already exists in his or her experience and knowledge base. Those who look down and to the right, however, are said to be less trustworthy.[2] They are accessing a creative part of the brain, making up information as they go along.

---

2. For more information on body language and deception, see http://changingminds.org/ techniques/body/parts_body_language/eyes_body_language.htm.

In Western societies, such as the United States, the person who gives and receives a large amount of eye contact is viewed as a respected and credible individual.

Photo courtesy of Karen Christensen.

Those versed in the scholarship of deception may simply work to form habits that will help them escape this self-betrayal of their dishonesty, right? Yes and no; sometimes deception is completely undetectable. Buy any book that tells you the opposite, and apply its methods with regularity; if you are never lied to again, you stand to make a great deal of money. Some people are great liars. This is especially true when they communicate with a person who has an unattentive eye. Having said that, Erving Goffman, author of the classic nonverbal communication text *The Presentation of Self in Everyday Life* (1959), says that the attentive eye might spot what are known as "micromomentary" lapses, wherein the liar's very body betrays him or her. Male or female, all humans are physically created to be honest.

There is no foolproof way to hide an untruth, unless one is simply unaware of the truth. The best way to detect deception, according to O'Hair, is long-term behavioral comparison. The longer you know someone, the more you get to know the person's patterns of behavior. Anything out of the ordinary can signal an attempt at deception. In fact, it does not always take long to establish such knowledge for comparison's sake. Karla once took her car in to a repair shop. The mechanic was predictably friendly and bantered back and forth with her about trading cars with him. Then the discussion moved to what needed repair in her own vehicle. The man literally failed to look at her again until that portion of the discussion was over. Then the banter reignited. But for some reason, she was no longer interested in doing business with him. His failure to maintain eye contact made her wary of him.

Proxemics and Territoriality

The next time you are standing close to another person, imagine there is a multilayered (like an onion), invisible bubble around each of you, guiding you to determine your level of comfort when a person moves beyond a new layer, moving closer and closer into your personal space. The study of our use of space can be subdivided into two categories: proxemics and territoriality. **Proxemics** relates to how we utilize and react to that invisible bubble, the space that travels with us, which determines our comfort or discomfort in relation to the location of others in our midst. In one episode of the blockbuster 1990s sitcom *Seinfeld,* Jerry's latest excuse for failing to stay in a relationship with a woman was that she was a "close-talker." Ever met one of those people? Did you back farther and farther away as the person approached nearer and nearer? Effective leaders make optimal use of space, and they realize that people will respond best to them when they stay at least 18 inches away from others, as a general rule—4 feet away, or more, and they are relatively unacquainted.

Territoriality is our use of space other than that within our bubbles—for instance, our homes, our offices, and our cars. Our spaces are so important to us that we will ardently defend them, not only against theft and invasion but even against territorial restrictions of our expressions of personal style. The leadership of the Tehama County, California, Department of Social Services learned this lesson the hard way when one of their employees actually filed suit to fight policy that prevented him from displaying personal items of a religious nature at work, even within the confines of his cubicle. The religious nature of the artifacts was cited by the court as the reason the employee lost his case. First Amendment rights of free expression must be considered before an employer considers restrictions on employee privileges to individualize the decor in cubicles with color, personal photographs, and houseplants.[3]

There is a parental philosophy that one benefits by saying yes whenever possible! Perhaps this advice applies to other forms of leadership as well. By forming a habit of saying "yes" in every instance where logic fails to provide reasoning for a "no," leaders may keep followers generally contented, such that followers will be less likely to commit mutiny when they don't get their way. Having said that, a recent article on Collegerecruiter.com (Aretakis, 2007) recommends keeping cubicle decor to a minimum, warning "your workspace is a 3-D business card. Think twice about your Paris Hilton bobblehead and Ludacris screensaver."

Next time you are in the library, take note of how people "mark their territory" in spaces that do not even belong to them. Backpacks, coats, laptops, and books "mark" whole tables, even when a table is occupied by a single student. Only an individual of unfortunately low social intelligence would even consider sitting in one of the several empty chairs at one of those tables without asking permission. However, research indicates that even those whose territory has been clearly marked are likely to flee such "space invaders," especially by someone dressed formally or considered as higher status than the "victim" of the invasion (Barash, 1973). Therefore, those who "look like leaders" are given great leeway in terms of the space they are allowed to, quite literally, take.

Consider, too, the uncanny similarity in the ways in which people enter and stand in an elevator, eyes facing front, avoiding touch if at all possible, standing in specifically designated spots, depending on in which order they entered (first person back right, second person back left, third person front right, fourth person front left, etc.). Now think about how this auto-pilot behavior fits with leadership. As a leader, watch for areas in which your followers' auto-pilot behavior serves them. It may save resources or waste them. It is your job to communicate when it is inefficient or problematic and to help find and apply solutions. But that communication,

---

3. For more information about this case, see http://www.kmtg.com/data/rc_articles/ article.php?useSpr=&IDD=1160692231.

itself, may be most powerfully delivered through nonverbal channels. For instance, even the construction, lighting, and arrangement of furniture in a room communicate. Architectural icon Frank Lloyd Wright's genius seems to have been in his amazing ability to communicate via the use of lighting, materials, form, and space. Karla once worked in a communication department housed in a building designed by a student of Wright. She noted that it was absolutely amazing how efficiently the darkened, narrow hallways channeled students and faculty like so many cattle until the hallways opened up into beautiful, spacious, naturally lit foyers, where people could congregate and converse. "It embraces you, then releases you," she would joke, yet it was true. Would you like to have your employees interact with one another more? Arrange the furniture to allow for "conversation spaces," with groupings of couches and chairs in various nooks and crannies around the office. Would you prefer to discourage the stereotypical "talk around the water cooler"? Put the water cooler closer to your own office or desk. It's amazing how much less thirsty people are when they have to walk past the boss to get a drink!

Haptics

Another area in which nonverbal communication has been vastly studied is that of **haptics,** or the communication of touch. Expectancy violation theory (EVT) by Judy Burgoon discusses some of the ways in which individuals interpret touch and other forms of communication. She says that one who touches you in a positive and unexpected way will enjoy enhanced credibility, and perhaps warmth ratings in your eyes. One who touches in negatively evaluated and unexpected ways, however, will suffer the consequences of lowered credibility. Burgoon states that women touch more than men but that women are resentful when touched on certain places, such as the top of the head, especially by men (Burgoon, 1994). Men, for some odd reason, very much enjoy being touched on the backs of the calves—by men or by women, it does not matter. Of course, keep in mind that the improper use of touch by a person in a leadership position has been the subject of many a professional reprimand, censure, or lawsuit. Beyond social or monetary consequences, however, are the relational consequences. How well can one follow a person for whom one has lost respect, much less trust?

Olfactics and Chronemics

There are some little known, little discussed areas of nonverbal communication that merit discussion. One such area is **olfactics**—the study of the communication of scent. Good leaders smell good. That's a given. As the Budweiser® ad says, "We're talking to you, Mr. Way-too-much-cologne-wearer." Then again, if you take the time to shower, you may negatively violate someone's chronemic expectations. **Chronemics** is the study of the communication of time usage. Some people, especially those in Western cultures, observe time in what is referred to as a displaced pattern, meaning that we view time as real; 1:00 P.M. occurs at 1:00 P.M. Other cultures do not share this displaced view of time but, rather, utilize what is known as a diffused time pattern. Think of a diffuser that spreads a concentrated amount of perfume into tiny droplets of spray—the same volume of liquid reaches a larger area of space. That is exactly the way time is viewed in many Latin American countries and Native

American cultures. Many tribes and villagers, for instance, refer to "Indian Time," which is the view that time is relative. When you are finished doing one task or talking to one person, then and only then do you move on to the next task. When Karla was in an Athabaskan village in Alaska, she and her family were often told that they would need to wait "an hour and a half" for the next meal, for the boat to arrive, for the store to open. This hour and a half meant, essentially, "I have no idea when you will get what you want, but I know you like to hear numbers, so I will give you one." Sometimes it meant a matter of several hours, sometimes only a few minutes.

Imagine a classroom where a 2:00 class begins whenever everyone arrives. Such is the case in many cultures. One rule that good leaders know about the use of time, and what it communicates, is that time is a construct that varies from culture to culture. Due to our ever-increasing global village, all other cultures may have their own expectations of time, but many of them know that Americans believe 1:00 is 1:00. Therefore, we are expected to be on time, even if it means we have to wait.

A strange irony about chronemic communication with regard to leadership is that on time is late and early is on time, but too early or too focused on timeliness can signal weakness as well. According to Certified Career Management Specialist Coach Deborah Walker, in a recent article on quintcareers.com, last accessed January 7, 2008, showing up too early is actually one of the "top ten interview bloopers." Prospective employees who show up more than five to ten minutes early to wait for their interviews are seen as overly anxious, nervous, and overall less credible than their five-minutes-early counterparts. Walker advises, "Don't diminish your desirability as a job candidate by appearing desperate. Act as if your time were as valuable as the interviewer's. Arrive on time, but never more than 10 minutes early."

It is a challenging balance, indeed, but well worth the work. When in a leadership position, it is rare that the literature will recommend that you take advantage of your position, but as Dr. Don Simmons, director of the McGovern Center for Public Service and Leadership, advises, "Do not call attention to slight lateness. Do not even look at your watch as you enter the room. You are the leader. Your actions will show that you are confident or unconfident in this role." He does note, however, that more than a minute or two is another story.

Time is one factor in how we are judged as credible or lacking in credibility by our peers, our followers, and our leaders. As the old saying goes, you never get a second chance to make a first impression. Also, you rarely get a second chance to destroy a negative impression. Not only can we not *not communicate,* but we cannot *uncommunicate.*

Artifacts

From our cars to our hair, to everything we wear, our personal artifact choices communicate, and one day's poor choices can make a lasting impression that is difficult to overcome. Do my clothing and personal style choices reflect my core values, attitudes, and beliefs? You might be surprised how many times such nonverbal choices literally define us in the eyes of others.

Of course, we all know that "the clothes make the man," but did you know that those who dress as if they already have the job they aspire to are more likely to achieve it eventually? It is also wise advice to dress one level above the style of dress you would wear on a prospective job when you go to the interview—unless, of course, the job requires a suit and tie, in which case you would be ill advised to show up in a formal.

Channel Effects

One area of nonverbal study that has not been included in the traditional typologies, such as that by Burgoon (1994), is that of **channel effects.** Communication scholar Marshall McLuhan (1964) said, "The medium is the message." This means that the invention of each new form of communication technology—from the Guttenberg Galaxy to the telegraph, telephone, radio, TV, and Internet—has drastically altered the communication of the era, and everyone thereafter. In the modern workplace, and in the halls of the academy, cell phones, blackberries, Powerpoint presentations, ipods, laptops equipped with wireless Internet, text messages, and emails overwhelm the airwaves, communicating with previously undreamed of frequency and speed. But the question is, just because we have this new technology, does that mean we should always use it?

Are we guilty of using technology for technology's sake, oblivious to the messages our channel choices send about us and our relationships with those to whom we send them? Like the lead character of Napolean Dynamite's brother Kip, "I still love technology." The authors of this chapter love technology, too. We just know the power of a face-to-face conversation and a firm handshake, a paper thank-you note with a snail-mail stamp on it, and an old-fashioned speech that relies on something deeper than a bunch of colorful slides. We have also witnessed and experienced the dark side of technology as a communication modality, sending embarrassing emails to unintended recipients and showing Powerpoint slides with credibility-crushing misspellings.

Some people will tell you, "It's not what you say; it's how you say it." The heart of McLuhan's message is that what you say is sometimes in how you say it. An old Hallmark card commercial used to say, "When you care enough to send the very best." Do I communicate much caring when I email rather than walking ten paces to a colleague's office door? Or when I have to look up my mother or father's telephone number on my cell phone? Technology is fun. Let's just keep sight of each other. Effective leaders know that interoffice emails cannot communicate nonverbal information, and emoticons are no substitute for genuine emotional connection.

■ CONCLUSION

This chapter began with a justification of why the study of leadership communication is a vital one, moved through the various things that good leaders know about vision and verbal messages, and concluded with a discussion of ways effective leaders can harness the knowledge of various nonverbal communication research.

Effective leaders are, above all, realistic about their own limitations. They have thoroughly inventoried their assets and liabilities as leaders, and as communicators. It is only in doing so that they become willing to call upon the aid of others who can complement their own leadership styles, or work to improve in their own weakest areas. A leader may find that he or she is not, for instance, a good manager of detailed scheduling information. An effective leader can work around that liability, and even capitalize on it by sharing power with able managers and staff members. In this way, the leader can obtain more widespread commitment from his or her constituents and, as is the reward of a good leader, maintain the privilege of leading for another day.

■ KEY TERMS

Channel Effects—The communication theory that the medium also sends a message.

Chronemics—The study of communication by time usage.

Default Face—The unique face each person makes when experiencing no emotion.

Haptics—The communication of touch.

Intermodal Matching—The process by which an infant learns appropriate facial expressions by matching the expressions of others.

Kinesics—A form of communication involving use of the body, commonly referred to as "body language."

Leadership Style—A preference regarding how one relates to others in a leader/follower dynamic.

Olfactics—The study of communication by scent.

Proxemics—The study of the use of personal space while communicating with others.

Territoriality—The study of the utilization of space by asserting domain over a given area.

Vocalics—A form of paralanguage involving rate, pitch, volume, tone of voice, and modulation.

X-Styled Leadership—Top down, task-oriented leadership.

Y-Styled Leadership—Relational leadership.

■ SUGGESTED READINGS

Hackman, M. Z. & Johnson, C. E. 2004. *Leadership: A Communication Perspective* (4th ed.) Prospect Heights, IL: Waveland Press.

Hesselbein, F., Goldsmith, M., & Beckhard, R. (eds.). 1997. *The Leader of the Future: New Visions, Strategies and Practices for the New Era*. San Francisco: Jossey-Bass.

Kalbfleisch, P. & Cody, M. (eds.). 1995. *Gender, Power, and Communication in Human Relationships*. Hillsdale, NJ: Erlbaum.

Knapp, M. L. & Hall, J. A. 2006. *Nonverbal Communication in Human Interaction* (6th ed.) Belmont, CA: Wadsworth/Thomson Learning.

Manusov, V. & Patterson, M. L. (eds.). 2006. *The SAGE Handbook of Nonverbal Communication*. Thousand Oaks, CA: Sage.

Morrison, T. & Conaway, W. A. 2006. *Kiss, Bow or Shake Hands: The Bestselling Guide to How to Do Business in More than 60 Countries*. Avon, MA: Adams Media.

■ REFERENCES

Aretakis, N. 2007. "12 Cube Etiquette Tips for 20-Somethings." Collegerecruiter.com (31 August). http://www.collegerecruiter.com/career-counselors/archives/2007/08/.

Barash, D. P. 1973. "Human Ethology: Personal Space Reiterated." *Environment and Behavior, 5,* 67–73.

Birdwhistell, R. L. 1955. "Background to Kinesics." *Etc., 13,* 10–18.

Burgoon, J. K. 1994. "Nonverbal Signals." In *Handbook of Interpersonal Communication* (2nd ed.). M. L. Knapp, & G. R. Miller, eds. Thousand Oaks, CA: Sage.

Burgoon, J. K., Buller, D. B., & Woodall, W. G. 1995. *Nonverbal Communication: The Unspoken Dialogue*. New York: HarperCollins.

Goffman, E. 1959. *The Presentation of Self in Everyday Life*. Garden City, NY: Doubleday.

Gudykunst, W. B. & Kim, Y. Y. 1984. *Communicating with Strangers: An Approach to Intercultural Communication*. Reading, MA: Addison-Wesley.

Hesselbein, F., Goldsmith, M., & Beckhard, R. (eds.). 1996. *The Leader of the Future: New Visions, Strategies, and Practices for the Next Era*. San Francisco, CA: Jossey-Bass.

McLuhan, M. 1964. *Understanding Media: The Extensions of Man*. Cambridge, MA: MIT Press.

Mehrabian, A. & Wiener, M. 1967. "Decoding of Inconsistent Communications." *Journal of Personality and Social Psychology, 6,* 109–114.

Metzloff, A. N. & Moore, M. K. 1983. "Newborn Infants Imitate Adult Facial Gestures," *Child Development, 54,* 702–709.

Morrison, T. & Conaway, W. A. 2006. *Kiss, Bow or Shake Hands: The Bestselling Guide to How to Do Business in More than 60 Countries*. Avon, MA: Adams Media.

O'Hair, H. D., Cody, M. J., & McLaughlin, M. L. 1981. "Prepared Lies, Spontaneous Lies, Machiavelianism, and Nonverbal Communication." *Human Communication Research, 7,* 325–339.

Riggio, R. E. 1986. "Assessment of Basic Social Skills." *Journal of Personality and Social Psychology, 51,* 649–660.

Walker, D. "Avoid These 10 Interview Bloopers." http://www.quintcareers.com/interview_mistakes.html.

Watzlawick, P., Beavin, J. H., & Jackson, D. D. 1967. *Pragmatics of Human Communication: A Study of Interactional Patterns, Pathologies, and Paradoxes*. New York: Norton.

CHAPTER SIX REVIEW QUESTIONS

1. Communication is described in this chapter as the key factor in maximizing the qualities of leadership. What are some examples of important leadership qualities and skills that require communication?

   _____

   _____

   _____

2. What are some of the reasons nonverbal communication is so vital when interacting with others?

   _____

   _____

   _____

3. Discuss two nonverbal forms of communication that you regularly utilize with success and two that you might want to improve. How might you work to improve in your areas of weakness?

   _____

   _____

   _____

4. Charisma and enthusiasm are tremendous assets, but they can also be stumbling blocks to success as a leader. Explain.

   _____

   _____

   _____

5. The role of eye contact in communication varies considerably, depending on the dominant culture. Describe some examples of how eye contact usage differs, depending on where you are in the world.

   _____

   _____

   _____

CHAPTER SIX SELF-TEST

1. Leadership _____ is one's preference in how you relate to others in a leader/follower dynamic.

2. If we _____ better, we wouldn't have to talk so much later, trying to correct our mistakes and misunderstandings.

3. _____ leadership is task-oriented, emphasizing a top-down approach.

4. _____ is the study of communication by one's use of time.

5. _____ is the study of touch communication.

6. _____ is one of the most important skills required in leadership.

7. _____ is the key factor in maximizing the indispensable qualities of leadership.

8. Task and people are the two types of leadership _____.

9. Unilateral and consensus are the two philosophies regarding a leader's _____ of his or her subordinates.

10. To be an effective leader, one must understand nonverbal communication, which comprises up to _____ percent of all communication, and how it impacts success and failure.

Women in Public Service and Leadership

7

Challenges and Lessons

Kate
Cadenhead

Robert P.
Watson

◼ OVERVIEW

The story of the struggle for equality by women in the United States has been filled with adversity. It has been a long journey and one in which many women have gained greater resolve and status along the way. It is also a story that continues, as women still face challenges in nearly all facets of society. Perhaps nowhere is this more profound and also more apparent than in public service. Quite simply, in our society leadership has often had a masculine connotation, if not a man's face.

From serving in elected office to holding senior positions in government and the military to leading community-based programs, the numbers present a grim picture for women. Women enjoy far less success in nearly every category of employment and public service than do men. But statistics present only part of the picture, as the fingerprints of women are found throughout American history and the country has benefited by the actions of many celebrated women leaders.

Real progress has, indeed, been made by women in leadership roles, as servant-leaders and otherwise. But women's contributions are not always easily measured by numbers alone. The status of women in public service and leadership is far more nuanced and raises a number of questions, five of which will be addressed in this chapter:

◼ What are the major challenges women have faced in pursuing and wielding leadership positions?
◼ Is there a gendered facet to leadership?
◼ How have successful female leaders overcome these challenges?
◼ What explains the progress made by women in public service and leadership?
◼ Do women lead differently than men and, thus, does it matter if women hold power?

■ A HISTORY OF INEQUALITY

Women's leadership and service are nothing new. Possibly the first recorded evidence of a woman ruler dates to the thirty-first century B.C. with Meryet-Nit. The great Egyptian civilization of antiquity had a host of female leaders who served in the capacity of queen or as wife or mother of a pharaoh, with the Cleopatras as but the most famous of them. Ahhotep, the queen of Thebes in the fifteenth century B.C. not only ruled but bore three more rulers, one of whom was a daughter, Ahmose Nofretari (Chauveau, 1997). Indeed, history has recorded the feats of a number of women leaders, both in the United States and throughout the world, from Saint Joan of Arc to Russia's Catherine the Great to Queens Elizabeth I and Victoria of Britain and Spain's Queen Isabella, yet far less attention has been paid to the struggles women have faced attempting to serve their communities and countries. While women have led and served, they have done so at great personal cost and in the face of severe discrimination and inequality (Liswood, 1996).

Before he was the second president of the United States, John Adams was an important figure in the revolutionary struggle for independence. While attending the meetings of the Continental Congress in 1776, Adams received a letter from his wife, Abigail, on the topic of gender and leadership, stating:

> In the new Code of Laws . . . I desire you would Remember the Ladies, and be more generous and favorable to them than your ancestors. Do not put such unlimited power into the hands of the Husbands. Remember all Men would be tyrants if they could. If particular care and attention is not paid to the Laidies [sic] we are determined to forment a Rebelion [sic], and will not hold ourselves bound by any Laws in which we have no voice, or Representation (Butterfield, 1975, p. 121).

To be sure, every one of the delegates gathered in Philadelphia to decide the future of the fledgling experiment in self-government was a man. At the time Mrs. Adams penned her famous words on behalf of women, every position of leadership in politics, religion, commerce, and education was held by a man. Despite the passionate words of Abigail Adams, it would be many years until anything resembling an organized movement on behalf of women would appear and before women began to attain positions of leadership in the public realm.

Indeed, women of Abigail Adams' time were denied the right to vote, could not legally divorce, and suffered limited educational opportunities. Careers in politics, the military, religion, higher education, law, medicine, and other institutions and occupations were closed to women. In addition to the formal legal and political barriers limiting a woman's opportunities for public service and leadership, a host of informal sociocultural barriers also impeded progress by women. Sex-role norms were such that it was seen as "unladylike" for women to work outside the home, express their opinions in public, or take an interest in politics. The benefits of family planning and women's healthcare as well as an understanding of violence against women would not even enter the public's consciousness for well over a century (Evans, 1989).

Accordingly, one of the few avenues to power and service open to women was spousehood. Likewise, given the prevailing attitudes on gender, women generally had to exercise their influence behind the scenes through the social realm, rather than directly in the public realm. And so, in both settings, they did, and did so with what might be seen as a distinctly feminine tone. Functioning as hostesses, confidantes to their husbands, teachers of their sons, and volunteers in the community, women found creative ways to impart their voices, fingerprints, and values on American history.

For instance, Martha Washington served her country beside her famous husband in each of his difficult winter encampments during the Revolutionary War, where she assisted the general with correspondence, mended uniforms, cared for the soldiers, and basically had a reassuring influence on her husband while "mothering" his troops. Similarly, Dolley Madison, wife of the country's fourth president, presided over White House social events with a political sophistication perhaps not seen since, charming both his enemies and the American public and strategically designing everything from the timing of events to seating arrangements to advance her husband's policies (Watson, 2000).

Martha Washington served her country beside her famous husband during the Revolutionary War and basically had a reassuring influence on her husband while "mothering" his troops.

Library of Congress.

The road to equality would be long and bumpy, and the struggle continues. Perhaps the first touchstone event in women's leadership in the United States occurred in 1848, when a group of women (and some men) gathered at the **Seneca Falls Convention** in a small community in central New York. Among those in attendance were pioneering feminists and leaders Elizabeth Cady Stanton, whose hometown was Seneca Falls, and Lucretia Mott. Just eight years before the landmark meeting at Seneca Falls, Stanton and Mott had traveled with their husbands to attend the World Anti-Slavery Society meeting in London. However, the women were prevented from participating in the meeting, which led to a vigorous debate about the role of women at the meeting and motivated the two leaders to begin planning a course of action.

A few years prior to the Seneca Falls meeting, the famous Grimke sisters—Sarah and Angelina—through their writings and lecture tours in northern states, raised consciousness about the need for social reform. Though born on a plantation in Charleston, South Carolina, to a father who was a noted judge, slave owner, and traditional thinker on matters of the status of women, the Grimke sisters became leading advocates for abolishing slavery and promoting equality for women.

The Seneca Falls Convention produced an important document modeled on the Declaration of Independence, known as the **Declaration of Sentiments.** The Seneca Falls Convention also provided a means for organizing opinions and the women who held them into political action for possibly the first time in the country's history. The conference and its declaration put forward to the public ideas such as ending legal discrimination against women, expanding educational opportunities for women, and challenging the repressive moral codes on the "proper" role for women in society and the belief that women who spoke out in public were somehow "unladylike" (Evans, 1989).

■ WAVES OF CHANGE

Scholars sometimes view both the women's movement—which sought, and continues to promote, equal rights for women—and the feminist movement—which seeks to empower women and move society beyond negative and restrictive concepts of gender—in three waves. The origins of the **feminist movement** date to the nineteenth and early twentieth centuries, while the "second wave" occurred in the 1960s through the 1980s. The period from the 1990s to present is generally seen as the "third wave" of the movement and is marked by changes in strategy and the issues in response to some of the shortcomings of earlier efforts.

The history of the women's movement dates to the Seneca Falls Convention of 1848, with the "first wave" running through the mid-1870s. This period marked the first efforts to organize a movement, identify leaders, and establish social organizations and events in order to advance a consciousness of the need for the basic rights that women were denied.

The "second wave" of the women's movement concerned itself with a number of issues facing women and larger concerns, such as social justice and children's welfare. The movement grew out of a rift in the first wave surrounding, in part, the question of whether to support the **Fifteenth Amendment** to the Constitution in 1870, which granted black men the right to vote. Women had played an important role in the long and bloody struggle to abolish slavery and enfranchise former slaves. But now the question arose of whether women should embrace the extension of suffrage to black men, when the right did not include women. But there was disunity even among women. White women's racism led to feelings of trepidation that black involvement would validate southern perceptions that their participation would undermine slavery. Hence, white **suffragists** rejected black women's attempt to collaborate in the common cause of **enfranchisement** (Dumenil, 2007).

In 1869, two distinct factions of the movement formed under the auspices of the National Woman Suffrage Association and the American Woman Suffrage Association. Ultimately, the two groups merged in 1890 into the National American Woman Suffrage Association (NAWSA), led by Susan B. Anthony and directed by Carrie Chapman Catt. NAWSA had difficulty reconciling the discrepancy between fighting opposition abroad during World War I while women protested the fight for democracy at home (Dumenil, 2007).

Like so many of the early leaders of the women's movement, Sarah Grimke, the older, more influential of the two sisters, was a woman of faith, whose social advocacy was tied to deeply held religious convictions—in this case, the pacifist teachings of the Quakers. Likewise, Stanton, Mott, and other women leaders cut their teeth advocating social reform and often with a religious fervor and from a moral basis. This was true of the writings of Harriet Beecher Stowe, whose *Uncle Tom's Cabin* gave a woman's perspective to the anti-slavery movement. It was also the case for the women who led the temperance movement against alcohol and a predecessor of modern domestic violence awareness, as well as the women who were the foot-soldiers in the social justice movements beginning at the turn of the twentieth century.

Such moral underpinnings of social advocacy and the sheer diversity of social issues championed reflect a broader base for the early women's movement than is generally depicted. So, too, did it provide many of the early leaders of the women's movement with valuable organizational and political experiences. Many of the organizations and causes benefited from cross-fertilization. For example, the Woman's Christian Temperance Union, established in 1874, soon began advocating women's suffrage. Although the women who assembled at the 1848 Seneca Falls Convention had little experience as political organizers prior to that time, by the end of the century they managed to establish a viable women's movement in the United States (McGlen, O'Conner, Assendelft, & Gunther-Canada 2002).

In general, the Progressive Movement of the turn of the twentieth century expanded the social and public activities of women, as the women's movement also helped promote the far-reaching and important agenda of progressivism. It was during the nineteenth and early twentieth centuries that women's demand for the vote joined the political climate for the ideas of social reform and justice. The campaign for social justice and the right to vote caught the attention of both upper- and middle-class white reformers, as well as working-class women, but excluded black reformers. And while many women supported the suffrage movement, they were far from a united front. Frequently, black women were rejected by the white-dominated suffrage groups (Dumenil, 2007).

The advent of an industrialized, urbanized society brought new opportunities and challenges for women. Many stepped forward and took on new roles as servant-leaders for their communities as they fought for reforms that would help those who could not help themselves. One of the distinctly feminine facets of progressivism was the settlement house movement. One of the first and largest settlement houses was **Hull House,** established in 1889 in Chicago by Jane Addams. Hull House and others like it offered to the poor and working class social, educational, and art programs; free lectures and job training; and some of the country's first public kitchens, gymnasiums, and playgrounds. They also promoted women's rights, child labor laws, and educational reforms. By the 1920s, there were an estimated 500 settlement houses in the United States, and Jane Addams, the epitome of a servant-leader, went on to become the first American woman to win the Nobel Peace Prize. Like her predecessors in the women's movement, Addams was committed to an array of social justice causes, including the peace movement and women's right to vote.

Jane Addams, the epitome of a servant-leader, was the first American woman to win the Nobel Peace Prize.

Library of Congress.

The women's movement remained committed to an ever-broadening agenda of social reforms. For instance, the Women's Trade Union League endeavored to improve working conditions. But it became increasingly apparent that women needed a voice in politics and the key to attaining reforms rested with the right to vote. United by struggles for social justice, the women's movement set its sights on universal suffrage. After many bitter disappointments, President Woodrow Wilson came out in support of women's suffrage in 1918—in part because of the influence of his late wife, Ellen Axson Wilson, and his new spouse, Edith Bolling Galt Wilson—and another proposal was initiated in 1919. On August 18, 1920, women finally gained the right to vote with the passage of the **Nineteenth Amendment** to the Constitution, roughly three-quarters of a century after the Seneca Falls Convention. Not one of the early mothers of the movement lived to celebrate the occasion or to cast a legal vote (Watson, 2000).

Both celebrating this achievement and assuring continuing participation by women in the political process, the pioneering leader Carrie Chapman Catt helped establish the **League of Women Voters** in 1920. Rather than support a specific political party or candidate, it was the league's mission, as the successor organization of NAWSA, to establish a nonpartisan group that supported active national involvement. The league now has active chapters in all fifty states and continues its mission as a nonpartisan advocate for voter education, voter registration, and fair election practices.

Marginality and limited power and influence continued to plague women even as their issues were recognized by both Democrats and Republicans. Women did, however, sometimes become political officeholders. Seven out of a total of 128 women who sought the office were elected to the US House of Representatives in 1920. Although not one woman served in the US Senate that year, hundreds served at the state and local level (Dumenil, 2007).

One factor in women's limited political participation was the patronizing premise still held by most men that women should not concern themselves with issues outside the home. Thus, despite women's political gains, female officeholders generally worked under constraints that their efforts be limited to women's issues. This form of "maternalism" refers to the idea that women are nurturers and that any work outside the home should encompass social reform, especially as it applies to poor women and children. Ironically, women's commitment to serve others, some might argue, hurt women's efforts to gain recognition as leaders in the political system and the workplace. The male-dominated society of the early twentieth century still believed that women were not capable of making the "tough calls" required of a corporate CEO, a general in a time of war, or the president in a time of national crisis.

The Second World War, however, changed women's roles in American society forever. Large numbers of women entered the American workforce for the first time. Because so many men were fighting the war, female workers were vital to the production of tanks, airplanes, ships, and other necessary military equipment. They also played a vital role as nurses and support personnel, both at home and abroad, helping win the war. The entry of women en mass into the workplace in place of the men on the frontlines would mark the first time women held such male-dominated jobs, made livable wages, and contributed so much to the economy in American history. Over 6 million women toiled in factories to produce the products of war and, by the end of the war in 1945, over 20 million American women were employed outside the home. This is best symbolized by the iconic **Rosie the Riveter,** a popular song, poster, and campaign during WWII that helped overturn negative images of women who worked outside the home. Despite the fact that women were equally as capable as the men they had replaced, once the war ended many women were fired. Returning servicemen replaced the women who had filled their jobs, leaving many women bitter. Gendered discrimination resulted in less pay for those few women who did remain in the public sphere of the American workforce.

During the 1950s, women did not fare much better. Before the 1960s, most women did not work outside the home. Seeing the kids off to school, running Girl Scout meetings, and making dinner were how many women passed their time. Psychoanalysts claimed women were overeducated and not adjusting to their proper role as women. Others asserted that educated women made better mothers for their children. For those women who did pursue higher education, the old joke was that female college students were simply earning their "MRS" degree (Friedan, 1963).

One of the key events in the new movement was the publication in 1963 of *The Feminine Mystique* by Betty Friedan. Friedan and other leaders recognized that, although a gradual change in social mores, religious and family perspectives on the role of women, and the status of women in the workplace had occurred, women still faced individual and institutional discrimination (Friedan, 1963). For example, Freidan's book contends that not all women feel fulfilled as mothers and wives at the expense of a traditional career. Career women were seen as threatening to the family unit. It was this threat that society wanted to thwart by accusing them of being out of their natural element as mothers and wives. However, the women's movement also supported the idea that women should be able to choose spousehood and motherhood as options, not as an inherent biological determination. Dismissing housework and motherliness was as equally discriminatory.

Feminists soon began to pressure the government to mandate occupational equality. Their first victory came with the passage of the Equal Pay Act of 1963. This law made it illegal for women to be paid less than men for performing the same work. The following year saw another victory, when Title VI and VII of the **Civil Rights Act** prohibited discrimination in employment based on race, sex, religion, and national origin. The passage of these laws did not change people's attitudes or behavior, however, and feminists realized that further steps would need to be taken to ensure full equality between the sexes (Friedan, 1963).

Much like the earlier movements, the modern movement includes many issues and organizations and has been led by women committed to social justice. Many leaders of the contemporary women's movement were involved in the civil rights and anti-war movements. Changing laws was part of the answer and women set about to promote anti-sex discrimination laws, affirmative action, equal pay, and so on. Likewise, women worked to make and later keep family planning and reproductive health legal and fight for women's healthcare and affordable and accessible childcare.

One of the notable setbacks of the movement was the failure to gain ratification of the **Equal Rights Amendment,** which was introduced in 1972. After a seven-year deadline, the proposed change to the Constitution was not ratified by 1979 or by the 1982 extension date. Although many states did support the ERA, others did not, a few even rescinded their support, and the proposal narrowly failed. It faced severe opposition in the South, by conservatives, and from Christian churches, even though the amendment stated simply that "equal rights not . . . be denied on account of sex."

However, changing the laws only impacts human behavior. While it might be illegal to discriminate, it is not illegal to have racist, sexist, or bigoted views. Certainly, racist, sexist, and bigoted views often lead to illegal acts, known as hate crimes. Crimes such as domestic violence, racial exclusion, and numerous biases often lead to cruelty and bloodshed. These are not uncommon occurrences. And so the women's movement has worked to achieve not only equality of condition and opportunity but also a new feminine consciousness and a change in the way society views and values women's work, service, and leadership.

■ CHALLENGES TO WOMEN'S SERVICE AND LEADERSHIP

Initially, it is important to differentiate between *sex* and *gender.* The former pertains to the fundamental biological and physiological differences between males and females, while the latter refers to society's social construction of possible or perceived differences between the sexes. Cultures exert pressures and expectations in terms of the roles, attitudes, and behaviors of men and women, which may or may not have anything to do with innate differences and aptitudes. In almost every society, females and males—on the basis of their sex—are assigned separate and specific roles: the sex roles. Sex roles are made up of a set of expected behaviors, with accompanying gender traits. Thus, gendered practices, jobs, and language are created.

Historically, leadership was considered a male domain. Men dominated the public sphere, while women were relegated to the private one. In the public sphere, leadership was thought of as a manly virtue, whereby men led battles, presidents led nations, and fathers led families. Women, on the other hand, nurtured children, kept a nice home, and took care in their appearance. Leadership was the stuff of the public realm and women were not socialized to participate in the activities of that environment.

The American presidency has been referred to as the most gendered office in the country (Clift & Brazaitis, 2000; Watson & Gordon, 2003). There are only three constitutional requirements for eligibility to be president—age, residency, and natural-born status—none of them having to do with a candidate's sex. To better understand why it has been difficult for women to acquire and wield political power—let alone dream of becoming president—one must examine some of the social, political, and environmental barriers that women have encountered. Even today, prevailing attitudes toward the role of women have erected a "glass ceiling" between women and positions of leadership.

Historically, women found themselves in service jobs, such as nurses, teachers, and social workers. As women began moving up in occupational status and into a wider spectrum of professions, so, too, have they experienced increasing levels of institutional barriers. While doors are beginning to open for women to move into nontraditional careers, they still experience the discrimination that society places on women who work outside the home.

Gender stereotypes do impact both service and leadership by women and there are perceived differences in how men and women obtain and wield such positions. Gender stereotypes have portrayed men as masculine and women as feminine. Such rigid depictions hinder the free expression of how to lead and be of service. For example, some people still think of women as too emotional, less intelligent, and less competent, while men are represented as in control, strong, and powerful. These stereotypes have limited the range of men's and women's abilities to be effective.

Women have been unable, for a variety of reasons, to enter many professions. In the past, women were channeled into occupations seen as "appropriate" for them. They are continuations of the roles females are expected to fulfill in the wider society: for example, secretaries, waitresses, nurses, childcare providers, receptionists, and airline hostesses (Ruth, 1995). Such jobs became known in a negative sense as **pink collar jobs** and were typically lower-paying and less valued employment experiences. Tangibly, the demands of child rearing, household maintenance, and other family roles "assigned" by society to women made it difficult for women to devote sufficient time to outside employment.

In contrast, it was assumed that males were better suited for paid labor in general and for leadership in particular. Leadership was associated with such masculine traits as toughness, decisiveness, authoritativeness, and so on (Ruth, 1995). However, there have been expanding notions of the definition of leadership, including such characteristics as being relational, process-oriented, and inclusive. What are perceived as "women's ways of leading" have often been dismissed as unimportant, when, in fact, many women have led quite competently and successfully.

With the advent of anti-discrimination laws, equal opportunity, job training, and equal pay legislation, women were assisted in their quest for both equal opportunity and equality of condition in the workplace. However, as women entered the workforce and leadership positions, existing male-centered customs continued to present challenges.

Leadership studies have sought to examine the socialization of women and men and to determine the impact of gender stereotypes. For instance, more men than women have been encouraged to acquaint themselves with public affairs and pursue political careers, yet there are the occasional exceptions. Former Texas governor, Ann Richards, overcame staunch resistance to her political campaign by successfully negotiating the male bastion known as "the good ol' boys" network.

While Richards was able to thrive in political office, studies still show men to be more aware of political affairs and men dominate public and elected offices. Women are less likely to engage in civic and community affairs or to pursue or hold public office. Thus, there is a self-fulfilling prophecy, as societal attitudes continue to work against women's leadership and enforce a male orientation to leadership. What exists is often described as a "gender gap" in public life (Delli Carpinin & Keeter, 1992; Verba & Nie, 1972).

Are there differences between men and women in leadership positions? The answer is both yes and no. It depends on how one defines *difference*. Historically, women are socialized differently than men by their families, schools, and society insofar as they were given less educational, nutritional, social, recreational, and occupational choices. They were told to be less assertive, less competitive, and to not take risks. Since risk taking is a critical factor of successful leadership, many women were left out of the political process. In short, women lacked many of the social ingredients necessary for success in a competitive, capitalistic economy and male-oriented leadership positions.

Although the results are inconclusive, studies suggest that there are differences in leadership styles. Stereotypes exist about the possible differences suggesting that men are more self-confident, forceful, and task-oriented. Similarly, studies suggest that women are risk averse, are emotional, and are more concerned with relationships. Men are reported to be more likely to engage in a "selling" style of leadership, while women are more likely to participate, listen, nurture, and communicate. Thus, a distinctly male style of leadership emerges that is more task-oriented, autocratic, and directive, while a female style is more sensitive, rewarding, meditative, and communicative (Applebaum Audet & Miller 2002; Heam & Parkin, 1986; McGlen, O'Conner, Assendelft, & Gunther-Canada 2002).

However, even though leadership is a gendered concept and women have faced considerable obstacles in pursuing leadership opportunities, such distinctly female approaches to leadership are now increasingly seen as positive and desirable. At the same time, studies now find that any differences between male and female leaders in terms of their background, age, religion, and other demographic factors, as well as their leadership style, are disappearing. Historically, it might also be said that women rulers such as Catherine the Great, Queen Elizabeth I, and Queen Isabella were just as powerful, effective, and ruthless as their male counterparts. The same might be said for nonmonarchical female leaders in modern times, such as India's Indira Gandhi, Israel's Golda Meir, and Britain's Margaret Thatcher.

There are, of course, a bewildering array of tangible, measurable barriers to women's leadership. For instance, leading scholars who study women in politics identify five basic challenges facing women (McGlen et al., 2002):

- Gender stereotypes
- Career choices and preparation
- The demands of raising a family
- Sex discrimination
- A host of institutional and structural obstacles in the political system

Noted scholar Kathleen Hall Jamieson describes what she terms **double binds,** or "double burdens," such as the expectation that women work like men yet assume primary responsibility for raising children and running the household (Jamieson, 1997). As such, women have role conflicts that make it hard for them to pursue elected office in the way men do. Women are expected to do both, yet when women run for office while raising children society deems them as neglecting their maternal responsibilities. Women thus often run for their first office at a later point in life or what is seen as an **empty nest syndrome**—that is, waiting until their children are grown before pursuing public endeavors and careers.

Relatedly, women face the double bind of the so-called **second shift syndrome.** Working women often return home from their paid jobs to begin a "second shift" involving the many challenges of domesticity. Moreover, even when working women are married, they still perform the lion's share of cooking, cleaning, diaper changing, shopping, and other household tasks. As such, men generally have far more leisure time to participate in community service and political activities than do women.

Arguably the foundation for each of the double binds faced by women is sexism from the electorate, their colleagues, and society in general. Studies have shown that less educated voters are less likely to support a woman, and prospective women leaders face different levels of support based on ideology, religious belief, geographic region, and so on. There is even the burden that women are not perceived to be as credible on national security, crime prevention, economic growth, and other "force" (masculine) issues, which often happen to be the very same issues that motivate voters.

In politics, incumbents have an advantage over their challengers in terms of name recognition among the electorate, free press coverage, and the ability to raise funds. The statistics on the high reelection rates of incumbents at all levels of elected office and among both parties are hard to refute, yet this, too, serves as another burden for women, who are far more likely to be pursuing elected office as challengers than incumbents. As outsiders in the political system, women also typically lack the institutional supports from the political parties or a network of mentoring from senior, often male political leaders.

One of the most frustrating obstacles for many women in political life is the biased coverage they receive from the media. This runs from the obvious, such as when Margaret Chase Smith, a Republican who served in both the US House and Senate from Maine, campaigned for the presidency in 1964 and was often referred to by the press as "Mrs." Smith rather than as "Senator" Smith. Her male opponents were called by their political titles, as is customary (Wallace, 1995). Occasionally, the media ask voters if a male candidate is tough enough to hold office, while women office seekers are always expected to prove their competency, strength, and experience. Other women have suffered either from less media coverage than their male opponents or from stories with "soft" messages that focus on their hairstyle, clothing, family, or favorite recipes. Such coverage does not make the recipient look like a serious candidate and, even though there is a preference in the media for personal stories over policy details, men are rarely asked about their shoes or holiday cookies (Kahn, 1996).

One final challenge facing women is that of fundraising. It takes money, lots of it, to win high office in the United States. The large donations to campaigns come from big business political action committees (PACs), which are more likely to support men than women. For example, some studies show that male candidates for the US Senate often receive upwards of 80 percent of their funds from corporate PACs, while their female challengers average less than 20 percent from that source. Given the perceived challenges facing women, other donors are rational actors who prefer to get the most "bang for their buck" and are thus less likely to donate to women, who are perceived to be outsiders, challengers, and underdogs (Farrar-Myers, 2003).

To paraphrase then-presidential candidate John F. Kennedy, who in 1960 faced questions about his Catholicism, prospective women leaders are often forced to pursue opportunities by downplaying their sex by running not as the female candidate but as the best candidate who happens to be a woman. For example, as a presidential candidate, Senator Hillary Rodham Clinton framed her campaign as not being about electing a woman but about being the best candidate. Unbelievably, Shirley Chisholm, the tough former congresswoman from New York, who was the first African American to run for president in 1972, stated that she encountered more opposition on account of her sex than her race (Chisholm, 1970). It is clear that women have made progress, but it is also apparent that it has been a long and arduous task and that masculine traits continue to be associated with leadership positions, especially in high office (Duerst-Lahti & Kelly, 2000).

■ PROGRESS AS LEADERS

Since the early 1970s and the success of the women's movement, assumptions about gender and leadership have been challenged. Volunteering and service, for example, even have feminine connotations. Perhaps society has accepted a human capital perspective whereby it does not make sense to underutilize half of the talent pool; to continue to do so is irrational and threatens an organization's competitiveness and bottom line. Indeed, today women's attributes do contribute to the bottom line. Much of society now values those things women bring to the political table.

Indeed, large numbers of women have entered the workforce and leadership positions in all occupations and levels. Women now comprise a viable and growing number of those enrolled in law schools, veterinary schools, medical school, and both MBA and Ph.D. programs. From corporate board rooms to college admissions, women have made gains in all areas of society. In the post–civil rights and women's movement era and with the advent of merit-based employment decisions and affirmative action programs, women have seen many of the traditional barriers to their success fall. Changes have occurred in the roles of women and societal views of gender, as well as with a general expansion of rights in areas such as reproductive health, equal pay, and sexual harassment (Freeman, 1975).

More women than ever are entering politics and public service. At the time of this writing, a woman (Nancy Pelosi) presides for the first time in American history as the speaker of the House of Representatives. Women have broken barriers by serving as secretary of state (Madeleine Albright, Condoleezza Rice), attorney general (Janet Reno), national security advisor (Condoleezza Rice), and US ambassador to the United Nations (Jean Kirkpatrick). So, too, are women now winning legislative campaigns in the United States with roughly the same frequency as men, and many women in legislative races are raising similar amounts of money as men (Kahn, 1996, Thomas & Wilcox, 1998). Organizations such as Emily's List, the

These young women at Hollins University are studying leadership at the Batten Leadership Institute. From corporate board rooms to college admissions, women have made gains in all areas of society.

Photo courtesy of Sarah Hazlegrove.

WISH List, and the White House Project are dedicated to promoting the election of women to high office, including the White House (Watson, 2003).

As a result, in 2007, nine women served as governors in the states of Alaska, Arizona, Connecticut, Delaware, Hawaii, Kansas, Louisiana, Michigan, and Washington. Eleven women functioned as lieutenant governor. Women headed twelve of the nation's Fortune 500 enterprises, held roughly 16 percent of the seats in the US House of Representatives and US Senate, and held just over 24 percent of statewide elected executive offices and just under 24 percent of state legislative seats. The progress by women, however, varies by region, with women doing well in the Northwest and Northeast but poorly in the "Bible Belt" of the Deep South (Norrander & Wilcox, 1998). Many of these numbers represent records and demonstrate the real progress made by women in leadership and public service.

While women have made much progress in all facets of life and in attaining elective office, women tend to fare better in legislative and support positions than in executive office and leadership positions. Nowhere is this more apparent than in the fact that, as of 2007, the United States had failed ever to elect a woman president. Nor has it ever come close to doing so. The closest that women came to achieving this goal was the selection of Geraldine Ferraro as the Democratic Party's vice presidential nominee in 1984, the only time a woman served on the ticket of a major party. In 2000, two women—both of color—were vice presidential nominees on third-party tickets: Winona LaDuke for the Green Party and Ezola Foster for the Reform Party. A number of women have, however, campaigned for the presidency, as is evident in Table 1.

◼ TABLE 1   Female US Presidential Candidates

Name	Date	Party	Race	State	Occupation
Victoria Woodhull	1872	Equal Rights	White	OH/NY	Stockbroker
Belva Lockwood	1884	Equal Rights	White	NY	Attorney/educator
Margaret Chase Smith	1964	Republican	White	ME	Educator/editor
Shirley Chisholm	1972	Democrat	Black	NY	Educator
Pat Schroeder	1988	Democrat	White	CO	Attorney
Elizabeth Dole	2000	Republican	White	NC	Nurse/attorney
Carol Moseley Braun	2004	Democrat	Black	IL	Attorney
Hillary Rodham Clinton	2008	Democrat	White	IL/NY	Attorney

The first public opinion poll to ask the question of whether voters were ready to vote for a woman for president was in the 1930s and was conducted by the Gallup organization. Some 37 percent of the public answered "yes" in that poll, and over the ensuing decades the numbers gradually increased to the point that, by the year 2000, just over 90 percent of the country indicated a readiness to vote for a woman and only 7 percent stated that they would not cast such a vote under any circumstances. However, the numbers supporting the election of a woman have fallen somewhat in the 2000s, perhaps because of the rise of the Republican Party to power, the growing influence of Christian conservatives, the onset of war in Iraq and Afghanistan, or the possible hostility by some voters to the prospects of electing Senator Clinton (Watson, 2006; Watson & Gordon, 2003).

Challenges exist for women because of the gendered nature of the presidency and because of the perception of a credibility gap by women on the issue of national security. This is especially evident during times of war. Surely, just like the men before her, the first woman president will make mistakes in national security, but she might be judged differently. A catch-22 "damned if she does, damned if she does not" scenario also faces women leaders whereby, if they are tough, then they are perceived as trying to establish "bona fides" or compensate for other weaknesses but, if they are not tough enough, then it is on account of their sex (Davis, 2003; Lansford, 2003).

While the United States has yet to elect a woman leader, such challenges are nothing new for women around the world. Several women have attained the pinnacle of leadership in Europe, the Americas, South Asia, and elsewhere. Not counting female monarchs, such as Queen Elizabeth II of Britain, Queen Margrethe II of Denmark, or the Maori queen Kuini, as of 2007, eleven women were serving as the heads of democratic governments. They are listed in Table 2.

Suhbaataryn Yanjmaa (1893–1962) was the widow of Mongolia's national hero and served as first deputy chairman and later chairman during a brief vacancy in the office from 1953 to 1954. This brief duty would likely make her the first woman political ruler in contemporary history aside from monarchs. Those women who did

▪ TABLE 2   Contemporary Female Leaders of Democracies

Michelle Bachelet (Chile)	Ellen Johnson-Sirleaf (Liberia)
Angela Merkel (Germany)	Tarja Kaarina Halonen (Finland)
Helen Clark (New Zealand)	Gloria Macapagal-Arroyo (Philippines)
Han Myung-Sook (South Korea)	Mary McAleese (Ireland)
Luisa Diogo (Mozambique)	Aung San Suu Kyi (Burma)
Pratibha Patil (India)	Cristina Fernandez Kirchner (Argentina)

serve as heads of government, as listed in Table 3, faced enormous challenges and some paid for the position with their lives. Not that it diminishes their service, but several women rose to power through family ties. Janet Jagan, for example, succeeded her husband, Cheddi Jagan, a few months after his death. Chandrika Kumaratunga was the daughter of Sirimavo Bandaranaike, the three-time prime minister of Sri Lanka. Her father, Solomon, was also prime minister and was assassinated; her husband, Vijaya Kumaratunga, was also assassinated. Megawati Sukarnoptri continues the family struggle as the daughter of the late President Sukarno. Other widows whose husbands were leaders include Corazon Aquino, the widow of Banigno Aquino; Violeta Chamorro, the widow of Pedro Joaquin Chamorro; Isabel Peron, the wife of Juan Peron; and Mireya Moscoso, the widow of President Arnulfo Arias Madrid. Gloria Macapagal Arroyo was the daughter of the late president Diosdado Macapagal, and Khaleda Zia was the daughter of the late dictator Ziaur Rahman. Familial ties surely have helped women, but there is no single path to power that has defined women's leadership (Watson Jencik, and Selzer 2005).

■ TABLE 3   Women Heads of Government Since 1945

Leader	Country	Office	Years
Sirimavo Bandarnaike	Ceylon	PM	1960–1965, 1970–1977, 1994–2000
Indira Gandhi	India	PM	1966–1977, 1980–1984
Golda Meir	Israel	PM	1969–1974
Isabel Peron	Argentina	Pres	1974–1976
Elizabeth Domitien	Cent Afr Rep	PM	1975–1976
Marie de Lourdes Pintasilgo	Portugal	PM	1979–1980
Lidia Gueiler Tejada	Bolivia	Pres	1979–1980
Margaret Thatcher	Britain	PM	1979–1990
Mary Eugenia Charles	Dominica	PM	1980–1995
Vigdis Finnbogadottir	Iceland	Pres	1980–1996
Gro Brundtland	Norway	PM	1981, 1986–1989, 1990–1996
Agatha Barbara	Malta	Pres	1982–1987
Milka Planinc	Yugoslavia	Pres	1982–1986
Maria Liberia Peres	Nicaragua	Pres	1984–1985
Maarie Liveria-Peters	Nether.Antilles	PM	1984–1986, 1988–1994
Corazon Aquino	Philippines	Pres	1986–1992
Benazir Bhutto	Pakistan	PM	1988–1990, 1993–1997
Violeta Chimorro	Nicaragua	Pres	1990–1997
Ertha Pascal-Trouillot	Haiti	Pres	1990–1991
Kazimiera Prunskiene	Lithuania	PM	1990–1991
Mary Robinson	Iceland	Pres	1990–1997
Edith Cresson	France	PM	1991–1992
Begum Khaleda Zia	Bangladesh	PM	1991–1996, 2001–present
Hanna Suchocka	Poland	PM	1992–1993
Susanne Camelia-Romer	Nether.Antilles	PM	1993, 1998–1999
Kim Campbell	Canada	PM	1993
Sylvie Kinigi	Burundi	PM	1993–1994
Marita Peterson	Faroe Islands	PM	1993–1994
Agathe Uwilingiyimana	Rwanda	PM	1993–1994
Tansu Ciller	Turkey	PM	1993–1996
Chandrika Kumaratunga	Sri Lanka	Pres	1994–2005
Claudette Werleigh	Haiti	PM	1995–1996
Sheikh Hasina Wajed	Bangladesh	PM	1996–2001
Ruth Perry	Liberia	Pres	1996–1997
Pamela Gordon	Bermuda	Prem	1997–1998
Janet Jagan	Guyana	Pres	1997–1999
Jenny Shipley	New Zealand	PM	1997–1999
Mary McAleese	Ireland	Pres	1997–present
Ruth Dreifuss	Switzerland	Pres	1998–1999
Jennifer Smith	Bermuda	Prem	1998–2003
Helen Clark	New Zealand	PM	1999–present
Mireya Moscoso	Panama	Pres	1999–2004
Vaira Vike-Freiberga	Latvia	Pres	1999–2007
Tarja Halonen	Finland	Pres	2000–2006

continues

■ TABLE 3   *Continued*

Leader	Country	Office	Years
Mame Madior Boye	Senegal	PM	2001–2002
Gloria Macapagal-Arroyo	Philippines	Pres	2001–present
Megawati Sukarnoputri	Indonesia	Pres	2001–present
Maria Das Neves de Sousa	Sao Tome	PM	2002–2003
Beatriz Merino	Peru	PM	2003
Luisa Dias Diogo	Mozambique	PM	2004–present
Natasa Micic	Serbia	Pres	2002–2004
Nino Burjanadze	Georgia	Pres	2003–2004
Barbara Prammer	Austria	Pres	2004
Yuliya Tymoshenko	Ukraine	PM	2005
Maria do Carmo Silveira	Sao Tome	PM	2005–2006
Angela Merkel	Germany	PM	2005–present
Portia Simpson-Miller	Jamaica	PM	2006–2007
Han Myung Sook	South Korea	PM	2006–2007
Ellen Johnson-Sirleaf	Liberia	Pres	2006–present
Michelle Bachelet Jeria	Chile	Pres	2006–present
Micheline Calmy-Rey	Switzerland	Pres	2007–2008
Cristina Fernandez Kirchner	Argentina	Pres	2007–present

Key: PM = Prime Minister
      Pres = President
      Prem = Premier

■ CONCLUSION

At a time when more and more women are climbing the career ladder, men's and women's leadership results are mixed. In the past few years, the United States has dropped several spots and now ranks seventieth in the world in terms of women's representation in politics. But women's leadership and service are not the only gender-based challenges they face. In fact, some would say social justice is just beginning for women. Hidden and not-so-hidden gender, racial, and ethnic biases are still all too common in our society. Sad to say, gender, racial, and ethnic biases are alive and well in America (Dana & Bourisaw, 2006).

But very real progress is starting to be made. American women's leadership and service are now becoming more the norm than the exception. Indeed, the future of women's leadership appears bright when one considers that college-aged individuals are far more accepting of the notion of women in power than their parents or grandparents ever were.

However, strong leadership may not be enough—at least in part because women's leadership style might differ from that of men. Women's engaging style of influence differs from traditional male notions. Men might not be as flexible or sociable and might rely more on force. Women, on the other hand, might employ qualities more conducive to workplace harmony, such as teamwork and collaboration (Miller, 2007).

Not all gender bias comes from men, however. Strong evidence exists that some women do not support other women in getting ahead. One study asked women employees if they would support a woman candidate for US president. Eighty-five percent of women said "no," and some women leaders have led like men perhaps because they have had little choice but to do so (Dana & Bourisaw, 2006). Many studies have suggested that men and women exhibit similar leadership styles (Frauehneim, 2007). But as more women emerge as leaders they might not feel as constrained in terms of their leadership style. Likewise, some men are leading in a way that is associated with women leaders, and differences between the sexes in many areas of political and leadership behavior narrow (Jaschik, 2007).

What does all this mean for women who lead and serve? The important lesson is to recognize that it is one of social justice. While female leaders remain plagued by gender stereotyping, they are beginning to blaze new trails in the media, education, entertainment, commerce, law, and politics. Perhaps more important, in prevailing mindsets about the status of women in society, progress is occurring.

■ KEY TERMS

Civil Rights Act—Keystone legislation passed in 1964 to prohibit legal discrimination.

Declaration of Sentiments—The document produced by early women leaders at the Seneca Falls Convention calling for women's rights.

Double Binds—The catch-22 dilemma facing many women on account of narrow views on gender.

Empty Nest Syndrome—The phenomenon in which women wait until their children are raised before becoming active in politics.

Enfranchisement—The extension of all the political rights and privileges to an individual or a group of people.

Equal Rights Amendment—An unsuccessful effort in the 1970s to amend the Constitution to preclude discrimination against women.

Feminist Movement—The effort to raise awareness of bias and discrimination against women and to advance equality.

Fifteenth Amendment—The amendment to the Constitution in 1870 extending the right to vote to black men.

Hull House—The most famous "settlement house" offering social services to women run by women in the early twentieth century.

League of Women Voters—A nonpartisan, nonprofit organization to promote fair elections and political participation.

Nineteenth Amendment—The amendment to the Constitution in 1920 extending the right to vote to women.

Pink Collar Jobs—Occupations traditionally held by women.

Rosie the Riveter—An iconic symbol of women workers during WWII.

Second Shift Syndrome—The phenomenon that working women still account for the vast majority of domestic work in their families.

Seneca Falls Convention—The gathering in 1848 in New York that first raised awareness of the inequality of women.

Suffragists—Women promoting the right to vote by women.

■ SUGGESTED READINGS

Jamieson, K. H. 1997. *Beyond the Double Bind: Women and Leadership.* New York: Oxford University Press.

McGlen, N. E., O'Connor, K., van Assendelft, L., & Gunther-Canada, W. 2002. *Women, Politics, and American Society.* New York: Longman.

Watson, R. P. & Gordon, A. eds. 2003. *Anticipating Madam President.* Boulder, CO: Lynne Rienner.

■ REFERENCES

Applebaum, S. H. Audet, L., & Miller, J. C. 2002. "Gender and Leadership? Leadership and Gender?" *Leadership and Organization Development Journal, 24(1),* 43–51.

Butterfield, H. L. Audet, L., & Miller, J. C. eds. 1975. *The Book of Abigail and John: Selected Letters of the Adams Family, 1762–1784.* Cambridge, MA: Harvard University Press; see page 121 for the March 31, 1776, letter.

Chauveau, M. 1997. *Egypt in the Age of Cleopatra.* Ithaca, NY: Cornell University Press.

Chisholm, S. 1970. *Un-bought and Un-bossed.* Boston, MA: Houghton Mifflin.

Clift, E. & Brazaitis, T. 2000. *Madam President: Shattering the Last Glass Ceiling.* New York: Scribner.

Dana, J. A. and Bourisaw, D. M. 2006. *Women in Superintendency: Discarded Leadership.* Lanham, MD: Rowman & Littlefield Education.

Davis, J. 2003. "Confronting the Myths: The First Woman President and National Security." In R. P. Watson & A. Gordon, eds. *Anticipating Madam President* (Boulder, CO: Lynne Rienner), pp. 189–200.

Delli Carpini, M. X. & Keeter, S. 1992. "The Gender Gap in Political Knowledge." *Public Perspectives, 3,* 23–26.

Duerst-Lahti, G. & Kelly, R. M. eds. 2000. *Gender, Power, Leadership, and Governance.* Ann Arbor: University of Michigan Press.

Dumenil, L. 2007. "The New Woman and the Politics of the 1920s," *OAH Magazine of History,* July, pp. 22–26.

Evans, S. M. 1989. *Born for Liberty: A History of Women in America.* New York: Free Press.

Farrar-Myers, V. A. 2003. "A War Chest Full of Susan B. Anthony Dollars: Fundraising Issues for Female Presidential Candidates." In R. P. Watson & A. Gordon, eds., *Anticipating Madam President* (Boulder, CO: Lynn Rienner), pp. 81–94.

Frauehneim, E. 2007. "Bias Study Sees Few Gains for Female Leaders." September 21, *Workforce Management* www.workforce.com.

Freeman, J. 1975. *The Politics of Women's Liberation.* New York: Longman.

Friedan, B. 1963. *The Feminine Mystique.* New York: Norton.

Heam, J. & Parkin, W. P. 1986. "Women, Men, and Leadership: A Critical Review of Assumptions, Practices, and Change in the Industrialized Nations," *International Studies of Management and Organization, 16(3–4),* 33–59.

Jamieson, K. H. 1997. *Beyond the Double Bind: Women and Leadership.* New York: Oxford University Press.

Jaschik, S. 2007. *Inside Higher Education Magazine,* May 22, www.insidehighered.com.

Kahn, K. F. 1996. *The Political Consequences of Being a Woman: How Stereotypes Influence the Conduct and Consequences of Political Campaigns.* New York: Columbia University Press.

Lansford, T. 2003. "A Female Leader for the Free World: The First Woman President and US Foreign Policy." In R. P. Watson & A. Gordon, eds., *Anticipating Madam President.* Boulder, CO: Lynne Rienner, pp. 177–188.

Liswood, L. A. 1996. *Women World Leaders.* New York: Pandora/HarperCollins.

McGlen, N. E., O'Connor, K., van Assendelft, L., & Gunther-Canada, W. 2002. *Women, Politics, and American Society.* New York: Longman.

Miller, C. 2007. "Are Women Creating a New Leadership Style?" *Hudson Valley Business Journal,* October, pp. 25–27.

Norrander, B. & Wilcox, C. 1998. "The Geography of Gender Power: Women in State Legislatures." In S. Thomas & C. Wilcox, eds., *Women and Elective Office.* New York: Oxford University Press.

Ruth, S. 1995. *Issues in Feminism.* Mountain View, CA.: Mayfield.

Thomas, S. & Wilcox, C. eds. 1998. *Women and Elective Office: Past, Present and Future.* New York: Oxford University Press

Verba, S. & Nie, N. H. 1972. *Participation in America: Political Democracy and Social Equality.* New York: Harper & Row; see page 83 in particular.

Wallace, P. W. 1995. *Politics of Conscience: A Biography of Margaret Chase Smith.* Greenwich, CT: Praeger.

Watson, R. P. 2006. "Madam President: Progress, Problems, and Prospects for 2008," *Journal of International Women's Studies, 8(1),* 1–20.

Watson, R. P. 2000. *The Presidents' Wives: Reassessing the Office of First Lady.* Boulder, CO: Lynne Rienner.

Watson, R. P. & Gordon, A. eds. 2003. *Anticipating Madam President.* Boulder, CO: Lynne Rienner.

Watson, R. P., Jencik, A., & Selzer, J. A. 2005. "Women World Leaders: Comparative Analysis and Gender Experiences," *Journal of International Women's Studies, 7(2),* 53–76.

Note: Emily's List at www.emilyslist.org; the WISH List at www.thewishlist.org; the Women's Campaign Fund at www.wcfonline.org; the National Women's Political Caucus at www.nwpc.org; the Center for Women, Leadership, and Management at Simmons College at www.simmons.edu/som; the Center for the American Woman and Politics at Rutgers University at www.rutgers.edu/cawp; Gallup Poll at www.gallup.org; and The Siena Research Institute Poll at Siena College www.siena.edu.

CHAPTER SEVEN REVIEW QUESTIONS

1. What challenges have women faced in attempting to gain positions of leadership?

_____

_____

_____

2. When did the women's movement first start advancing women's rights?

_____

_____

_____

3. What successes did the women's movement have in promoting political participation by women?

_____

_____

_____

4. How have women had success in the United States and around the world in gaining positions of political leadership? Cite specific examples.

_____

_____

_____

5. Do women lead differently than men? Explain your answer.

_____

_____

_____

CHAPTER SEVEN SELF-TEST

1. The great _____ civilization of antiquity had a host of female leaders, with the Cleopatras as the most famous of them.

2. The Seneca Falls Convention produced an important document modeled after the Declaration of Independence, known as the _____.

3. The _____ sisters became leading advocates for abolishing slavery and promoting equal rights for women.

4. The National Woman Suffrage Association and the American Woman Suffrage Association merged into a single organization in 1890, which was led by Susan _____.

5. During _____ large numbers of women entered the American workforce for the first time.

6. The term _____ refers to the expectation that women work like men and assume primary responsibility for raising children and running the household.

7. As of 2007, the United States had not yet elected a woman as president, but _____ women were serving as the heads of democratic governments in other countries.

8. One of the stumbling blocks to a united suffrage movement during the early twentieth century was the _____ views of white-dominated suffrage groups.

9. Settlement houses promoted _____, _____, and _____.

10. In 1963, Betty Friedan published _____, which heralded the "second wave" of the feminist movement.

The Greater Good
Ethics and Leadership

Michael J. C.
Taylor

■ HOW INDIVIDUAL BELIEFS SHAPE SOCIETY

In the history of seafaring, the tale of Edward Collins, the founder of the Collins Line, is one of both success and tragedy. More important, it is a lesson in the moral conduct of one's life.

Throughout the 1840s, Collins claimed America had an interest in the transatlantic passenger trade. After accepting a hefty government subsidy, he built four 282-feet, 2,860-ton steamers that were considered the finest of their time. However, they possessed one fatal flaw: At a time when his British rivals were building iron-hulled liners—which had proven to be more resistant to weather and collision—Collins had forged his vessels out of wood. By the launch of his fleet in April 1849, the line's namesake was wholly convinced that his were the finest ships afloat protected by the divine hand of God himself.

On September 25, 1854, in the midst of a thick, ominous North Atlantic fog, the Collins liner *Artic* collided with the iron-hulled French steamer *Vesta*. Only forty-five passengers and crew survived, and among those drowned were Collins' wife and two of his children. A year later, the Collins liner *Pacific* struck an iceberg and sank without any survivors. Within a few months of the latter disaster, the Collins Line—the foremost American transatlantic passenger carrier of its time—ceased to exist (Wall, 1977, p. 124).

Collins' story is a cogent reminder that actions resulting from one's beliefs invariably affect others. The basic question is whether Edward Collins had the right to hold to his convictions in lieu of prevailing evidence to the contrary, which made him culpable for the deaths of his passengers. Social interaction is inevitable. No judgment or action, no matter how miniscule, is made in a vacuum. Our decisions and what we believe have an effect on others. To quote philosopher William Clifford, "No simplicity of mind, no obscurity of station, can escape the universal duty of questioning all that we believe" (Clifford, 1984, p. 150). When one is occupying a leadership role, one's value judgments are vital. However, they demand a standard because our beliefs and actions influence the long-term progress of humanity.

The USM steamship *Baltic* was one of the oldest and most dependable ships of the Collins Line. It was sold at auction with the remainder of the fleet in 1859.

Library of Congress.

The very foundation of philosophy was stated by Socrates nearly three millennia ago in his *Apology:* "[T]he unexamined life is not worth living" (Segal, 1986, p. 22). In human existence, it is not enough to believe in something, for most of what we conceive to be true is based on the experiences of our lives. A philosophical exploration of what constitutes virtuous or willful conduct is **ethics,** the discipline whose goal is to differentiate genuine knowledge from mere opinion through objective reasoning. It requires a full commitment to discerning the intrinsic good, something desirable for its own sake, and the instrumental good, a means to something else that is desired, for the benefit of self and of others. If philosophy is concerned with perceptions of the world, ethics are concerned with the actions wrought from it. Ethics provide a standard to aspire to, goals to pursue; in striving toward their full realization, we become more conscientious human beings.

■ ETHICAL CONCEPTS AND MORAL CONSEQUENCES

The primary responsibility of a leader is to exemplify **morality** and, thus, inspire others to follow likewise, yet the definition of an intrinsic good for a single individual is difficult enough, never mind in a communal setting. In a media-driven age of instant analysis and interpretation of issues and events, careful reflection requires time that many consider better spent on other, more pressing matters related to daily life. Furthermore, such a self-examination sometimes involves questions—many of them—questions to which there are no easy answers. The best place to begin is often with an examination of the basic philosophies and concepts of ethics and their criticisms. The following is a brief introduction to these concepts.

The first of these abstract concepts is **relativism,** the view that there are no moral values or standards applicable to *all* peoples, cultures, and societies. Within such a context, moral practices can be *actually* right in one society yet be *actually* wrong when forced onto another. However, by appealing to the detrimental consequences of moral intervention, there are objective value judgments being made that have universal applications. To assume otherwise is to define what is right as merely socially acceptable, rather than what is objectively valuable and defensible. Under such standards, cultures could neither pass judgment on one another as inferior or superior nor gauge moral progress or call into doubt the questionable practices of others. Such openness and toleration would demand a strict policy of nonintervention even in cases of human atrocity, yet any ethical standard that valued human dignity would obviously demand otherwise.

The second of these abstract concepts is **utilitarianism,** the view that the utility for society is *the* intrinsic good. Because every society evolves in its unique manner, the determination of social good cannot be guided by a "one-size-fits-all" moral code; therefore, the principle of utilitarianism must be applied according to each circumstance. What if, however, the rules were specifically designed by a small group of people, as in an oligarchy, bent on social control? Or what of a dictatorship in which the mere whims of a single individual determine what is best for the society as a whole? And what role do the polar opposite concepts of justice and revenge play in the making of such edicts? Is the utilitarian paradigm best represented in the establishment or the implementation of the moral imperative?

The third of these abstract concepts is **egoism,** the view that human nature is so constructed that a person cannot help but act out of self-interest. When one acts out of generosity, it causes one to feel self-satisfaction; therefore, even when acting out of kindness one is always selfish. Furthermore, society is better off when each person pursues his or her own interests exclusively, for altruism is degrading to human beings, as it makes one the servant of the other and submerges individual initiative through dependency. Though the primary argument of egoism is that human beings are incapable of acting out of nothing more than selfishness, one cannot deny that multitudes of people throughout human history have answered calls to human responsibility and duty. Through personal gestures from donating to neighborhood food drives or attending local benefit dinners to participating in national events, such as Live Aid, or volunteering for military service, people have responded to human need on a level that transcends mere self-interest. Paradoxically, how would an egoist explain a "death wish," a conflict between self-interest and the pursuit of pleasure in which one's compulsive behavior acts against self-interest? Thus, egoism provides what some would consider a false dichotomy, in that it proposes there are but two options in life—self-concern and altruism—while assuming there is an incompatibility between the two.

The fourth of these abstract concepts is **hedonism,** the view that all pleasures are intrinsically good and that all intrinsic goods involve pleasure. In a manner similar to egoism, because pleasure is the root of human happiness, good is equal to the pleasure it carries. However, the human race has been enriched by the reflection on the entire spectrum of emotion. One of the best examples is artistic expression, in which the wide expanse of feeling and intellect melds to produce works that move us in a manner not rooted in pleasure alone. From the paintings of Vincent Van Gogh to those of Edvard Munch, from the writings of Edgar Allan Poe to those of Virginia Woolf, from the music of classical composer Hugo Wolf to that of alternative rocker Kurt Cobain, the articulation of emotional pain has led to breathtaking and haunting works of art. To judge what is intrinsically good based solely on what is pleasurable is to ignore experiences that sometimes provide inspiration and insight, which produce the great works of art, personal growth, and reflection that feed our souls.

The fifth of these abstract concepts is **natural law,** the view that what occurs in nature is an intrinsic good and, therefore, provides the universal standard to which all social and moral systems must be consistent. In turn, all human-made law that is not uniform with nature is illegitimate and, thus, immoral. The most apparent problem with this view is that it has the potential to thwart human progress by demanding a strict adherence to natural processes. If all new discoveries must be consistent with nature, it would deny the development of medicines and technology, for they are the products of humanity's manipulation of nature. Furthermore, not everyone interprets what is "natural" in the same manner. Due to this difference, often justified by the commandments of a "supreme being," by what manner can a universally applied "natural" law be determined and applied?

The sixth of these abstract concepts is the **categorical imperative,** the view that one should always act on that maxim that can be defined as universal. In making such a determination, one must have comprehendible reasons that can be easily stated and understood. The problem with the categorical imperative is that it reduces complex moral principles to inflexible rules. Once these laws are institutionalized, morality becomes a mere game of abstractions, rather than a practice based on a living and flexible ethical code. Another problem arises when there are conflicting duties that require unique considerations outside of a staid code of law. Finally, this paradigm assumes that all human beings are wholly rational and that all logical assumptions lead to the same universal conclusion, when rarely this is the case.

The seventh, and final, of the abstract concepts to be explored in this chapter is **existentialism,** the view that there is no ethereal structure involved with human existence; therefore, it is up to each individual to assemble a reality based on personal perception. This structure is a fluid amalgam of ideas regarding intrinsic goods that changes and reshapes itself over time. In tandem, it also demands complete personal responsibility for one's actions and their consequences, yet the immediate problem is that there is no universal law that is applicable, because all moral perceptions are arbitrary. Under such a paradigm, neither an individual nor a society can hold others accountable for immoral behavior. Furthermore, in order to secure a code of conduct for an ordered society, others must cede their individual moral sense or code to that of the group or a ruling individual, even if they perceive it to be a false one. Though it is clear that all moral philosophies are the product of human perception and thus are flawed, what is important is that the application of personal moral principles be consistent.

■ DUTY TO THE STATE VERSUS DUTY TO SELF

Perhaps the foundational question of public leadership is whether a citizen's foremost duty is to the community or to one's own conscience. In modern society, it is self-evident that no one exists as an island, for all necessary goods and services of contemporary life are intertwined in such a way that one break in this dependent chain will cause chaos. Without recognition of innate human individuality, however, humanity's existence is little more than a cog in a much larger machine—vital for its operation yet replaceable at a moment's notice when perceived as broken. But the machine is rendered inoperable once any part has ceased to perform its function properly; therefore, any effective maintenance requires attention paid both to the machine as a whole and to each mechanism.

The quandary, then, becomes which is of greater value for the survival of a community or, for that matter, a nation. Every machine is accompanied by a set of instructions that tells the user how to operate it properly. Laws accomplish this function within a society and are based on both the goals of its citizens and what the society perceives to be its standards of conduct. Are we obligated to obey an unjust law? By what authority does one defy such social edicts, and to what degree are we morally beholden to the social consequences of our actions?

There is much precedent to support the adage that the needs of the community outweigh the needs of the individual. The English political philosopher Thomas Hobbes argued in his book *Leviathan* that, in order to promote stability, citizens enter into a social contract in which they trade a portion of their liberty for a degree of safety. In doing so, they pledge their loyalty to a political authority and the laws it mandates (Hobbes, 1996, pp. 122, 143, 153, 231). Within the US Constitution, this notion is codified in Article VI § 1, which states that this governing charter represents "the supreme law of the land." Furthermore, the US Supreme Court's unanimous ruling in the case *Jones v. Van Zandt* (1847) mandates that an American citizen is bound to uphold the Constitution and the laws that have proceeded from it, even if those edicts conflict with their conscience.

However, a nation is comprised of individual citizens, distinct from one another in goals, beliefs, and worldview. Within this context, how can *any* governmental authority compel all people to adhere to a common objective? Should not the leader of a nation allow the individual to flourish and thrive as ambitions and conscience dictate? The French political philosopher Jean-Jacques Rousseau put forward in his social contract theory that any government that did not guarantee the liberty of the individual was illegitimate (Rousseau, 1973, p. 5). Furthermore, the US Constitution, in its Ninth and Tenth Amendments, guarantees that the rights and privileges left unclaimed by the federal government are to be given back to the citizens. This was made clear in the case of *Grannis v. Ordean* (1914), in which the US Supreme Court ruled that the Constitution's amendments—the Fifth and Fourteenth, specifically—assure every individual American citizen of "[t]he fundamental requisite of due process"—in other words, not even the federal government can run roughshod over the rights of individual citizens.

Though a leader may philosophically favor one side of this argument over the other, he or she must tread the fine line between these two diametrically opposed paradigms. Unfortunately, there is neither a magic formula nor a moral equation that when readily applied would accomplish this goal. It is up to the individual to find such equilibrium and, using his or her own moral code as a guide, to navigate these often treacherous waters. A leader must not be deterred by the fact that not all under his or her charge will agree with the course of action chosen; however, if such a course is the product of moral reflection and contemplation of outcomes, it is wholly defensible.

■ WHAT IS RIGHT VERSUS WHAT IS POPULAR

When he made the decision not to fight a war with France over the X-Y-Z Affair, President John Adams sacrificed both his extraordinary political career and his historical reputation. Following the president's public disclosure of the incident involving a French minister demanding tribute from a delegation of American representatives, members from both the Federalist Party, led by Alexander Hamilton, and the Democratic-Republican Party, led by Vice President Thomas Jefferson, called for immediate military action. Adams resisted such cries, convinced that such a conflagration would lead to certain defeat for the young nation. As a result, both parties castigated President Adams during his bid for reelection in 1800, a defeat that was wrought primarily by the fact that even his own party abandoned him (Smith, 1962, pp. 1038–47, 1059–63).

Within a few months of his inauguration the following year, newly elected President Thomas Jefferson initiated a military conflict with pirates stationed at Tripoli who were sponsored by the French government. The hostilities proved disastrous, in that it cost the United States what few naval vessels it had constructed for its fledgling fleet (Randall, 1993, pp. 560–63). John Adams may have been on the wrong side of popular opinion, but many today would argue that he was not on the wrong side of history.

The essential element of any republic is that public policy is determined by the support of the majority of its citizens. When any bill is first proposed in Congress, the public becomes engaged in an honest discussion relating to its morality, administration, and pertinent repercussions. Following a prolonged debate, the public registers their assessment through either written or verbal correspondence that instructs their elected representatives as to the appropriate course of action. In the end, a law will rise or fall on the will of the populace, yet this process begs an important question: Is a mere numerical majority the indispensable element of democratic leadership? What safeguards are there for a vocal minority who challenges such group decisions by a social or political majority? Most important, is the majority *always* right? Eminent political scientist Kenneth J. Arrow spent the bulk of his five-decade career studying this problem and ultimately concluded that, given the choice between supporting policies that supported their community and supporting those that benefited their own selfish interests, without fail the public would choose the latter (Arrow, 1983, p. 49). These implications are staggering, for, given that it is the majority of engaged citizens who determine public policy, if the benefit to self matters more than community, what are the implications for the latter's long-term survival?

Most historians believe that President John Adams sacrificed his political career when he decided to ignore popular opinion and refused to go to war with France, but they also believe that history has proven his decision correct.

Library of Congress.

Leadership Challenge

Reflect on a time in your life in which you were encouraged by peer pressure to do something that you would not typically do. Did you follow the crowd or follow your own path? If you followed the crowd, why did you do so? If not, why didn't you?

In the wake of the Panic of 1893, President Grover Cleveland took a brazen stand that cost him both the presidency and his historical reputation. Within three months of taking office for the second of his nonconsecutive terms, Cleveland was faced with a national economic meltdown brought on by a dangerous mixture of the uncontrolled government purchasing of silver and a highly protectionist tariff, both enacted in 1890. To keep the country from sliding into a long-term depression, the president called the Congress into special session and demanded the repeal of the Sherman Silver Purchase and the McKinley Tariff acts—even threatening to refuse its adjournment until it had accomplished what he wanted done. Against the mainstream of his political party, President Cleveland championed the return to the gold standard as the means by which the national currency could be stabilized. In 1896, during his bid for a third term, the Democrats abandoned the incumbent president of their party in favor of Nebraska congressman William Jennings Bryan, who energized convention delegates with his blistering attack against Cleveland and the steps he had taken to repair the nation's failing economy. Ironically, the policies enacted by President Cleveland during that crucial time laid the foundation for his successor, William McKinley's, successful first term (Brodsky, 2000, pp. 305–9).

Grover Cleveland acted on what he viewed as the best interests of his country, but in doing so he forfeited his future political career. The president of Princeton University and future president of the United States, Woodrow Wilson, acknowledged the caliber of leadership Cleveland had provided for the nation when he made the following statement:

> In the midst of the shifting scene Mr. Cleveland personally came to be seen as the only fixed point. He alone stood firm and gave definite utterance to principles intelligible to all. (Wilson, 1903, p. 220)

Within the hindsight of history, and a thorough examination of his record by a generation who have no direct memory of him, Cleveland is now regarded as one of the American nation's finest chief executives (DeGregorio, 1984, p. 329).

In the arena of leadership and service, one must be ever mindful of the timbre of discussion and debate and perpetually ask the following question: Are the options presented either ethical or expedient? Policy that results from rumination on the outcomes and their moral viability are dependent on how they provide the greatest good to the greatest number. President Cleveland demonstrated this adage when he charted a national course wholly unpopular with the members of his own political party and the majority of American citizens. Too often, the option that gains the desired outcome in a timely manner is also that which causes the greatest long-term carnage. Furthermore, a leader's moral authority is undercut when decisions are made for the sake of immediate public acclaim, for in its wake paths are taken and allies are gained that, under normal circumstances, would have been reprehensible. The intrinsic good for the greatest number, for both enemy and ally, is often lost for the sake of popular appeal and expediency.

During World War II, the United States entered the fray to bring down the Nazi regime of Adolf Hitler, a government that had implemented a policy of mass ethnic genocide, which summarily ended the lives of millions of Jews, Slavs, Gypsies, and others, yet in that cause the United States made binding political agreements with the Soviet Union under its premier, Josef Stalin, who was responsible for the execution of over 30 million of his own people (Hart, 1970, pp. 310–12, 523). In the postwar era, the United States offered aid to the devastated countries of Europe, but only if they promised not to adopt political systems that were similar to our perceived enemies (Hamby, 1995, pp. 396–98, 510). Soon after, the United States participated in covert missions under the authority of the Central Intelligence Agency throughout the Middle East, Central America, and South America that assassinated popularly elected leaders who supported socialism and then installed puppet capitalist governments favorable to American economic interests (Woodward, 1987, pp. 362, 389). Finally, after President Harry S Truman announced his policy of Communist containment within his 1949 inaugural address, Soviet Premier Stalin, seeking to repair the Soviet Union's shattered relations with its former ally, called for two-party talks, which were completely rejected by the Truman administration (McCoy, 1984, pp. 191–93).

Events such as these beg for further discussion with regard to their ethical viability. First, why did the United States forge a wartime political alliance with a tyrannical Communist regime against an equally tyrannical National Socialist regime, especially when both were involved in mass genocide? Why were human lives within the Soviet Union more expendable than those within Nazi Germany? Where is the morality in offering necessary humanitarian aid in return for loyalty? How can such relief be truly "altruistic" if it comes with a political price tag? What is ethical about a "democratic" government that thwarts another country's popular will by exterminating democratically elected leaders and installing governments loyal to its own interests, rather than that of a supposedly sovereign nation's own people? Finally, where is the morality in choosing confrontation over peace, especially toward a nation with which a peaceful alliance already exists?

Had any one of the above questions been pondered with the aim of producing an ethical outcome, the course of American history in the post–World War II era would have been radically different. The pertinent query regarding American policies toward the Soviet Union during this period should be focused on the premise of the necessity of such a military and political alliance. Could the Nazi regime, the mutual enemy of both the United States and the Soviet Union, have been defeated without the fusion of their military efforts? Did conditional humanitarian aid ultimately produce reliable allies in the fight against communism? Was American intervention into the political affairs of other sovereign nations and the murder of their leaders morally defensible? Was communism the pervasive threat that the American government contended it was? All of these queries do much to prove that contemporary political leadership is not based on ethical reflection but on the Machiavellian paradigm that the ends justify the means. Furthermore, few, if any, contemporary leaders are willing to follow in the footsteps of John Adams and Grover Cleveland and sacrifice their own political careers for the sake of doing what is best for the long-term good of the nation, especially if it means saying, "The public be damned."

■ THE CHOICES WE MAKE

When it comes to choices in life, we are conceived and born without one, and we die only after making a plethora of them. When it is critical to make choices, we either jump at the opportunity to get them over with quickly or postpone them to the last possible minute. In the necessity to optimize them, we routinely miss the best prospect to enjoy their benefits. We make choices because ultimately nobody else can make them for us, yet not every choice has to be the right one. Humans are prone to error, but such mistakes are often the means by which we experience personal growth, learn, and progress. Ultimately, our responsibility is to keep our own personal destiny, as well as the destiny of those we lead, from entering the realm of tragedy.

The 1850s were a perilous time in American politics, for it was an era in which the interests of "self" superseded those of "nation." Elected president of the United States in 1852, Franklin Pierce sought to enact policies of expansion in trade and territory, coupled with the strident reform of both the military and the civil service; during the fourteen months between his inauguration in March 1853 and May 1854, he achieved much of it, yet Pierce's accomplishments will be forever shadowed by one controversial act: his signature on the Kansas-Nebraska Act.

President Pierce never wanted the Kansas-Nebraska Act to become law, primarily because he was opposed to the "popular sovereignty" clause, which effectively repealed the 1820 Missouri Compromise. The president's position was that, if the compromise was to be eliminated, it should be through a decision of the US Supreme Court, rather than a legislative act, for it would lend it an air of legitimacy. Though he actively sought to thwart the bill's passage, going so far as to draft the "popular sovereignty" clause in a way that made this law unamendable by Congress, his efforts came to naught in May 1854, when both houses of Congress overwhelmingly passed it. Pierce was then faced with a dilemma: Should he veto the act and risk the secession of the South—and with it inevitable civil war—or should he enact it into law, hold the Union together, but effectively end his political career? As history records, the president did the latter and, as a result, the nation degenerated into violent chaos and he gained an ignoble place within American history (Nichols, 1931, pp. 333–38).

When one occupies a position of leadership, situations arise that do not always present an obvious ethical and moral path. The solution to such matters often requires deep inner reflection and a contemplation of every option that will produce an ethical outcome—coupled with the knowledge that throughout human history many decisions based on sound ethical and moral choices, in the end, produced discordant and devastating consequences. Thus, the soundest test of any personal and societal code of ethics occurs when one is faced with a decision in which every outcome will inevitably produce harm.

In the waning months of World War II, following the surrender of Germany, President Harry S Truman was faced with the ultimate dilemma: whether to drop the atomic bomb. With the surrender of Germany a few months before, the commander-in-chief had at his disposal a vast and effective military force that could successfully effect a land invasion of Japan, yet such an incursion of the

Japanese mainland would be long and costly. There was also a further and more deadly option open to the president. On assuming the presidency with the death of his predecessor, Franklin Delano Roosevelt, President Truman was made aware of a powerful weapon, which had been developed by the fusion of atoms, that had the capability of leveling highly populated metropolitan centers (Hart, 1970, pp. 691–98). On weighing the options carefully, President Truman came to the conclusion that, though hundreds of thousands of lives would be lost in its use, it would force a timely end to the war and, as such, save millions of both American and Japanese lives (Truman, 1955, p. 419).

Though at first glance President Truman's choice to use the atomic bomb on Japanese civilian targets may seem inconceivable in any ethical assessment, in real terms it achieved the desired goal—the end of war and with it the further slaughter of human life. What this serious moment in history demonstrates is that, for a leader, sometimes difficult choices, right or wrong, crucial or ephemeral, are inescapable.

On the surface, the mere existence of such dilemmas seems to undermine the purpose of ethical decision making, for the goal of a moral code of conduct is to lead and serve all justly. In facing off against an enemy, such as the genocidal regime of Germany under Nazism or a tribal civil war between the African nations of Rwanda and Burundi, what path can a leader take that will not allow the nation he or she represents to become the embodiment of what the nation is fighting against? During World War II, Mahatma Gandhi was posed this question with

President Harry S Truman's decision to use the atomic bomb was one of the most difficult in human history. He was faced with a decision in which every outcome would inevitably produce incredible human suffering.

Library of Congress.

regard to an enemy such as Adolph Hitler; recognizing the dilemma within the query itself, he replied that one must be willing to accept many defeats until, in the end, good would triumph over evil (Fischer, 1954, p. 215). If, in seeking a moral end to conflict, for expediency's sake a leader must engage in actions that are morally questionable, is that leader not the moral equivalent of his or her enemy? And, as such, where is the moral validation of actions if a nation must become the moral and ethical mirror image of what it is struggling to defeat?

■ COMPLACENCY VERSUS ACTIVISM

A consistent code of ethics is an impossible course to maintain unless it is demonstrated in the everyday conduct of one's life. To proclaim a life philosophy as your own, and then to act in conflict with it, is little more than intellectual self-gratification. This planet can be ruthless to those who possess a confident sense of self, and even more so to those who do not; thus, we are devastated when our highly esteemed leaders are found to be nothing more than mere mortals. Though the path of leadership and service to others is rarely glorious, it is vital for one very important reason: Progressions throughout human history have been wrought not by people who have submitted to the system for the sake of order but by those who have acted on their ethical and moral beliefs and refused to back down until their issue was seriously addressed.

One such application has been the fight against the governmental restriction of a guaranteed right, such as the liberty of speech and expression. The fundamental question to be posed here is whether in a truly free society there are subjects that are too obscene or dangerous to be discussed in a public forum. One who actively challenged the preconceptions of social hypocrisy on this issue was comedian Lenny Bruce. Using a cutting-edge combination of outrageousness and "blue" language, Bruce's social commentary confronted established social definitions of untouchable concepts of decency, obscenity, faith, and class. Throughout the last six years of his life, he was a favorite target of moralists on both sides who used the law to stifle expression—a struggle that cost him his life. Bruce's crusade against arbitrary definitions of the Constitution's First Amendment opened the door for such controversial commentators, critics, and satirists as Bill Maher, Rush Limbaugh, Al Franken, George Carlin, Richard Pryor, Chris Rock, and Richard Belzer, who not only engage, entertain and sometimes make audiences laugh but also force the public to ponder the dysfunction of society (Collins & Skover, 2002).

Another abstract idea that challenged popular preconceptions was the definition of peace, championed by singer/songwriter John Lennon and embodied by his composition "Imagine." After attaining international superstardom as one-fourth of the Beatles, Lennon later used his immense fame to put forward complex intellectual treatises, set to popular music, on themes such as the meaning of peace, the mistreatment of human beings within social institutions, and the outcomes of violence and discrimination. The most salient question posed by Lennon was simple: Is "peace" merely the lack of violence between enemies or the result of people freeing themselves from the elements that cause friction within human society?

He asked his audience to ponder a utopian world, stripped of all intellectual complexity, in which race, religion, class, and gender issues did not exist. Though he was assassinated by a disgruntled fan on December 8, 1980, over a quarter-century later his music and his message endure (Coleman, 1984, pp. 441–65).

On a deeper examination of history, there are a myriad of events and people who, through their spirited actions, fought for causes greater than themselves and enriched the awareness of the human condition. In the case of discrimination and segregation based on the color of skin, one needs only to study the extraordinary lives of Dr. Martin Luther King, Jr., and the Reverend Ralph Abernathy and the popular civil rights movement they commanded for well over three decades. In tandem, seeking a goal of gender equality were courageous women such as Alice Paul, Betty Friedan, Eleanor Smeal, and Gloria Steinem. Within the pages of her 1962 book *Silent Spring,* none were more influential in warning the world against the impending danger caused by pollution than Dr. Rachel Carson, who implored us to take a further look at how our arrogance was destroying our fragile planet. Then there are the stories of those who championed the plight of the less fortunate, not only in their own countries but around the globe—men and women such as Senator George McGovern, Mother Teresa, Florence Nightingale, and musician Harry Chapin. And there are a myriad of other issues and the champions who were willing to sacrifice for them—so numerous, in fact, that to give them the credit they so richly deserve would be impractical within the parameters of this tome.

The salient point here is that, if one leads by example, the code of ethics by which they live will be readily apparent. One has to lead and serve by action, not by mere assertion.

■ CONCLUSION: A PEBBLE IN A POND

In 1871, future president James Garfield stated, "I would rather believe something and suffer for it, than to slide along into success without opinions" (Peskin, 1978). Garfield won the presidency in 1880 by the slimmest popular majority in American history—fewer than 9,500 votes out of 9 million ballots cast—primarily because he was a highly vocal and controversial political reformer at a time of dominance by political machines (DeGregorio, 1984, p. 300). During his brief term in office, Garfield challenged the stalwarts of his own party and toppled the boss of New York's Tammany Hall political machine, Senator Roscoe Conkling. He was shot in the back by a disgruntled office seeker four months into his term on July 2, 1881, and died in agony two months later (DeGregorio, 1984, pp. 302–3). As a tribute to Garfield's leadership, his successor, Chester Arthur, a former machine politician, signed into law a sweeping reform bill that both destroyed the endemic "spoils" system of patronage and established the modern civil service (Karabell, 2004, pp. 104–7). As a result, the standard by which all public servants are held to is an ongoing testament to President Garfield and the moral principles by which he lived his life.

When one takes a pebble and tosses it into a pond, what results is a small wave that spreads outward until it reaches the bank. In the same manner, every life touches others. Throughout the cycles of our lives, tragedy and comedy pass in front of us in clearly recognizable patterns that provide ample opportunities for growth and tears, based on the choices we make. Because we do not live in isolation, every choice we make profoundly affects the actions of other people, and it is because of this that the choices we make take on a greater importance than any of us could ever imagine. In human existence, there is no choice but to choose; however, through a clear understanding of which is moral, the benefit to the world might someday be immeasurable.

This chapter has attempted to explain the importance of ethics in leadership and service to humanity by examining the actions of leaders who have acted on their moral convictions. As such, it has led this author to conclude that there are specific tenets by which those in positions of leadership and service can conduct themselves:

- Be cognizant of the difference between what is best for both the group *and* each individual within it and, with soundness of judgment, seek options that maintain a balance between group and individual needs.
- Act in the pursuit of opportunities that achieve long-term good for the greatest number, even if it means the sacrifice of short-term popularity.
- Be ever aware of the benefits of maintaining ethical and moral consistency and never sacrifice it or be tempted by the lure of expediency.
- Recognize that choices are the inevitable by-product of leadership and must not be avoided—and do not be fearful of changing direction when new evidence or circumstances dictate such a change.
- If under normal circumstances the goal of ethical leadership is to consistently act for the greatest good for the largest number, then it follows that, in the face of a dilemma, one must assure the least harm to the smallest number or those who have no voice.
- It is not enough to verbalize foundational principles or ideas; they must be consistently demonstrated through action, for only a public display of those core personal values provides a cogent example for others to follow.

The true significance of ethics and moral principles, especially in the realm of leadership, are the lessons they teach both to us and to future generations, for in the most vital sense our world is but a pond and our lives the pebbles waiting for a place within it. Should we decide to take advantage of this moment in history, perhaps generations to come will demonstrate their gratitude by following in our footsteps.

■ KEY TERMS*

Categorical Imperative—An absolute, unconditional requirement that exerts its authority in all circumstances, both required and justified as an end in itself.

Egoism—The worldview that it is necessary and sufficient for an action to be morally right if it maximizes one's self-interest.

Ethics—A branch of philosophy that studies the moral perceptions of a person or group, employing the analysis of concepts and perceptions of right and wrong, good and evil, and responsibility.

Existentialism—The worldview that individual human beings create the meanings and essence of their own lives.

Hedonism—The worldview that seeking pleasure is the most important pursuit of humanity.

Morality—A code of conduct held to be authoritative in matters of right and wrong, whether by society, philosophy, religion, or individual conscience.

Natural Law—The worldview that the existence of a law whose content is set by nature has validity everywhere.

Relativism—The worldview that no universal standard exists by which to assess an ethical proposition's truth.

Utilitarianism—The worldview that the moral worth of an action is solely determined by its contribution to overall utility.

■ SUGGESTED READINGS

Aristotle. 2004. *Nicomachean Ethics.* Trans. J. A. K. Thomson. New York: Penguin.

Hobbes, T. 1996. *Leviathan.* Ed. R. Tuck. New York: Cambridge University Press.

Kant, I. 1993. *Grounding for the Metaphysics of Morals.* Trans. J. W. Ellington. Indianapolis: Hackett.

Maguire, D. C. & Fargnoli, A. N. 1991. *On Moral Grounds: The Art/Science of Ethics.* New York: Crossroad.

Marino, G. (ed.) 2004. *Basic Writings of Existentialism.* New York: Modern Library.

Oord, T. Jay. 2007. *The Altruism Reader: Selections from Writings on Love, Religion, and Science.* Philadelphia: Templeton Foundation Press.

Rosen, F. 2003. *Classical Utilitarianism from Hume to Mill.* London: Routledge Books.

Tännsjö, T. 1998. *Hedonistic Utilitarianism.* Edinburgh: Edinburgh University Press.

Wong, D. B. 1984. *Moral Relativity.* Berkeley: University of California Press.

*The definitions have been paraphrased from the *New Oxford Dictionary,* Wikipedia, and the *Stanford Encyclopedia of Philosophy.*

■ REFERENCES

Arrow, K. J. (ed.) 1983. *Collected Papers of Kenneth J. Arrow, The Volume One: Social Choice and Justice.* Cambridge, MA: The Belknap Press of Harvard University Press.

Barker, E. (ed.) 1960. *Social Contract.* New York: Oxford University Press.

Bourke, V. J. (ed.) 1960. *The Pocket Aquinas.* New York: Washington Square Press.

Brodsky, A. 2000. *Grover Cleveland: A Study in Character.* New York: St. Martin's Press.

Burke, E. 1987. *Reflections on the Revolution in France.* J. G. A. Pocock (Ed.). Indianapolis: Hackett.

Burr, J. R. & Goldinger, M. 1984. *Philosophy and Contemporary Issues* (5th ed.) New York: Macmillan.

Calhoun, J. C. 1953. *A Disquisition on Government and Selections from the Discourse.* C. Gordon Post (Ed.), New York: Liberal Arts Press.

Campbell, J. with Moyers, B. 1988. *The Power of Myth.* New York: Doubleday.

Carey, G. W. & J. McClellan (eds.) 2001. *The Federalist.* The Gideon Edition. Indianapolis: The Liberty Fund.

Coleman, R. 1984. *Lennon.* New York: McGraw-Hill.

Collingwood, R. G. 1946. *The Idea of History.* New York: Oxford University Press.

Collins, R. K. L. & Skover, D. M. 2002. *The Trials of Lenny Bruce: The Fall and Rise of an American Icon.* Naperville, IL: Sourcebooks MediaFusion.

Countryman, E. 1996. *Americans: A Collision of Histories.* New York: Hill & Wang.

DeGregorio, W. A. 1984. *The Complete Book of the Presidents.* New York: December Books.

Edwards III, G. C. & Wayne, S. J. 1990. *Presidential Leadership: Politics and Policy Making.* New York: St. Martin's Press.

Fischer, L. 1954. *Gandhi: His Life and Message for the World.* New York: Mentor Books.

Frazier, J. G. 1922. *The Golden Bough.* New York: Collier Books.

Gellner, E. 1983. *Nations and Nationalism.* Ithaca, NY: Cornell University Press.

Grannis v. Ordean, 234 U.S. 394 (1914).

Hamby, A. L. 1995. *Man of the People: A Life of Harry S. Truman.* New York: Oxford University Press.

Hamilton, E. 1942. *Mythology.* Boston: Little, Brown.

Hart, B. H. L. 1970. *History of the Second World War.* New York: G. P. Putnam's Sons.

Hobbes, T. 1996. *Leviathan.* Ed. R. Tuck. New York: Cambridge University Press.

Jones v. Van Zandt, 5 How (46 U.S.) 221 (1847).

Karabell, Z. 2004. *Chester Alan Arthur.* New York: Times Books.

Kettner, J. H. 1978. *The Development of American Citizenship.* Chapel Hill: University of North Carolina Press.

Kurland, P. B. & Lerner, R. (eds.) 1987. *The Founder's Constitution.* Indianapolis: The Liberty Fund.

Locke, J. 1960. *Two Treatises on Government*. Ed. P. Laslett. New York: Cambridge University Press.

Lucretius. 1951. *The Nature of the Universe*. Ed. R. Latham. Baltimore: Penguin Books.

Maguire, D. C. & Fargnoli, A. N. 1991. *On Moral Grounds: The Art/Science of Ethics*. New York: Crossroad.

Malcolm, J. L. (ed.) 1999. *The Struggle for Sovereignty: Seventeenth-Century English Political Tracts*. Indianapolis: The Liberty Fund.

Maritain, J. 1951. *Man and the State*. Washington, DC: The Catholic University of America Press.

McCoy, D. R. 1984. *The Presidency of Harry S. Truman*. Lawrence: The University Press of Kansas.

Montesquieu, Baron de. 1989. *The Spirit of the Laws*. Cohler, A. M., Miller, B. C., & Stone, H. S. (Eds.). New York: Cambridge University Press.

Neustadt, R. E. 1980. *Presidential Power and the Modern Presidents: The Politics of Leadership from Roosevelt to Reagan*. New York: Free Press.

Nichols, R. F. 1931. *Franklin Pierce: Young Hickory of the Granite Hills*. Philadelphia: University of Pennsylvania Press.

Ober, W. (ed.) 1964. *Intellectual Origins of American National Thought: Pages from the Books Our Founding Fathers Read*. New York: Corinth Books.

Peskin, A. 1978. *Garfield*. Kent, OH: Kent University Press.

Randall, W. S. 1993. *Thomas Jefferson: A Life*. New York: Henry Holt.

Rousseau, Jean-Jacques. 1973. *The Social Contract and Discourses*. C. D. H. Cole (ed.). Rutland, VT: Charles E. Tuttle.

Saint Augustine. 1958. *City of God*. V. J. Bourke (ed.). New York: Image Books.

Segal, E. (ed.) 1986. *Dialogues of Plato*. New York: Bantam Books.

Sheehan, C. A. & MacDowell, G. L. (eds.) 1998. *Friends of the Constitution: Writings of the "Other" Federalists*. Indianapolis: The Liberty Fund.

Shirer, William L. 1979. *Gandhi: A Memoir*. New York: Simon & Schuster.

Sidney, A. 1996. *Discourses Concerning Government*. Thomas G. West (ed.). Indianapolis: The Liberty Fund.

Smith, P. 1962. *John Adams*. Garden City, NY: Doubleday.

Strout, C. 1974. *The New Heavens and New Earth: Political Religion in America*. New York: Harper & Row.

Suárez, Francisco. 1994. *On Efficient Causality: Metaphysical Disputations 17, 18, and 19*. A. J. Freddoso (trans.). New Haven, CT: Yale University Press.

Taranto, J. & Leo, L. (eds.) 2004. *Presidential Leadership: Rating the Best and the Worst in the White House*. New York: Wall Street Journal Books.

Tocqueville, Alexis de. 1990. *Democracy in America*. P. Bradley (ed.). New York: Vintage Books.

Truman, H. S. 1955. *Memoirs by Harry S. Truman, Volume One: Year of Decisions*. Garden City, NY: Doubleday.

Voltaire. 1994. *Political Writings*. D. Williams (ed.). New York: Cambridge University Press.

Wall, R. 1977. *Ocean Liners*. London: New Burlington Books.

Whittemore, R. C. 1964. *Makers of the American Mind: Three Centuries of American Thought and Thinkers*. New York: William Morrow.

Wilson, W. 1903. *History of the American People*. New York: Harper & Brothers.

Woodward, B. 1987. *Veil: The Secret Wars of the CIA 1981–87*. New York: Simon & Schuster.

Name: _____   Date: _____

CHAPTER EIGHT REVIEW QUESTIONS

1. Do ethics require that a leader must pursue policies that reinforce the intrinsic good of his or her charge even if those policies are unpopular?

_____

_____

_____

2. Do ethics require a rational basis for religious beliefs, especially of those in leadership positions?

_____

_____

_____

3. To whom does a person owe his or her greatest allegiance: the state in which he or she lives or him- or herself?

_____

_____

_____

4. Is it appropriate for a leader to utilize unethical means to achieve an ethical end?

_____

_____

_____

5. If you could select only one of the basic philosophies of ethics on which to base your life and work, which would you choose and why?

_____

_____

_____

CHAPTER EIGHT SELF-TEST

1. The story of the Collins Line is a reminder that actions resulting from one's beliefs invariably_____.

2. According to _____, "The unexamined life is not worth living."

3. _____ is the view that there are no moral values or standards applicable to all peoples or societies.

4. _____ is the view that all pleasures are intrinsically good.

5. English philosopher _____ argued that, in order to promote stability, citizens entered into a social contract.

6. Political scientist Kenneth Arrow concluded that, given a choice between what is best for the community and self-interest, the public would choose

   _____.

7. The true test of a code of ethics occurs when all outcomes will inevitably produce _____.

8. _____ is the belief that one can't help but act out of self-interest.

9. If you accept the concept of _____, you believe that it is up to each individual to assemble a reality based on perception.

10. In the case *Jones v. Van Zandt,* the Supreme Court unanimously ruled that American citizens are bound to uphold the Constitution and the laws that have proceeded from it, even if those edicts conflict with their_____.

Leadership for the Common Good

9

John S. (Jack)
Burns

■ INTRODUCTION

Leadership for the Common Good is the noblest kind of leadership. Unfortunately, many obstacles conspire to make it rarely practiced and poorly understood. Our hope is that this chapter will help students of leadership both understand this concept and aspire to conduct Leadership for the Common Good. We begin with the central thesis of this chapter: It is possible to conduct Leadership for the Common Good. A subtext to this thesis, however, is also important: While it may be possible to conduct Leadership for the Common Good, it is so difficult that it seems impossible! To work through this thesis, the chapter will develop a working understanding of three essential terms: (1) leadership, (2) **The Common,** and (3) **The Good.**

■ A WORKING UNDERSTANDING OF THE TERM *LEADERSHIP*

In 1978, James MacGregor Burns wrote *Leadership,* one of the most important leadership books ever published. This book established the study of leadership as a unique discipline related to, but independent of, the disciplines of political science and management. In the Prologue, Burns stated, "Leadership is one of the most observed and least understood phenomena on earth" (p. 2). Although millions of words have been written on the topic, there is still no commonly accepted definition of *leadership.* Some writers simply avoid defining the term, assuming that, like good art, "you'll know it when you see it." Joseph Rost criticized those authors in his book *Leadership for the 21st Century.* He suggested responsible scholarship demands that authors always develop a working definition of *leadership* in their writing (Rost, 1991).

Developing a definition of *leadership* is no easy task. Consider for a moment various ways the word *leadership* is used. Advertisers try to enhance the perception of their products and services by linking them to the word *leadership,* such as "Channel 6 News Team—Journalistic Leadership." Sometimes the word is a noun used as a synonym for a person or persons at the top of an organizational hierarchy, such as "The leadership decided to fire half of the workforce." Most often, we associate the word *leadership* with the behavior of leaders who are effective in their positions. But is leadership simply a function of filling a slot somewhere on the upper level of an organizational chart and being effective in that position? Many people have been in charge of many types of organizations, and some of those people have been extremely effective in those positions. Does that mean they have conducted leadership? For example, think about Nazi Germany. Hitler was the leader, and he was certainly effective. Did he "do" leadership? Scholars have long argued over definitions of *leadership* that have either included or excluded Hitler's actions as an example. Though Hitler was the head of an organization and was effective in that position, Burns argued that it is inappropriate to use the term *leadership* to describe what Hitler did. Burns assigned the term *tyranny* to Hitler's actions, not *leadership;* the behavior of a tyrant is not leadership (Burns, 1978).

To move the definition beyond an assessment of the efficacy of a leader's actions, Burns described a leadership continuum ranging from transactional to transforming processes and outcomes. **Transactional leadership** is an exchange between leaders and followers that facilitates the accomplishment of some goal or purpose shared by both parties. Transactional leadership is relatively easy to conduct. Examples include a person writing a check to a charity he or she supports and a citizen choosing to give a politician a vote, so that the politician will pursue a political goal that the citizen supports. After the transactional exchange, each party continues with his or her life, which may or may not involve future transactions. According to Burns, these transactions fall on the leadership continuum if they are the result of a free choice devoid of the abuse of power by all parties in the exchange. The abuse of power, which eliminates the opportunity for choice, moves the transaction from Burns' leadership continuum into the realm of tyranny. Thus, Hitler was a tyrant because the transactions he forced on the German people deprived them of choice.

The other end of Burns' continuum, **transforming leadership,** is at once far more difficult to conduct on a large scale but also has greater potential to produce significant, lasting change for everyone involved. Burns said transforming leadership occurs when "one or more persons engage with others in such a way that leaders and followers raise one another to higher levels of motivation and morality" (Burns, 1978, p. 20). Let X^1 represent an honest assessment of where an organization is with regard to fulfilling its mission and values. Let X^2 represent what the organization would look like and what it would be doing if it were fulfilling the organization's mission and values in every possible way. If X^2 could be achieved easily through some sort of a simple transaction, then the gap between X^1 and X^2 would be inconsequential. Indeed, if a hypothetical organization could operate at X^2, there would be no need for transforming leadership because there would be no need for anything or anyone to change.

Unlike hypothetical organizations, real organizations must learn to transform or adapt if they are to survive and thrive. The transforming journey to X^2 is like climbing a huge mountain. On the plain miles from the mountain, one sees the challenges of the climb in grand relief. As one begins to climb the lower slopes,

Miles from the mountain, one sees the challenges of the climb in grand relief, but, as one begins to climb the lower slopes, immediate obstacles appear.

Library of Congress.

immediate obstacles appear to obstruct the path to the summit. Each obstacle conquered reveals many more that were never visible from a distance. Indeed, for most of the climb, the obstacles are so great that the way view of the summit itself is rarely clear. Much like climbing a mountain, the transforming path from X^1 to X^2 is fraught with obstacles, many of which seem impassable.

Mountain climbers reach the summit if they are able to make successful adaptations to overcome everything the mountain environment throws at them. In the world of organizations, the perfection of X^2 (summit) can never be reached. Organizations live in dynamic, fluid environmental contexts where critical variables are constantly changing. As an organization approaches X^2, new challenges from its turbulent environment will always pop up like the sudden storms that can keep even the best mountain-climbing teams from reaching a summit. Organizations die if they are unable to adapt to the new challenges.

In order to meet these challenges, people and their organizations must learn, adapt, and implement effective problem-solving strategies. Ronald Heifetz (1994) suggests that problems—or, in this case, the obstacles between X^1 and X^2—are of three major types. Type I problems are technical problems with technical solutions. These kinds of problems fit nicely near the transactional end of Burns' leadership continuum. For instance, when it snows in mid-October on I-90 in Montana, the Montana Highway Department sends out its snowplows and sanders to clear the road and sand the icy spots. Such an event hardly fazes Montana drivers. Their vehicles are well equipped for winter driving, and Montanans possess the skills required to maneuver efficiently and safely on wintry roads, even when winter

Transforming/Adaptive Leadership

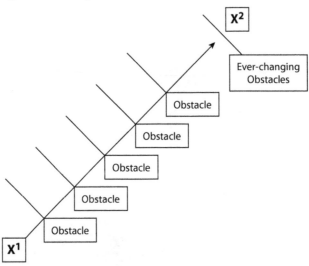

starts in October. If the only problems we faced on the path to X^2 were Type I problems, the journey would be relatively simple as we employed a series of readily available technical fixes for each obstacle.

Heifetz also identifies Type II problems, which are a bit more difficult. They are still technical problems with technical solutions, but the technical solutions may not be readily available or may require significant learning (adaptation/transformation) before implementation. The October snowstorm in Montana is a technical problem with readily available technical solutions for people who live in that state. For a person from Florida enjoying a fall vacation in Glacier National Park, the sudden October snowstorm becomes a Type II problem. The same snowplows will clear the roads and sand the icy spots, but the Florida driver, who has never driven his or her 35-foot RV (Recreational Vehicle) on a snowy interstate, is a long way from being able to take advantage of the highway department's technical fix to the snow problem. The Florida driver will have to make adaptive transformations to work through this obstacle. The driver may have to purchase winter tires or tire chains, and practice driving on an empty, snow-covered parking lot. Fortunately, Montana is a huge state, and the Florida driver may indeed master the skills necessary (adaptive transformation) to continue confidently through the snowy Midwest on the way back to the Sunshine State. On the journey from X^1 to X^2, we can work through Type II problems with relative ease if we are willing to adapt or transform by learning and implementing new technical solutions.

Heifetz's Type III problems are the most difficult of all. Type III problems are not technical problems with technical solutions. These problems require learning and subsequent adaptive transformation by everyone involved. There is an endless list of Type III problems: racism, transportation gridlock, dependence on fossil fuels, global hunger, hate crimes, global poverty, drug addiction, out-of-control consumerism, voter apathy, and so on. No matter how much faith we put in science and its offspring, advanced technology, and technical fixes will not fully solve Type III problems. These are the most difficult obstacles on the journey from X^1 to X^2. This is the heart of Burns' transforming leadership. When an obstacle is a Type III problem, people and organizations must transform or, in Heifetz's terminology, do the adaptive work necessary to overcome the obstacle.

Adaptive work is difficult, and organizations and individuals are adept at avoiding the work required to achieve a successful transformation. There is a great temptation to settle for relatively easy cosmetic technical or transactional Band-Aids posing as solutions, instead of doing the deep adaptive work Type III problems require. Organizations cannot remain the same and still make progress toward X^2. Transforming leadership creates an organizational climate where people and the organization can undergo significant transformations.

This transforming journey from X^1 to X^2 has other important qualities. If you look at Burns' definition, you will see that on this journey leaders and followers must raise one another to higher levels of motivation and *morality*. It is not difficult to imagine people getting more and more motivated as they approach a goal. Psychologists, social scientists, teachers, coaches, parents, and anyone else who observes human performance support the notion that, as people achieve success in moving toward a goal, they become more motivated. Raising one another to higher levels of motivation is not the challenge in Burns' definition.

Burns' requirement for moral elevation, however, raises important and difficult questions. Scholars were critical of Burns when he introduced the requirement for moral elevation in his definition of *transforming leadership*. They argued that there is no moral standard on which to base Burns' moral requirement. Therefore, they reasoned, transforming leadership must be amoral. For these scholars, organizational transformation from *any* X^1 to *any* X^2 is transforming leadership. We will address the question of moral leadership in some detail later when we develop our understanding of the term *The Good*.

While our deeper examination of morality rests on a back burner for now, we can discuss how, at the surface, Burns' principle of moral elevation is appealing. For example, Hitler's actions resulted in a major transformation of Germany. Indeed, Germany can be said to have moved from *an* X^1 to *an* X^2, but this transformation was immoral, no matter whose morality is employed (save that of a dedicated Nazi). Most of us have difficulty labeling Hitler's actions leadership in the same way we call the actions of Mohandas Gandhi and Martin Luther King, Jr., leadership. At this visceral level, Burns' moral requirement has utility, so for now we will give Burns the benefit of the doubt and agree with his requirement for moral elevation in leadership. *Leadership* may indeed be far too noble a term to assign to the actions of Adolf Hitler, Idi Amin, or any of the other countless bullies who have ruled their turfs at the expense of others, for the exclusive benefit of themselves and their toadies.

What, then, is our working understanding of the definition of *leadership?* James MacGregor Burns' fundamental principles in his definition form the basis for our understanding. First, leadership is a journey from an honest assessment of where we currently are (X^1) toward fulfilling our ultimate purpose and honoring our highest values (X^2). We will have to work through every obstacle on this journey. Some

According to James MacGregor Burns, Adolph Hitler's use of power to force people toward organizational goals was tyranny, not leadership.

Library of Congress.

obstacles will be relatively easy, Type I kinds of problems, which transactional or technical fixes will resolve. Every Type II and III obstacle we encounter will require us to transform or adapt, or these obstacles will arrest our journey and our subsequent development. This transforming journey must also be morally elevating for all who are engaged in the process.

Second, abusive power and leadership are not compatible. Using power abusively to force people to move toward organizational goals or in the transactional or transformation processes is called tyranny, not leadership.

Third, leadership cannot be isolated and assigned to the effective behaviors of a person or persons at the top of a hierarchy. No matter where a person is on an organizational chart, if that person has the best understanding of the current obstacle, he or she is the one who can best conduct the skills of the others to develop effective adaptive strategies. Leadership in this sense is collective and dynamic. Each member of the organization must step up and use his or her skills to make a unique contribution in the face of ever-changing adaptive challenges.

Fourth, a major task of leadership is to challenge everyone in the organization to always keep in mind the organization's purpose and values (X^2), especially when the journey becomes ensnared by seemingly overwhelming Type III obstacles. Remembering the organization's ultimate purpose and honoring its values will free everyone to become creative and to undergo personal and organizational transformation in order to move past seemingly insurmountable obstacles.

In summary, our working understanding of the term *leadership* has four major components:

1. Leadership is a transforming journey from X^1 to X^2, which is morally elevating.
2. Power cannot be abused to get people to take the journey or in the various transactions and adaptive processes along the way.
3. Leadership is conducted broadly throughout an organization.
4. Leadership requires us to focus on our ultimate mission and values, even in the midst of dynamic turbulence.

■ A WORKING UNDERSTANDING OF THE TERM *THE COMMON*

There is not much controversy or debate about the definition of *The Common*. The Common is something shared by everyone. There are difficulties, however, with linking The Common with leadership in North American culture. Our culture's systemic individualism, postmodernism's influence on the general North American worldview, and consumerism all pose threats to conducting leadership for The Common.

Systemic Individualism

Individualism takes precedence over concern for The Common in North American culture. We can trace the roots of this central characteristic of the culture at least as far back as the early sixteenth century and the Protestant Reformation in Europe. Before the Reformation, through centuries fraught with political, economic, and social chaos, Europe had one, common, enduring, stabilizing institution: the Roman Catholic Church. The universal acceptance of the authority of the Church was the mortar that held the turbulent European culture together.

When Jean Calvin and other Reformation leaders endorsed the idea of "a priesthood of all believers," they opened the floodgates of radical change that would eventually undermine the authority of the Church and shatter the unifying common worldview of Christian Europe. Instead of submitting to the Roman Catholic tradition that authorized an intermediary (a Catholic priest and the Church) between humanity and God, Reformation leaders encouraged every individual to develop a personal and intimate relationship with his or her God. In the fertile soil of political and economic disaffection with the Roman Catholic Church, the Reformation took root and thrived, especially in Northern Europe. As the authority of the Church crumbled, a new worldview emerged based on individualism and the authority of human reason.

Humanism, science, capitalism, and new political ideas, such as individual freedoms and rights, became significant features of the Age of Enlightenment. When the seeds of ideas from the Enlightenment germinated in the North American colonies, they thrived. Protecting the rights of individuals became a systemic influence on the fundamental tenets of the emerging culture. The founding documents of the United States became the canon for these ideas. Over time, the westward expansion into the frontiers of the new continent only reinforced the American ethos of individuality. Mythology grew that celebrated ascendancy of individuals and their accomplishments in politics, industry, and nearly every other sphere of human activity. Individual achievement has become far more important than the accomplishments of a group.

Individualism has become so tightly woven into the fabric of the culture that people rarely give it a second thought. On the following list, which items do people value most? Why?

- Flying first-class
- Public housing
- Country club
- Public swimming pool
- Stadium luxury box
- Bus terminal
- Public pay phone
- General admission
- Personal trainer
- Public defender
- Gated community
- School uniforms
- iPhone®
- Public restroom

Viewed pejoratively, The Common is an unavoidable necessity, needed most by those who cannot make it on their own. The Common equates with average or worse. The systemic influence of individualism teaches one to maximize individual potential, to be above average, hopefully way above average. The Common provides an acceptable refuge for "others" whose existence is comparatively substandard, but it is not for "us," the high achievers who can provide for ourselves. Thus, serving The Common takes on the connotation of charity or community service work.

Postmodernism and The Common

Postmodern philosophy is a response to modern philosophy (modernity), which, from the Enlightenment through much of the twentieth century, posited rationalist theories intent on uncovering fundamental truths intended to answer all essential worldview questions. In 1979, Jean-Francois Lyotard wrote *The Post-Modern Condition,* in which he described postmodern philosophy as a deconstruction of the assumptions of the "meta-narratives" and their "truths." Postmodernism thrives in contemporary North American culture, and it poses another challenge to The Common. Postmodernism claims that throughout history the powerful have been able to develop meta-narratives composed of stories, ideas, rules, and myths that define the standards and history of the culture. The result is that the less powerful are marginalized or persecuted because the meta-narrative of the powerful declares other groups' narratives to be substandard. The powerful are thus able to assure their continued ascendancy at the expense of the less powerful, many of whom are from racial or religious minorities or other targeted groups.

One of the reasons the founding of the United States was so unique is that the US Constitution includes the Bill of Rights. Even so, it does not take much digging around in the history of the United States to unearth how constitutionally guaranteed rights have been systematically denied to various segments of society. It has become a postmodern obsession to venerate individual rights and freedom as a protection against the historic abuse by the powerful. Over the last several decades, postmodern philosophy has helped generate important cultural reforms that make the culture far more inclusive. However, the promotion of individual rights can also fragment the culture, isolating people into smaller and smaller homogenous groupings of like-minded individuals. In a Balkanized society, it can become very difficult to establish The Common, to unify all people around a shared purpose and values (X^2). Social isolation and fragmentation present a major challenge for those who would conduct Leadership for the Common Good.

Consumerism

Joining the culture's systemic individualism and the social isolation and fragmentation that can result from the postmodern obsession with individual rights is a third and perhaps the most menacing of all the impediments to The Common: rampant consumerism.

What were the top three things you hoped to get as presents on your last birthday? If you got them, how did you feel? How did you feel if you did not get them? Perhaps the most important question of all is: Why did you *feel anything* about the *things* you did or did not receive? Why is it that we assign so much meaning to mere things that they are able to elicit feelings ranging from depression to ecstasy?

In the Declaration of Independence of the United States, Thomas Jefferson wrote about the inalienable rights to life, liberty, and the pursuit of happiness. This was a modification to seventeenth-century English philosopher John Locke's original discussion of humanity's right to life, liberty, and property. In the United States, the pursuit of happiness and the acquisition of more and more things (property) go hand-in-hand; nothing should stand in the way of one's inalienable right to seek personal fulfillment through selfish consumption. Rampant selfish consumerism, it might be argued, is the culture's ultimate expression of individualism.

Benjamin Barber is a scholar who has examined global social challenges associated with excessive consumerism. He has suggested that institutional and economic forces, which are for the most part unquestioned, create a self-absorbed desire to consume. He has coined the term *McWorld,* which he describes as the

> onrushing economic, technological, and ecological forces that demand
> integration and uniformity and that mesmerize peoples everywhere
> with fast music, fast computers, and fast food—MTV, Macintosh, and
> McDonald's—pressing nations into one homogenous global theme park,
> one McWorld tied together by communications, information, entertain-
> ment, and commerce. (Barber, 1995, p. 4)

Does this scene look familiar? It could be almost anywhere in America. Countries, citizenship, public, and The Common are of little relevance to McWorld marketers, to whom people everywhere in the world are merely consumers tied to markets.

Photo courtesy of Diana Goldammer.

McWorld succeeds because it is able to tap into the psyche of individual consumers, convincing them that the acquisition of things can bring meaning and purpose to their lives, satisfying their very souls. For example, Toyota® promotes its cars with the slogan "Oh, what a [good, satisfying] feeling" and Nike® convinces consumers they can rise above their relatively insignificant existence because there is a link joining them as individuals with superstars, such as Tiger Woods, if they buy products with the Swoosh symbol.

Countries, citizenship, public, and The Common are of little relevance to McWorld marketers. People everywhere are merely individual consumers tied to markets. In the market niche, "community" is where consumers can have relationships centered primarily on their things and it is where they can observe and compare the things others are obtaining. The consumerist mentality slops over to other segments of the society beyond markets. For example, Barber has suggested that consumers have little need to fulfill their responsibilities as citizens:.

> Markets simply are not designed to do the things democratic polities do.
> They enjoin private rather than public modes of discourse, allowing us as
> consumers to speak via our currencies of consumption to producers of
> material goods, but ignoring us as citizens speaking to one another about
> such things as the social consequences of our private market choices (too

much materialism? too little social justice? too many monopolies? too few jobs? what do *we* want?). They advance individualistic rather than social goals, permitting us to say one by one "I want a pair of running shoes" or "I need a new VCR" or "buy yen and sell D-Marks!" but deterring us from saying, in a voice made common by interaction and deliberation, "our inner city community needs new athletic facilities" or "we should rein in the World Bank and democratize the IMF!" Markets preclude "we" thinking and "we" action of any kind at all, trusting in the power of aggregated individual choices (the invisible hand) to somehow secure the common good. Consumers speak the elementary rhetoric of "me," citizens invent the common language of "we." (1995, pp. 242–243)

Daniel Kemmis, a Harvard educated attorney, public scholar, and sometimes politician is the former minority leader and speaker of the Montana House of Representatives, as well as the former mayor of Missoula, Montana. Over the years, Kemmis has observed how the notion of citizenship has been relegated to the status of consumer. He illustrated his point with the following excerpt (unedited) from an electronic chat room that was set up to collect citizen comments about a tax increase in Missoula.

[You] are not alone in your frustrations with the city. all thay want is more tax money so thay can do less. thay can't take care of what thay have now what can we look forward to when thay inlarge the city, more potholes, more taxes. thay (the people in power of the city, these are not the taxpayers) will vote in a rase for themselves when the #$%& is about to hit the fan. (Kemmis, 1995, p. 8)

Kemmis suggests this frustrated citizen's lament represents the thoughts and feelings of people who might be far more articulate. The misspelling of the word *thay* underscores the disconnection citizens feel from those who are in government. Further, the writer chooses the word *taxpayer* as the appropriate label for his or her role in the system. Taxpayers are consumers of government services. Taxpayers believe politicians who turn hard problems back to the taxpayers to solve are failures. Taxpayer consumers no more expect their political leaders to have problems turned back on them for the hard work of resolution than they expect a fast-food worker to have them come behind the counter and fry up their own burgers after they have ordered them. Leadership for the Common Good is nearly impossible in a culture where taxpayers' consumerist demands for government services take precedence over personal involvement in solving community needs as engaged citizens.

Leadership for the Common Good must address the challenge to The Common from our culture's individualistic roots, our postmodern social fragmentation, and our proclivity toward selfish consumption of goods and services from the economy and government, and away from our responsibilities as citizens participating in a democracy.

Martin Luther King, Jr., is often referred to as one the preeminent examples of moral leadership, The Good.

Library of Congress.

▪ THE GOOD

Earlier, we discussed James MacGregor Burns' requirement for moral elevation in transforming leadership. We suggested that most people have a visceral objection to labeling as leadership the behavior of Hitler. Our objection is based on a moral assessment of his behavior. Thus, our discussion of The Good is essentially a discussion about morality. However, postmodernism's influence on the concept of The Good is even more significant than its impact on The Common.

A major tenet of postmodernism is the rejection of the notion of absolute or objective truth, which means there is no basis for universal moral judgments. Postmodern philosophy charges that the powerful invent a meta-narrative that imposes "objective" truths that are favorable to the powerful. The powerful receive moral authority for sustaining these truths and perpetuating the meta-narrative. When a segment of a culture has not only the means to power but also the moral authority, it is far easier to keep minority and other less powerful groups in their subordinate positions. Postmodern adherents rightly see the need to check the ability of any worldview to subjugate others, especially when they use moral absolutes to justify their hegemony.

In the late seventeenth century, Isaac Newton "discovered" the laws of motion in what he considered an orderly and knowable universe. Newton's ideas led to the paradigm of a mechanical universe, a universe that worked like a wonderful, complicated machine invented by a master mechanic (God). The job of scientists and mathematicians was to discover the objective facts of the universe, as well as the certainty about how and why things are the way they are. People believed these scientific and mathematical insights would also help humanity better understand the God who put everything into motion. For more than four centuries, while this paradigm guided scientific exploration, it also influenced the ongoing development of theology and philosophy. In the late nineteenth century, Newton's mechanical universe began to crumble when physicists began to explore quantum theory.

The mechanical universe paradigm gave way to quantum descriptions of reality. Chaos theory in physics and complexity theory in biology also described a universe that established limits to the utility of Newton's linear equations. Objective facts gave way to the subjectivity imposed by the investigator's perceptions and technology. These new ideas uncovered troubling uncertainties found in probabilities and potential (e.g., in physics, Heisenberg's uncertainty principle). The parallel development of postmodernism's moral subjectivity seems to draw support from the sciences where chaos and complexity theories destroyed basic Newtonian assumptions about the mechanical universe's foundation based on objective facts. The postmodern concept of The Good, therefore, is not an absolute capital *G* Good but, instead, *good* takes on a subjective character. There can be no absolute Good, only locally constructed relative goods.

Postmodernism wreaks havoc with the thesis of this chapter, that there can actually be Leadership for the Common (capital *G*) Good. Postmodernism might suggest an alternative to our chapter thesis: leadership for a locally constructed relative good. This isn't a bad thesis, but it may not be the best thesis. Just as Newtonian physics continues to have tremendous utility in the context of certain kinds of applications in math and physics, leadership for a locally constructed relative good can also offer benefits in some circumstances. However, this limited view of The Good constricts our ability to conduct leadership broadly and meaningfully. Transient public opinion or a locally constructed morality becomes the basis for moral leadership if there is no absolute Truth or The Good. Our thesis requires the possibility of absolute Truth or The Good.

In this section, we will explore the possibility of The Good with the caveat that our discussion will not offer a comprehensive apologetic for moral absolutes. Philosophers and theologians are arguing those fascinating questions, and space will not permit us to even scratch the surface of the debate. Our strategy here is to open up the possibility for the existence of absolute Truth, or The Good. If it is possible that absolute Truth exists, then we can lead in a way that is consistent with that Truth; we can indeed conduct leadership for the Common Good.

Tank Man

Beijing's Tiananmen Square, The Gate of Heavenly Peace, is the world's largest public space. Google it anywhere in the world, except in China, and multiple pages of images of June 3, 1989, will appear. These images chronicle the massacre of Chinese students, workers, and other citizens who gathered to protest against the economic and social oppression of the Chinese central government. For several weeks before June 3, all over China, tens of millions of Chinese had taken to the streets to protest the government's oppressive policies. The Berlin Wall was the symbolic center of protest that led to the collapse of the Soviet Union. In China, the symbolic focal point of the nationwide protest against communist totalitarian rule was Tiananmen Square. After weeks of protests, hardliners in the Chinese government feared that the country was on the brink of a collapse, similar to what had been happening to the Soviets.

On the evening of June 3, The People's Army moved in from the suburbs to take control of the square, which had been the site of peaceful but massive protests. Along the way, people tried to stop the army's advance to the square by taking to the streets and forming a human blockade. This strategy had worked previously, bringing the army to a halt in its advance toward Tiananmen Square, forcing it to retreat to the suburbs. On this fateful night, the army was told that failure was not an option. When the people took to the streets to block the army's advance, they were indiscriminately slaughtered. Once the army reached Tiananmen Square, the soldiers instructed the protestors massed there to leave immediately or face live fire. Many left. Others were arrested, some escaped into the city, and some stood their ground and came under fire. Official reports of minimal casualties fly in the face of Western video that showed massive human devastation. In the weeks and months after the massacre, the government arrested and punished thousands of dissidents nationwide. No one from the West has any way of knowing the human toll for this massive expression of the desire for freedom and justice.

On June 5, 1989, the army was beginning its redeployment away from Tiananmen Square. A tank column left the square using a street in front of a hotel where many Western journalists were staying. A photojournalist named Charles Cole shot an unauthorized video of a single Chinese worker who walked into the street, stood in front of the exiting column of tanks, and brought them to a halt. The footage recorded how this man, knowing he would likely be crushed, as so many had been a few days earlier, stood his ground against the tanks as they tried to creep forward. Repeatedly, the tanks started, stopped, feigned to the right and left, stopped, tried forward again, and stopped. Finally, the tanks turned off their engines and the man scampered on top of the lead tank, yelling something to the occupants. Hatches opened and closed. Engines started up again and he retook his position, blocking them. Finally, the footage shows four people emerging from the crowd, talking with the man, and then helping him scurry back into the crowd.

No one from the West knows who this man was. People have speculated whether those who helped him into the crowd were rescuers or secret police. No one knows, and the man has certainly never come forward. The Western press has named the man "Tank Man." He has come to symbolize the universal desire to stand against abusive power in the name of freedom and justice. Except for the powerful in the Chinese government, almost every culture in the world acknowledges The Good of Tank Man's actions and the ideals for which he risked his life.

Thin Morality, Thick Morality, and the Tao

Why do people universally see Tank Man's actions and ideals as an example of The Good if there is no absolute Truth or objective Good? Michael Walzer writes about how some philosophers have developed a description of what they call "thin" and "thick" morality (Walzer, 1994). Thin morality defines right and wrong at the most basic, core level. Thick morality refers to how the thin, "core morality is elaborated in different cultures" (Walzer, 1994, p. 4). We become aware that some situations represent moral dilemmas because of the underlying cross-cultural presence and intensity of the thin morality. With cultural elaboration, moral dilemmas take on the character of thickness and are subject to "qualification, compromise, complexity, and disagreement" (Walzer, 1994, p. 6). The universality of the thin morality provides us with the moral basis for identifying with people outside our own small sphere when they experience injustice, oppression, and other violations of deep moral values. If The Good (thin morality) exists, our localized thick elaboration of The Good allows us to recognize and take action consistent with the universal Good. The danger posed by postmodern moral relativism is that the thin morality is declared nonexistent, and a culturally elaborated thick morality, estranged from the thin morality, becomes the only available moral base.

Christian author C. S. Lewis also discussed cross-cultural universal moral values. He called these constructs "the *Tao*" (Lewis, 1947, p. 29). He was writing to those who, like today's postmodern philosophers, believed that values were innovations of a particular culture and not related to any kind of universal values. His argument was succinct:

> The rebellion of new ideologies against the *Tao* is a rebellion of the branches against the tree: if the rebels could succeed they would find that they had destroyed themselves. The human mind has no more power of inventing a new value than of imagining a new primary color, or, indeed, of creating a new sun and a new sky for it to move in. (Lewis 1947, pp. 56–57)

As an appendix to his book *The Abolition of Man,* Lewis identified several universal "laws" that illustrate the *Tao*. For each law, he provided cross-cultural examples of how the law is elaborated or, in Walzer's terms, how the thin universal value becomes thickened in different cultures. Much like the illustration of Tank Man, the list of Lewis' universal values illustrates the possibility that universal moral values exist and are the basis for the moral tenets of all cultures.

It is possible to conduct Leadership for the Common Good because it is highly likely The Good exists. Cultural elaborations of The Good (thick morality) are important and can guide much of what moral leadership needs to do. It is also important to understand that the thick, culturally elaborated good is based on the thin, universal Good. There is a basis for morality. Deep down, there is a basis on which we can judge whether leadership is indeed honoring The Good. Indeed, transforming leadership can be morally elevating.

■ DISCOVERING COMMUNITY: THE KEY TO CONDUCTING LEADERSHIP FOR THE COMMON GOOD

Leadership for the Common Good is the noblest form of leadership and, though it is incredibly difficult to conduct, it is not impossible. It is not difficult to envision conducting effective transforming leadership that promotes The Good in many kinds of circumstances, ranging from intimate personal relationships to organizations with global reach. Leadership for The Good, the kind of morally elevating transforming leadership James McGregor Burns discussed, is paradoxically common and uncommon:

> *Common,* because acts of leadership occur not simply in presidential mansions and parliamentary assemblies but far more widely and powerfully in the day-to-day pursuit of collective goals through the mutual tapping of leaders' and followers' motive bases and in the achievement of intended change. It is an affair of parents, teachers, and peers as well as of preachers and politicians. *Uncommon,* because many acts heralded or bemoaned as instances of leadership—acts of oratory, manipulation, sheer self-advancement, brute coercion—are not such. Much of what passes as leadership . . . is no more leadership than the behavior of small boys marching in front of a parade, who continue to strut along Main Street after the procession has turned down a side street toward the fairgrounds. (Burns, 1978, pp. 426–427)

The most challenging obstacle we face in conducting Leadership for the Common Good is the qualifier: The Common. Our culture's systemic promotion of individualism, postmodernism's influence on social fragmentation, and selfish consumerism all conspire to convince us to settle for leadership for the good *in our parochial circumstances.* Leadership for the Common Good, noble leadership, demands that we move beyond individualism and the parochial in order to serve The Common.

Amatai Etzioni is a scholar who has written extensively about the notion of community. He documents the dangers of isolation to human development:

> In short, communities are essential for our full constitution. We can survive without them, but we can neither achieve nor sustain a full measure of what is considered a "fully functioning" human being without some measure of community. (Etzioni, 2004, pp. 20–21)

When we move beyond the easy path to the selfish consumer communities of McWorld into the real communities where we live, we have the opportunity to engage with one another as citizens and neighbors. When we engage with one another, we create what Robert Putnam calls **social capital.** Societies that nurture rich connections between its members become rich in social capital. Social capital is like any other economic capital. When it is created and invested, it produces private and public benefits (Putnam, 2000).

As citizens and social capitalists, we move beyond the role of mere "taxpayers" to become participants in governance of The Common. Citizens derive meaning and purpose from their association with The Common, seeking to nurture that which we all share. It is in our communities where we come together and at once relate to each other and retain our unique identity. It is in these relationships in the community where we develop both our individual and collective meaning and purpose.

As our communities grow and our collective needs are met, our defensive need to promote our individual rights diminishes. Etzioni recognizes the postmodern veneration of individual rights and its propensity to fragment society. He challenges us to think about rights existing in a kind of hierarchy. Universal rights are those that are shared throughout society and they prevail over the expression of individual rights. Even so, if individual rights are not in conflict with the universal rights, they can find legitimate expression. No society can function for long, however, without some sort of understanding of what is honored together in community. These shared values become the mortar that holds together the various subcommunities of a larger cultural community (Etzioni, 2004). It is in this community where we discover our collective vision as citizens, our X^2. Citizenship, therefore, requires individuals and subcommunities to subordinate themselves to the larger community—The Common.

Communities need more than citizens; they also need people to live together as neighbors. Etzioni and Kemmis are two of many, broadly classified as communitarians, who are urging people to respond to a deep human need to be in active relationships as neighbors. Discovering and becoming engaged with our neighbors is at once incredibly simple and very complicated. It is simple because our neighbors are literally outside our front doors. It is complicated because of the nature of our culture. We put on our iPod®, walk out of our front door, and are immediately on the move to other spaces, often miles away, where we may work, recreate, and otherwise engage (often superficially) with other humans. Even without leaving our homes, we substitute face-to-face human contact with virtual human connections through various electronic devices. Jodi R. Cohen has written about how electronic media have helped isolate us from each other, even as they remove communication barriers of time and space between humans. She relayed a personal incident that illustrates how complicated technology makes it for developing community right where we live:

> While we once gathered together into a physical place, such as a courtyard, a schoolhouse, or a church, to define ourselves and the issues of the day, today we are nowhere and everywhere. A series of conversational exchanges between my landlady and me illustrates this paradox. She disapproved of my volunteer work at a soup kitchen just three blocks from where we lived. Her disapproval took the form of snide remarks about the people who ate there. She hollered from her back door whenever I returned home from working at the kitchen. One day as I was climbing the steps to my apartment, she called me into her home to share her grief over an earthquake on another continent. She had seen the pictures of people on television and was now crying and setting out her canned goods to send to the people there. Clearly, she identified with people living on another continent more than with those living in her neighborhood. (Cohen, 1998, p. 44)

There are myriad reasons we have estranged ourselves from our natural communities, some of which we have already discussed. What we fail to recognize is that this is a relatively new sociological phenomenon. As few as fifty years ago in the United States, it was common for neighbors to know one another, socialize with one another, watch out for each other's children, join together in celebrations, grieve with one another, and otherwise meet one another's needs. These thick neighborhood communities were woven into larger communities of towns and cities, which also gave a sense of belonging and identity.

In the twenty-first century, our culture is pushing us into even more fragmentation and away from those with whom we share our physical space. Instead of chatting with a neighbor over a backyard fence, we chat with people on the Internet, who may live on another continent or next door. Where participants are physically is not important in an Internet community.

Though estranged from our neighbors, we have still noticed needs people have in our neighborhoods. Unlike the response of our grandparents and earlier generations, where neighbors were involved with one another and joined to meet those needs, now we often expect government services to address these issues. If our notion of building community is to make government more efficient at providing services that meet our neighbors' needs, we miss the most important part of The Common, the development of a supportive and responsive community, in which community members are fully engaged. Communities have historically provided for the needs of the human condition in ways far superior to what economic entities or government institutions can generate. Etzioni writes:

> The more the state takes over functions once discharged by communities, voluntary associations, and families, the weaker society will become. In contrast, the more the state generates opportunities for social actors to initiate and sustain their own action, the more viable the society will become. But if, for instance, the government starts sending professional grief counselors, licensed and trained by the state, to the homes of people who have lost a loved one, this is likely to weaken friendship ties: those of neighbors, of religious groups, and of extended families. (Etzioni, 2004, p. 149)

It requires individual initiative to step away from our protective isolation and into engagement with the lives of our neighbors. Each community will have unique catalysts for development. For some, it might be a glaring community need, such as a deteriorated school, that facilitates community engagement. Sometimes it only takes a common recreational activity to bring people together. In other instances, a neighbor might have limited physical capabilities and other neighbors can join to provide transportation, clear snow, or do regular yard maintenance. Children are also great teachers about forming community. In neighborhoods where kids are still free to roam around, they get to know neighbors far better than the adults do. Deep down we actually know how to develop community; lately, our culture simply has not allowed us to have much practice.

Leadership for the Common Good cannot happen if we do not lead in a manner that helps develop our communities—The Common. Kemmis reports Hannah Arendt's perspective on community as she wrote about the public realm:

To live together in the world means essentially that a world of things is between those who have it in common, as a table is located between those who sit around it. . . . The public realm, as the common world, gathers us together and yet prevents our falling over each other, so to speak. What makes mass society so difficult to bear is not the number of people involved, or at least primarily, but the fact that the world between them has lost its power to gather them together, to relate and to separate them. (Kemmis, 1990, p. 6)

Robert Putnam is optimistic about our ability as a society to regain our commitment to The Common. He maintains that the American commitment to The Common has ebbed and flowed throughout its history. He has suggested the need to increase social capital in America, restoring it to levels enjoyed by previous generations. He identified the following seven action steps that will facilitate this process over the coming years and challenged Americans to find ways to ensure that:

1. . . . "the level of civic engagement among Americans then coming of age in all parts of our society will match that of their grandparents when they were that same age, and that at the same time bridging social capital will be substantially greater than it was in their grandparents' era."
2. . . . "America's workplace will be substantially more family-friendly and community-congenial, so that American workers will be enabled to replenish our stocks of social capital both within and outside the workplace."
3. . . . "Americans will spend less time traveling and more time connecting with our neighbors than we do today, that we will live in more integrated and pedestrian-friendly areas, and that the design of our communities and the availability of public space will encourage more casual socializing with friends and neighbors."
4. . . . "Let us spur a new, pluralistic, socially responsible 'great awakening,' so that by 2010 Americans will be more deeply engaged than we are today in one or another spiritual community of meaning, while at the same time becoming more tolerant of the faiths and practices of other Americans."
5. . . . "Americans will spend less leisure time sitting passively alone in front of glowing screens and more time in active connection with our fellow citizens: Let us foster new forms of electronic entertainment and communication that reinforce community engagement rather than forestalling it."
6. . . . "significantly more Americans will participate in (not merely consume or 'appreciate') cultural activities from group dancing to songfests to community theatre to rap festivals. Let us discover new ways to use the arts as a vehicle for convening diverse groups of fellow citizens."
7. . . . "many more Americans will participate in the public life of our communities—running for office, attending public meetings, serving on committees, campaigning in elections, and even voting." (Putnam, 2000, pp. 404, 406, 408, 409, 410, 411, 412)

Leadership for the Common Good requires us to step out and once again build communities large and small where people can gather, relate to one another, and find meaningful ways to develop and respect their separate identities. Is this difficult? It is very difficult. But that is precisely why Leadership for the Common Good is the noblest kind of leadership.

■ KEY TERMS

Social Capital—Human interaction in a given community that produces, or has the potential to produce, private and public benefits.

The Common—That which is shared by everyone.

The Good—That which is morally elevating and transforming.

Transactional Leadership—An exchange between leaders and followers that facilitates the accomplishment of some goal or purpose shared by all parties.

Transforming Leadership—Leadership that occurs when one or more persons engage with others in such a way that leaders and followers raise one another to higher levels of motivation and morality.

X^1—An honest assessment of where an organization is with regard to fulfilling its mission and values.

X^2—What the organization might look like if it were fulfilling the organization's mission and values in every possible way.

■ SUGGESTED READINGS

Etzioni, A. 2004. *The Common Good.* Malden, MA: Polity Press.

Putnam, R. D. 2000. *Bowling Alone: The Collapse and Revival of American Community.* New York: Simon & Schuster.

Walzer, M. 1994. *Thick and Thin: Moral Argument at Home and Abroad.* Notre Dame, IN: University of Notre Dame Press.

■ REFERENCES

Barber, B. R. 1995. *Jihad vs. McWorld.* New York: Random House.

Burns, J. M. 1978. *Leadership.* New York: Harper & Row.

Burns, J. S. 2002. "Chaos Theory and Leadership Studies: Sailing Uncharted Seas." *Journal of Leadership and Organizational Studies,* Vol. 9. No. 2, pp. 42–48.

Cohen, J. R. 1998. "The Significance of Critical Communication Skills in a Democracy." In *The Public Voice in a Democracy at Risk,* by P. M. Sias & M. Salvador. Westport, CT: Praeger, pp. 39–51.

Etzioni, A. 2004. *The Common Good*. Malden, MA: Polity Press.

Heifetz, R. M. 1994. *Leadership Without Easy Answers*. Cambridge, MA: The Belknap Press of Harvard University.

Kemmis, D. 1990. *Community and the Politics of Place*. Norman: University of Oklahoma Press.

———. 1995. *Good City and the Good Life*. New York: Houghton Mifflin.

Lewis, C. S. 1947. *The Abolition of Man: How Education Develops Man's Sense of Morality*. New York: Macmillan.

Putnam, R. D. 2000. *Bowling Alone: The Collapse and Revival of American Community*. New York: Simon & Schuster.

Rost, J. C. 1991. *Leadership for the Twenty-First Century*. Westport, CT: Praeger.

Walzer, M. 1994. *Thick and Thin: Moral Argument at Home and Abroad*. Notre Dame, IN: University of Notre Dame Press.

CHAPTER NINE REVIEW QUESTIONS

1. What are some of the significant challenges associated with transforming leadership?

    _____

    _____

    _____

2. What is the author's working understanding of leadership?

    _____

    _____

    _____

3. Summarize the three challenges to "The Common."

    _____

    _____

    _____

4. Why is it difficult in the postmodern world to conduct leadership in support of "The Good"?

    _____

    _____

    _____

5. Describe seven action steps Robert Putnam has identified that can facilitate the development of "The Common."

    _____

    _____

    _____

CHAPTER NINE SELF-TEST

1. _____ leadership is an exchange between leaders and followers that facilitates the accomplishment of some goal or purpose shared by parties.

2. _____ leadership raises both leaders and followers to higher levels of motivation and morality.

3. Type II problems require adaptive _____ in order to overcome obstacles.

4. According to the author, in contemporary North America, serving The Common takes on the connotation of _____ or community service work.

5. According to Benjamin Barber, institutional and economic forces create a self-absorbed desire to _____.

6. Three obstacles to The Common Good are systematic _____, postmodern fragmentation, and rampant _____.

7. The author contends that a postmodern assumption is that there can be no absolute or universal Good, only _____ constructed relative goods.

8. Benjamin Barber coined the term _____ to explain the forces that press nations into one homogenous global theme park.

9. According to Putnam, when _____ capital is created and invested, it produces private and public benefits.

10. Type III problems require _____ and subsequent adaptation and transformation by all involved.

Global Leadership in the Twenty-First Century

Daniel N. Huck

■ THE COMPLEXITIES OF GLOBAL LEADERSHIP

A serious effort to think critically about any phenomenon of contemporary human society requires an initial effort to define the "it" to be examined. As demonstrated by the variety of approaches in earlier chapters of this book, simply defining *leadership* as one such phenomenon is a difficult enough task. An attempt, then, to define *global leadership* and from that definition analyze the dimensions of that experience across all human boundaries would seem to be impossible. Most would agree that any effort to formulate a theory about "global leadership," and to model a way of thinking about it in the present century, demands agreement on the key principles that shape such considerations. Unfortunately, as with "leadership" in the first instance, a precise agreement on its "global" proportions will require an examination of competing views, which the student of leadership will have to consider, balance, and choose among. In addition, because the discussion in this chapter is brief, the text here can at most model a beginning point for a consideration of leadership on a global scale, not fully deliberate its complexities.

"Leadership" Is Leadership

Before considering a more academic approach to defining *global leadership,* a basic critical analysis of that label will yield some clarity. In terms of "leadership" in the present context, perhaps the best approach is to think of the underlying human activity connoted by that word. Much effort has been devoted in the recent past to defining *leadership,* with whole books published on that single subject. These "definitionalist" thinkers proceed from a premise that a human phenomenon can be defined apart from the daily scope and press of human activity. This type of reasoning is deductive, seeking to define leadership *a priori* and then declaring each potential occurrence of human activity as either within or outside that definition. Advocates of this approach often describe how they believe leadership *should* arise among humans, thereby creating the attendant risk that their definitions will suffer from normative predispositions—that is, they see any particular incidence of leadership as either "good" or "bad."

An opposite approach is to look at "leadership" inductively, deriving its definition from how that phenomenon shows itself among humans as they relate to each other in the contemporary world. For purposes of the present chapter, wherein knowledge of "leadership" is sought over the entire horizon of human relationships, this inductive approach will be used. Taking this *a posteriori* approach of looking at actual events, there seems to be minimum, general agreement among those who study the subject that "leadership" arises among humans when one person or a group of people is able to influence another person or group of people to believe or act in a way that they would not otherwise have considered or chosen without that influence. Considered another way, most serious thinkers believe that "leadership" is a human "phenomenon"—that is, an occurrence jointly perceived and experienced by all humans—that excites the interest and curiosity of individual humans. Although the words chosen by various thinkers to denote "leadership" might differ, they seem to agree on a conceptual level that it is a phenomenon of influence, so the discussion here will adopt that inclination.

■ WHICH "GLOBAL LEADERSHIP"?

The more difficult issue derives from the use of the word *global* in discussions of the leadership phenomenon. Two connotations of *global* are available for inclusion in a potential definition of the term *global leadership,* and those who think and write in the leadership field use both those connotations. A clear analysis of the subject requires distinguishing clearly at the outset between these two usages. The first definition of *global* that impacts the present discussion derives from the concept of taking all the different aspects of a situation into account with a single approach. In everyday communication, this meaning is demonstrated in a phrase such as "let's find a global solution to this problem," by which the author or speaker means that the best method for resolving an issue will be one on which all individuals involved can agree. The second definition of *global* describes the idea that something relates to or happens throughout the entire, joint experience of human beings. The most common and clearest use of this term at present is contained in the phrase "global warming," by which authors and speakers mean that the entire earth is impacted by the single, clearly understood phenomenon of a human-made temperature increase. Those who study leadership have used both these meanings of the term *global* to modify the subject, so a review of each is important to considering how to approach the "it" of the present topic.

Global as Suggesting a Universal Perspective

Several significant attempts in the contemporary era have approached the study of leadership from the perspective that a universal framework—one that applies to every human circumstance—exists for thinking about that influence phenomenon. In these efforts, the idea has been pursued that a set of "global" principles is available for interpreting and predicting what each human being in every place will do when encountering an attempt to influence his or her actions. Stated differently, these advocates propose use of a universal analytical framework, believing that contemporary humans across the globe experience leadership in ways that are fundamentally alike. While most contemporary academic literature on leadership derives its conclusions from this "universalist" approach, two efforts in particular demonstrate this influence.

The first of these "global" efforts came in 1978 with the publication of the book by James MacGregor Burns entitled *Leadership*. Burns had won the Pulitzer Prize for a book on President Franklin Roosevelt, so his effort on leadership was received as a serious undertaking. The publication of Burns' book has had perhaps the single most significant impact on the study of leadership in the contemporary era, spawning an entire, new discipline of leadership study at colleges and universities throughout the United States. In his 540-page volume, Burns attempts to create a digest of all the ideas he believes should go into consideration of leadership as a structured area of study.

While Burns lamented that "no school of leadership, intellectual or practical" existed, he proposed that the state of research in the many social sciences allowed for a new discipline to arise and begin addressing the phenomenon (Burns, 1978, p. 3). He suggested new frameworks within which leadership could be considered with some intellectual rigor and brought to bear various insights from the various social sciences. As a Western political scientist, his analyses tended toward considerations of power and political authority, but his work is most often cited for its distinction between "transforming" and "transactional" leadership. One clear theme derived from this distinction is a focus on the person of the leader rather than the phenomenon of reciprocal influence, and a second is an effort to create a normative foundation for the interpretation of leadership. A much less discussed assertion in the book was Burns' belief that it was "possible to generalize about the leadership process across cultures and across time," the promotion of which he declared as "the central purpose" of his book (Burns, 1978, p. 3). This last contention has earned Burns the role as primary advocate for the universalist methodology.

A second, more recent effort to define the study of all human leadership through a single framework came out of an effort in the United States initiated in November 2001 at the Jepson School of Leadership Studies at the University of Richmond. Over the course of the next two years, leadership scholars from universities that had focused on developing leadership as an academic discipline during the 1990s met to pursue what they initially termed a "Global Theory of Leadership." The results of this effort were reviewed in a collection of essays written and edited by participants in these meetings and published using the term *General Theory of Leadership* (Goethals & Sorenson, 2006). While these essays provide an exciting array of viewpoints on the analytical foundations of leadership, the original effort was ultimately deemed a failure. The group found that they could not even agree on a single intellectual structure of theory because of disputes over whether to take an *a priori* or an inductive approach to considering leadership (Wren, 2006, pp. 6–11). Many scholars resisted any agreement on a "global" theory target, in the sense of a universal perspective, because of their essential belief in the need for culturally defined parameters when assessing the phenomenon of leadership (Wren, 2006, pp. 29–34).

Global as Suggesting Multiple Perspectives

The second definition of *global* used by contemporary thinkers to modify the study of leadership seeks to describe a phenomenon that extends across the entire human experience. A thinker who adopts this usage of *global* accepts the premise that the influence phenomenon of leadership will arise and demonstrate itself in different ways across different human communities. The key element that differentiates the "global leadership" of multiple perspectives from that of the universal approach is the concept of culture. The universalist thinker on leadership believes that **culture** is an increasingly ephemeral element of analysis in a contemporary human world where individual wants and desires are coalescing in unprecedented ways. Representing a contrary position, the **perspectivist approach** to leadership is rooted in the belief that culture has become the paramount lens through which to view human interaction, especially the leadership phenomenon.

The great limitation of the contemporary literature that considers culture as a key conceptual underpinning of leadership is the narrow focus of that analysis on organizational management of business concerns in a world economy. While the titles of such works often include the term *global leadership,* the analysis contained within them is narrowly focused on the for-profit sector's needs in pursuing the overseas initiatives of U.S.-based multinational corporations. Often, these efforts are divided into chapters specific to particular nation-states (e.g., Peru, China, India) and seem focused on cultural minutia, such as proper etiquette in greetings, at meals, and as part of business undertakings in a foreign country (Moran, Harris, & Moran, 2007). Other efforts that attempt to work with the culture concept become so focused on the task of cultural description that the consideration of particular phenomena, such as leadership, are not separately analyzed.

Unfortunately, beyond the limited field of international management, no serious academic effort has been made to apply the multiple perspectives approach of a cultural analysis to contemporary human leadership as a societywide phenomenon. For instance, outside the meeting room of the corporate office tower in Shanghai, China, how does the typical Chinese human experience leadership? Beyond the production floor of the assembly plant outside Thonburi, Thailand, how does the typical Thai human experience leadership?

The limitations of the present perspectivist literature are understandable, given the complexity of any potential effort to approach leadership outside the conveniently defined boundaries of modern commercial enterprise. Unfortunately, those boundaries have produced a Western bias that dominates the leadership literature of multiple perspectives. In fact, the existing structure of thought in this area often promotes its counterpart—the universalist approach—because Western cultural precepts are seen as dominant, and indeed transcendent, in interpreting the contemporary human world. Stated differently, most of the literature that seeks to describe global leadership's multiple perspectives proceeds from the unexamined premise that a Western cultural model of free markets and endless consumption has proven itself best. With such a predisposition, that literature becomes an undemanding attempt to accommodate the perceived shrinking of cross-cultural differences that still exist among Western and non-Western market participants in the present era (House, Hanges, Javidan, Dorfman & Gupta, 2005).

However, the result of identifying the limitations from prior studies of global leadership, whether from a universalist or perspectivist viewpoint, is to recognize not just a predisposition toward Western thinking or toward private enterprise. At a more fundamental level, what is missing from the discussion of leadership as something "global" is an analysis of the fundamental assumptions that have dominated the discussion of that phenomenon. In philosophy, this line of analysis would be called a search for "first principles," referring back to the approach of the Greek philosopher Aristotle. In searching for such principles, the central question for Aristotle was what a thinker takes as *a priori*—as given to be true—when he or she considers a topic such as global leadership. Thought of from this perspective, the central problem at present in considering global leadership is that there is no "metaphysical" foundation for critical analysis of that influence phenomenon. Establishing a metaphysic of global leadership requires explaining the ultimate nature of being human in the world, and in a rigorous critical analysis of human activity such explanations are a necessary part of any serious discussion.

■ A "PARADIGM" FOR GLOBAL LEADERSHIP

Following in the footsteps of Aristotle, contemporary thinkers in many academic disciplines have recognized the need for the metaphysical step of establishing "first principles" when pursuing critical inquiry of the modern world. The most influential among these recent thinkers was Thomas Kuhn, a historian of science, who wrote a groundbreaking book titled *The Structure of Scientific Revolutions.* Kuhn introduced into academic discourse the highly regarded concept that a **paradigm** influences and limits all research and thinking. In employing the word *paradigm,* Kuhn meant to connote more than the original meaning of the word, which was "an example or pattern." Kuhn instead was interested in demonstrating that every natural science inquiry—whether in physics, biology, or otherwise—was contained within a prevailing pattern of thought ascribed to and maintained by all practitioners in that discipline (Kuhn, 1996/1970, pp. 43–52).

As a historian of science, Kuhn found that a particular paradigm dominates almost all scientific inquiry in a historical period. That dominant paradigm provides rules about the types of problems natural scientists may investigate and dictates the way they should go about solving those problems. Kuhn also came to understand that these dominant rules of thought do not evolve slowly and predictably over time, leading from a less sophisticated and antiquated vision of a particular science to a more rational and modern approach. Instead, his research revealed that the paradigms influencing scientific inquiry at a particular point in history almost always are undermined in revolutionary ways by anomalies that cannot be solved under the constraints of that existing paradigm. To solve these anomalies, some scientific thinkers will suggest answers that only can be derived by adopting a wholly new structure for thinking about the challenges faced by that scientific discipline. When this structure proves viable, it becomes the new dominant paradigm for thinking through problems, and the old paradigm disappears rapidly and forever (Kuhn, 1996/1970, pp. 77–92).

Thus, what relevance should a leadership student find in Kuhn's thinking about the creation, dominance, and eventual disintegration of paradigms in natural science? The significance of Kuhn's insight for a discussion of global leadership is twofold. First, Kuhn's thinking has had significant consequences well beyond the boundaries of the natural sciences, influencing as well the structure of thinking in many social science disciplines. Historians, sociologists, psychologists, and serious thinkers in other branches of the social sciences have considered Kuhn's paradigm concept as a key tool in developing the study of contemporary human societies and individual relationships within them. As a new field of inquiry in the social sciences, leadership cannot ignore Kuhn's insight and every serious thinker within the discipline must be prepared to consider its implications.

A second, more compelling answer to the significance question relates to the particular challenge presented to leadership thinkers in the early twenty-first century. If the most recent past has demonstrated anything about the common human experience around the globe, it has shown that the prevailing patterns of thought about where humanity is headed have changed in radical ways. Within the brief lifetime of even the newest undergraduate who is reading this text, the long-standing and seemingly immutable paradigm of ideological struggle in the twentieth century—captured in the label of "The Cold War"—has abruptly ended, a second paradigm of apparently permanent peace—labeled "The New World Order"—has come and gone in less than a decade, and a third paradigm of cross-cultural struggle—"The War on Terror"—has been declared and pursued for almost all of the first decade of this new century. Such dramatic shifts have caught most social scientists unprepared and have caused the serious thinkers among them to throw out the theories, models, and rules they had depended on for learning about humanwide phenomena.

Various social science thinkers have attempted to define a new paradigm for human interactions in the wake of the close of The Cold War, the passing of The New World Order, and the advent of the new conflicts generated by the attacks on September 11, 2001. There are many sources available for review, making any summary a wide-ranging task well beyond the scope of the present chapter. Unfortunately, none of them have dealt effectively or specifically with the effect of these historic changes on the influence phenomenon of leadership, but the constructs of two authors have so far stood up as viable competitors in the search for a new paradigm of human relationships in the twenty-first century. The first model for a new paradigm is described by Samuel Huntington in his book *The Clash of Civilizations and the Remaking of World Order,* and its direct challenger is authored by Francis Fukuyama in his book *The End of History and the Last Man.* If the leadership discipline is to keep pace as a serious social science, with relevant contributions at the level of global theory, then its students must embrace this new struggle for a new paradigmatic framework. As a starting point in that effort, the following analysis will build from the powerful foundations established by Huntington and Fukuyama.

■ THE "EMERGENCE PARADIGM" OF GLOBAL LEADERSHIP

If those who previously advocated the **universalist approach** to understanding contemporary global leadership were looking for a successor paradigm, they would find it in Fukuyama's discussion of "the end of history." While that work is complex in its ideas and references, Fukuyama essentially argues that, when global communism collapsed at the end of the Cold War, the surviving ideology of liberal democracy combined with market capitalism was clearly victorious after a long struggle. Moreover, he asserts that no other ideological competitors remained when that conflict ended that might offer a viable alternative paradigm for human social existence. Fukuyama argues that the modern history of humanity has progressed from a beginning to an end, with modern science and consumerism as the engines of this progression. The result now is an "end" to the conflicts about which cultural system will prove universally beneficial to all humans in all places for all time. The paradigm emerging from those battles is liberal democracy and its free markets, and its progenitor and parent is Western civilization (Fukuyama, 1992/2006, pp. 3–54).

Having declared an end to the clash of ideological disputes, Fukuyama presents the possibility that this declaration represents both good news and bad news for humanity. The good news is his belief that the serious conflicts that produced world wars and massive destruction in the twentieth century will no longer be fought. Instead, all human societies will continue to pursue—or move inexorably toward pursuing—the liberal democratic paradigm. Fukuyama's bad news is that humans in such a passionless world will become soft, meaningless "last men" who live and exist but strive for nothing (Fukuyama, 1992/2006, pp. 287–341). This evaluation has had a significant impact on other thinkers who have accepted Fukuyama's premise and its enhanced efficacy, given the tremendous growth of global communications technology (Friedman, 2007). They see the emergence of a single pattern for all contemporary human relationships, and more fundamentally the growing emergence of a universal human culture.

If this "emergence" paradigm is true, what does it mean for the student of leadership? Certainly, the most obvious conclusion is that, if Western cultural systems have prevailed as a humanitywide paradigm, then there is no utility in pursuing a multiple perspectives approach. Instead, the proper inference is that the universalist thinkers within the leadership discipline were prophetic in tracking its "globalness" as the manifestation of a distinct, communal phenomenon of humankind. Western liberal democracy, combined with its attendant market approach, has now emerged victorious, carrying with it the ideas of leadership that best fit that ascendant culture's needs. Since all other cultures now are striving toward that same "end," all they need do is adopt those leadership approaches as part of their overall migration to the universal human experience.

The central difficulty in accepting a Fukuyama-inspired paradigm of global leadership is that it does not appear to be coming true. While its currency seemed powerful at the dawn of the twenty-first century, the attacks of September 11, 2001, and the subsequent advent of a cross-cultural war between the United States and Islamic cultural entities, such as Iraq, the Taliban, and al-Qaeda, have shaken the foundations of the universalist approach. To be fair to Fukuyama, he predicted that his overall vision of ideological conflict's demise would not be a quick or linear convergence. In fact, he cautioned that continuing conflicts would appear in the world even as humanity moved toward its "end." What Fukuyama and the other universalist advocates seem not to have considered is the potency and resilience of cultural allegiances that would spawn such devastating conflict. While the apparent dominance of The War on Terror may not fully dismiss the universalist approach, it certainly has brought into doubt many of its suppositions.

■ THE "CULTURAL IMPERATIVE PARADIGM" OF GLOBAL LEADERSHIP

An alternative paradigm candidate for the human experience in the twenty-first century was authored by Samuel Huntington, and it has attracted a steady following since the events of September 2001. Like Fukuyama or any other serious historicist thinker, Huntington's analysis is daunting in its full scope and complexity. At its core, though, Huntington's work suggests that the new paradigm for humanity is one of conflict between the major "civilizations" of the contemporary world. By using the term *civilization* Huntington makes clear that he means the major human groupings that were competitors for human allegiances well before the onset of the ideological battles of the twentieth century. Huntington argues that these civilizational conflicts were suppressed by ideological conflicts but that they have always remained at the center of human identity. When the Cold War ended, conflict across a single ideological divide between liberal democracy and communism may have ended, but for Huntington that end simply released the pent-up conflicts that always have existed between civilizations (Huntington, 1996, pp. 19–56).

Huntington is a sharp critic of those who would see a coalescence of human beliefs and activities around a single contemporary core. He sees, instead, a "clash" between human civilizations based primarily on multiple and competing core paradigms of religious belief and historical identity. He views each of these civilizational units as a "culture writ large" that serves as the "values, norms, institutions, and modes of thinking to which successive generations in a given society have attached primary importance." He bases his analysis on the assumption that humans, by nature, seek self-identification by deciding who is "us" and who is "them," and once decided they seek to associate with the same and dissociate with the dissimilar. Huntington does not deny that there are forces of integration—such as technology and economic expansion—that are bringing civilizations into closer contact than ever before. Instead, while agreeing that such contacts are multiplying, he believes that those exchanges only fuel the "counterforces of cultural assertion and civilizational consciousness" (Huntington, 1996, pp. 56–81).

Interpreting Leadership as a Cultural Imperative

The debate between the emergence and cultural imperative approaches to defining a phenomenon of "global leadership" among humans in the twenty-first century will not be resolved here. Perhaps a universal momentum has begun to emerge that will lead to the end of a previous history where humans competed across cultural divides. If that is so, then it is not a difficult paradigm to model, and the analytical structures built over the past three decades by Western, especially American, academics will suffice to track the phenomenon of leadership in that new world. Stated differently, if Fukuyama is right, then the contemporary era will witness the coalescence of the human experience—including the influence phenomenon of leadership—into a single, shared, and rather bland consumer utopia. If the emergence paradigm is to dominate all social science inquiry, then students of leadership can expect their intellectual challenge to be rather prosaic. Under the **emergence paradigm,** the primary intellectual exercise will focus on applying the liberal democratic, market-driven models of leadership to those cultures that have not yet accepted that paradigm. Since the outlines of those models have been examined earlier, the remainder of this chapter will focus on deriving a cultural imperatives framework of analysis.

In contrast, if the universalist viewpoint is not the future of human social analysis, then the emerging leader should take a moment to consider the humbling prospect of pursuing the cultural imperative paradigm. This search for a single interpretive framework describing any human leadership across highly developed civilizational boundaries presents a seemingly overwhelming task. Reared, educated, and committed to the principles of one cultural tradition, can a human living within those civilizational boundaries then map a fair, critical consideration of how influence relationships arise within the permanent contraints of another human's culture? Even more daunting, can a human immersed in one cultural tradition find a method to fairly compare leadership as expressed inside his or her own civilization to the same phenomenon as expressed inside another? The primary intellectual pursuit from this perspectivist view of "global leadership" is to recognize and define the many different and permanent cultural iterations of the leadership phenomenon across contemporary civilizations, and to consider how they will clash or correspond.

Moreover, there is a risk in developing a critical framework for thinking about leadership in the contemporary human world that, as with all macro-scale social analysis, the framework's development will become a rather esoteric exercise. In a longer, treatise-style academic work, such framework development would require generating a new vocabulary of analysis and a much more extensive consideration of the metaphysical issues dealt with in this chapter. That type of exposition may come along at some point and provide the emerging leader with an even greater challenge of how to truly design the "first principles" of leadership in the twenty-first century. For purposes of the brief consideration in this chapter, other analytical devices seem the better choice for a leadership student considering the issue for the first time. Specifically, a key analogy and an easy mnemonic should prove more useful in considering the broad outlines of a global leadership understood within the cultural imperatives paradigm.

The Refraction Analogy and the Cultural-Organizational-Idiosyncratic Model

Emergence thinkers who have approached the question of leadership as "global," in the sense of finding a single model to apply to all human experiences of that phenomenon, have proposed interpreting leadership at various levels of inquiry. Even though some of these scholars might emphasize a psychodynamic approach that focuses on the individual leader, they would not deny the additional impact of modern organizational life on that leader. Similarly, those scholars who emphasize the organizational approach to analyzing leadership would not deny the impact of individual factors. A cultural imperatives thinker goes much broader in a search to comprehend leadership, but that thinker cannot deny the important analytical insights provided at the levels of the organization and the individual in society. A synthesis of all three in a single analogy would offer the potential for a truly comprehensive model that the cultural imperatives approach requires. The analogy of clear sight, and the process of adding refractive adjustments to clarify that vision, offers a powerful metaphor for understanding the cultural imperatives approach.

This refractive metaphor emphasizes the probability that any one human's view of a particular incidence of human leadership is imperfect, and thus must be adjusted through various analytical magnifications. If the view of a leadership incident is to be seen accurately at the macro level of civilizational impact, then that view must be shaped through a wide cultural "lens" that sees a great number of factors all at once, but only from a significant analytical distance above an entire culture. However, an interpretation of any one incidence of leadership could not fully magnify the more immediate impacts of human associational life within that culture. Even if a second, more polished lens of organizational considerations were added to the magnification already provided by the cultural lens, the particular predispositions of the individuals involved in a particular incident of leadership could not be ignored. Therefore, a third lens refined by knowledge of the most micro, individual factors would have to be installed within the frame of analysis as well.

The three levels of refraction, or "lens" magnification, can be labeled for analysis purposes as the "idiosyncratic" for considerations at the individual level, "organizational" at the level of modern associational relationships, and "cultural" at the level at which humans group themselves by identifications that are beyond their capacity to choose or control. The analogy invokes a telescopic image wherein the minute details of leadership can be observed as individual phenomena, but with such observations always related to a broader context of immediate constellations and to the overall context of a broad phenomenological horizon.

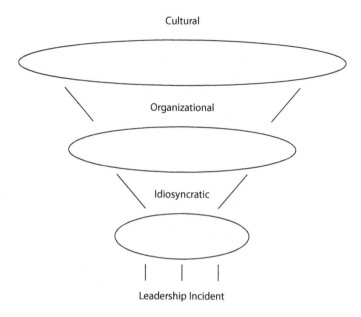

Cultural

Organizational

Idiosyncratic

Leadership Incident

The idiosyncratic level of the metaphor focuses on those physiological or behavioral observations that arise from the unique individuals involved in the particular incident of leadership. These observations would be related to gender, race, conduct, or psychodynamic testing, and they provide a method for rough prediction of how the individuals would interact in an influence relationship if they were viewed in isolation. The organizational "lens" extends the analogue by magnifying for the same individuals the immediate social structures through which they cooperate with other humans to pursue some interest, activity, or purpose. These observations magnify the influence phenomenon among those individuals to include their associational lives, including those civic, fraternal, political, and artistic groups that overlap and affect how they experience leadership. The cultural magnifier rests above the two smaller lenses and brings into specific relief the total spectrum of patterns, beliefs, and other products of conscious design that express the central differences among human communities at any particular time in history. Seen from this macro perspective, individuals involved in an incident of leadership will reflect in their reactions to that phenomenon the learned biases that have been inculcated in them.

If the model ended with just the refraction metaphor, a fair assessment would find it overly simple and of limited use as an analytical tool. At one level, this critique would be based on the generally accepted principle that reasoning about human action by analogy to laws in nature (such as the laws defining the nature of refraction of light) is always a weaker approach than measuring human actions by human standards. At another level, an appraisal of this analogy would find it lacking the complexity necessary to account fully for the contemporary context of leadership on a humanitywide basis. To meet these shortcomings, there is a taxonomy of human civilizational identifiers that provides greater depth to a cultural imperatives analysis of the leadership phenomenon.

The CHARLIE Taxonomy of Civilizational Identifiers

The seven elements of the civilizational taxonomy are *customs, history, ancestry, religion, language, institutions,* and *ethic.* The mnemonic of CHARLIE provides a simple device for remembering and applying that **taxonomy,** a pre-determined system of classification, but its components are a complex derivative from the collected works of Huntington and other historicist, or civilizational theorist, thinkers. Their insights, as discussed earlier, provide the fundamental building blocks of the cultural imperative paradigm of global leadership. Understood as part of the refractive three-lens metaphor for understanding the global context of leadership in the contemporary era, the seven elements of the **CHARLIE taxonomy** might best be viewed as "polishing agents" used to shape those lenses. Just as an optic technician might modify a microscope lens by using powders to grind it to a particular refraction, by analogy the CHARLIE elements serve as factors that enhance and refine the merged analysis available through the cultural, organizational, and idiosyncratic model.

For instance, while it may serve a cultural imperative leadership analysis to magnify an individual participant's psychodynamic profile through the idiosyncratic lens, that insight would remain obscured from a cultural imperative approach if his or her allegiances built on personal **ancestry** were not considered. Similarly, examining through the organizational lens the associational commitments of leadership participant group members would remain murky if the impact on their activities of educational, public service, or other long-established cultural institutions were not considered. In addition, no cultural imperative observation would come into full focus through the cultural lens without the refining insight of how the relevant civilization's unique history has affected the predispositions of its members participating in a leadership influence event.

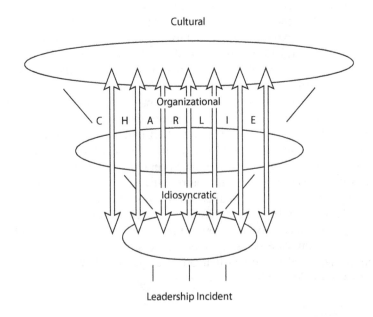

Leadership Incident

To highlight the potential application of all seven elements in the civilizational taxonomy to the cultural imperative framework, the definition of each element must be considered in turn. Given that approach, the question that links the analysis of the refractive analogy and the CHARLIE elements now can be stated clearly: When viewing any occurrence of leadership among humans through the cultural-organizational-idiosyncratic model, how do the key elements of civilizational identity (i.e., CHARLIE) affect the application of that model?

There is no preferred or linear approach to applying the seven civilizational identifiers, since each impacts the cultural imperatives analysis in different ways and all at the same time. To ease an initial consideration of the content contained in each element, it seems reasonable to take each in the suggested mnemonic order. If individuals experiencing leadership are encompassed by the patterns of a particular civilization, then they will demonstrate an allegiance to certain **customs.** By referencing customs, the central idea is that all individuals in a given group share certain habitual patterns of behavior, not biologically determined, that are transmitted from one generation to another. This element would not include the short-lived fads or fashions of a single generation but, rather, the accepted rules of behavior that a human society informally regulates. For instance, in Western civilization the custom of waiting one's turn is accepted and practiced, such as when patients at a doctor's office sign in and wait, customers at a deli take a number and wait for it to be called, or patrons at a theater line up neatly to purchase tickets. If someone violates the order of turn, others who are waiting will complain and even attempt to ostracize the violator. This custom derives from a cultural norm of "fairness," or perhaps "privilege," but it is known and enforced as a custom without the use of any formal legal mechanism.

A civilization's history offers another element that clarifies the complexities of the cultural imperative model. At one level, the history of a particular culture is a record of chronological events that a recognizable subset of humanity has shared. At another level, a history is the shared telling of a common narrative of experience that transcends many generations of humans who perceive themselves as a common people. Both these approaches point to an element that is inculcated into each human who participates in a relationship of influence that produces leadership. The "story" of a culture's development includes many subplots of how the phenomenon of leadership has arisen to affect that overall chronicle. The individuals drawn into contemporary influence events in a culture cannot easily escape their commitment to that civilization's storyline and its impact on the perception of the leadership phenomenon.

Leadership Challenge

What are some customs that are unique to your family? Identify at least three. Ask a friend about customs that are unique to his or her family. What are some fads that are unique to your generation that will probably be short-lived?

While in the West, especially in North America, there is a desire to believe that ethnicity and family origin hold no significant value, the real experience in that civilization and all others proves the persistence of ancestry as a key cultural marker. Ancestry used in this sense certainly includes the level of family, both immediate and extended, but it also encompasses extended attachments generated by affiliations across time and space in a culture. While the Smiths and the Joneses take separate pride in their own lineages, they also find a broader common bond on a cultural level that they will not easily or fully share with the Guptas and the Singhs, or with the Shahbandys and the Hassans. A key underpinning to the cultural imperatives paradigm of leadership is that humans will look to dissociate the "other" and assort with the "akin" in making choices to influence or be influenced. Given that supposition, the element of descent is a necessary rub in the effort to accurately magnify the leadership phenomenon under the cultural-organizational-idiosyncratic model.

In the view of the key historicist/civilizationist thinkers referenced in this chapter, religion is the foremost element of cultural differentiation in the contemporary world. While action motivated by faith may be fading in Western culture, the evidence seems clear that it is an increasingly central motivation for social initiative in most other civilizations. For instance, Christianity has become such a powerful force in Sub-Saharan Africa that modern governmental structures are giving way to the influence of traditional and nontraditional church structures and their leaders (Jenkins, 2002, pp. 79–107). Islam's resurgence also has impacted the contemporary world in ways that are obvious at the level of the intercivilizational conflict, but also in less apparent ways down through the levels of organizational life and individuality. While individual governments nominally rule subparts of the

The university setting is often the first opportunity for students to get to know people from other cultures.

Photo courtesy of Diana Goldammer.

Muslim civilization, the organized faith of Islam has reasserted its role as social welfare agent, healthcare supplier, educational provider, and lawgiver. In an era when most humans look more often to their faith than to their government, religion will be a necessary focus of any serious leadership evaluation.

Considered alone, the taxonomy identifier of language might not seem a valuable analytical element for analyzing the phenomenon of human leadership. After all, an undergraduate student or full-time businessperson from the West who has traveled outside Western culture knows that English is spoken almost everywhere. From this viewpoint, English is becoming so "global" that, if anything, it is an indicator of how human relationships are converging in the world, not diverging along cultural lines. The available statistics do not support this view but, rather, show a marked tendency for various cultures to reassert their native tongues as part of their civilizational identity. The available evidence in the early twenty-first century indicates that humans are not moving to English as a first language for intracultural communication. Mandarin Chinese far outpaces English in present usage and growth of usage, and Hindi and Spanish are often listed above English in terms of native speaking worldwide (Wallraff, 2000). The idea of ubiquitous English derived by the Western traveler is rather an encounter with its use as a lingua franca for the business of intercultural communication, such as tourism, industrial production, and air traffic control. When faced with how to respond to an appetizer order, a non-native speaker may summon some business English to accomplish the transaction. When faced with the influence offer of leadership, a human being will more likely find common cause with another speaker of his or her innate idiom.

Including the element of institutions to the taxonomy adds more than simply another aspect of the organizational level in a particular culture. While consideration of organizational commitments implies a voluntary set of associations, the concept of institution points to obligatory parameters established by a larger human culture, of which the individual is a part. In this sense, an institution can be an entity or an activity that establishes rule boundaries and standardized behavior patterns for all members of a culture. Institutions exist to address persistent problems of human interaction that every culture will face, such as childrearing, knowledge dissemination, and power relationships. Hence, human cultural institutions include the family, the education system, the legal system, political parties, and the economy. For instance, both East Asian and Islamic cultures maintain the institution of family to facilitate a new generation, but the status of male and female members in such families, as well as the extended or more nuclear nature of such family units, will have an important effect on the idiosyncrasies of the individuals involved in an influence event of leadership.

The final element of the CHARLIE civilizational taxonomy is **ethic.** By employing this term, it is important to note that it is not synonymous with the term *values*. If values were the seventh identifier of cultural affinity, then this portion of the refractive adjustment would focus only on the accepted moral principles—that is, the choices of what is "right" and what is "wrong"— adopted by a person or group within a culture. The use of the term *ethic* goes further to seek out what rules or habits of conduct are in place within a culture to monitor and enforce such choices. For instance, adultery and usury might be adopted as "wrong" by a culture based on a set of moral codes that is upheld through a predominant religion in the culture and preached in the key institution of a particular church, mosque, or temple. But those "wrongs" may not be enforced by rule or habit throughout a culture, and therefore no ethic against adultery or usury exists within the culture. However, the presence of the moral evaluation and the absence of rule or habit to enforce it can be said to create an ethic in and of itself, that of not interfering in the private choices or business transactions of individuals in that culture—an ethic that might be described informally as "live and let live." For purposes of interpreting how a particular instance of leadership will be affected, if adultery were an ethic in a culture, then a full analysis under the cultural imperatives model would require information about the private affairs of a married person involved in the influence phenomenon of leadership.

An Analysis Framework for Applying the Cultural Imperative Model

Having converted the cultural imperative paradigm into a rough model using an analogy with interpretive elements does not mean that its application will be simple. A key complication derives from the obvious insight that the model is not based solely on applying one set of polished lenses to evaluate leadership. Rather, each civilization must have its own culturally specific magnifying array in order to assess each incidence of leadership. For example, Huntington argues that there are at least eight major civilizations—including the West, Islam, and Sub-Saharan Africa—that are clashing along the boundaries defined by his insights. If Huntington is right, at least eight different refractive mechanisms must be identified and applied when assessing leadership across the contemporary global experience. An influence event in the Congo River delta, then, must be viewed through a cultural-organizational-idiosyncratic arrangement—with the seven taxonomy elements as civilizational clarifiers—that is specific to the Sub-Saharan African civilization. An instance of leadership in the Arabian Peninsula must be viewed through a separate arrangement of the three lenses that is specifically calibrated to the Islamic civilization. With this type of approach, the complexities of applying the cultural imperative paradigm to global leadership become apparent, but the model allows some ability to begin to manage these complexities for purposes of useful analysis.

In addition to the model of the cultural imperative approach, a student of leadership could consider using an analysis framework in applying the model. That framework should include an inventory of questions aimed at collecting adequate data to identify and refine each of the three main lenses and the seven civilizational taxonomy identifiers. In its most effective format, that framework also would suggest the integrated nature of the model, so that the resulting analysis of leadership is a synthesis and not a scorecard. That synthesis will not be self-evident, however, but will develop only from thoughtful assessment of the data collected and from the application of human judgment. The following effort is an example of what such an inventory might look like.

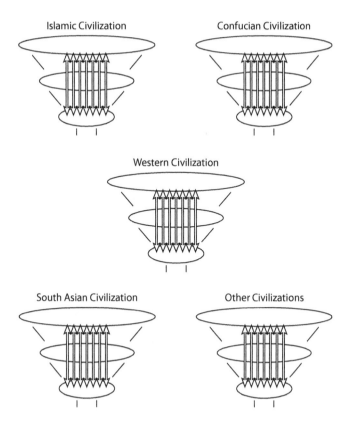

AN INVENTORY FOR THE CULTURAL IMPERATIVE MODEL

The Presence of Leadership

Is one person or a group influencing another person or group to act?
Does the influence cause action not otherwise considered or chosen?

The Refractive Analogy

A. The Cultural Lens
Do individuals involved in the influence event exhibit shared patterns of activity?
What are those patterns?
Is there a conscious design underlying those patterns?

B. The Organizational Lens
Do the individuals involved in the influence event belong to any associations?
What are the names and purposes of those associations?
Do those individuals belong to any of the same associations?

C. The Idiosyncratic Lens

Do the individuals involved in the influence event demonstrate behavioral patterns that are distinct?

What gender and race are the individuals? What ages are the individuals?

The Civilizational Taxonomy

A. Customs

Do the individuals involved in the influence event perform routines that are so repetitive that they have become the unconscious habits of those individuals?

Are those routines related to human biological needs?

If an individual deviates from these expected routines or habits, what is the reaction of others affected by that deviation?

B. History

Do the individuals involved in the influence event emphasize a particular record of chronological events?

Do they share with other individuals a common narrative of experiences that has been perpetuated over many decades or centuries?

How are the stories of individual leaders recounted?

C. Ancestry

Do the individuals involved in the influence event look to a particular lineal set of attachments in describing themselves?

How do they describe these attachments?

Do they reference those who are considered "we" and others who are considered "they"?

D. Religion

Do the individuals involved in the influence event ascribe to a defined set of spiritual beliefs?

Do they consider those beliefs in deciding which initiatives and solutions to pursue?

E. Language

Do the individuals involved in the influence event speak the same first language?

Do they use any second language?

In their discussions, is there a difference between the subject matter they discuss in their first language and their second?

F. Institutions

Do the individuals involved in the influence event recognize fundamental rules and behaviors?

What are those rules and behaviors?

Are those rules and behaviors enforced and promoted by systems established to deal with enduring human issues in society?

What are those systems and what methods do they employ to enforce or promote such rules and behaviors?

G. Ethic

Do the individuals involved in the influence event demonstrate a clear commitment to certain moral principles of what human choices are "right" and those that are "wrong"?

By what rules or habits do those individuals conduct themselves that demonstrate such a commitment?

How do those individuals monitor and enforce such rules and habits in other individuals?

■ CONCLUSION

The central issue addressed in this chapter could be summarized in one key question: Is there one leadership phenomenon in the human world or are there many? Leadership students in North America and the broader West tend to believe that a single account of that influence phenomenon is adequate to describe its reflection across all humanity. Even the brief overview provided in this chapter of the dramatic paradigmatic debate among scholars of the human world should give those students reason to pause and reconsider their universalist-inspired assumptions. Experts in the new field of leadership studies have not yet come into full engagement with the contemporary macro debates of social science, but the cultural imperative interpretation seems a more probable paradigm candidate as civilizations continue to clash with increasing intensity in a complex new century. If that is so, then the even more daunting message for leadership study is this: It will not be easy. Completing a framework such as the inventory set forth in this chapter will be time intensive in itself, but deriving from it an interpretation of any particular occurrence of leadership will require a new level of intellectual commitment. If there is an appropriate position for the modifier of "global" in the study of leadership, it may be as a description of the broad knowledge base and insight that the contemporary student will have to bring to the study of that complex phenomenon.

■ KEY TERMS

Ancestry—Extended family, both immediate and family identifications, across time in a culture.

CHARLIE Taxonomy—Customs, history, ancestry, religion, language, institutions, and ethic.

Culture—The totality of all learned and socially transmitted behavior patterns shared by a distinct people.

Customs—Habitual patterns of behavior transmitted from one generation to another.

Emergence Paradigm—Patterns and evidence that indicate a universal human culture is emerging.

Ethic—Accepted moral principles adopted by a person or group within a culture.

Paradigm—An example, a model, or a pattern that dominates analysis of a phenomenon.

Perspectivist Approach—A theoretical framework based on the assumption that leadership is influenced by the human community from which it evolves.

Taxonomy—A classification according to a predetermined system.

Universalist Approach—A theoretical framework based on the assumption that humans across the globe experience leadership in similar ways.

■ SUGGESTED READINGS

Chua, A. 2003. *World on Fire: How Exporting Free Market Democracy Breeds Ethnic Hatred and Global Instability*. New York: Anchor Books.

Ferguson, N. 2004. *Colossus: The Price of America's Empire*. New York: Penguin.

Smith, H. 1991. *The World's Religions*. New York: HarperCollins.

Stiglitz, J. E. 2003. *Globalization and Its Discontents*. New York: Norton.

Zakaria, F. 2004. *The Future of Freedom: Illiberal Democracy at Home and Abroad*. New York: Norton.

■ REFERENCES

Burns, J. M. 1978. *Leadership*. New York: Harper & Row.

Friedman, T. L. 2007. *The World Is Flat: A Brief History of the Twenty-First Century*. New York: Picador.

Fukuyama, F. 1992/2006. *The End of History and the Last Man*. New York: The Free Press.

Goethals, G. R. & Sorenson, G. L. J. (eds.) 2006. *The Quest for a General Theory of Leadership*. Northampton, MA: Edward Elgar.

House, R. J., Hanges, P. J., Javidan, M., Dorfman, P. W., & Gupta, V. (eds.) 2004. *Culture, Leadership, and Organizations: The GLOBE Study of 62 Societies*. Thousand Oaks, CA: Sage.

Huntington, S. P. 1996. *The Clash of Civilizations and the Remaking of World Order.* New York: Simon & Schuster.

Jenkins, P. 2002. *The Next Christendom: The Coming of Global Christianity.* New York: Oxford University Press.

Kuhn, T. S. 1996. *The Structure of Scientific Revolutions.* Chicago: University of Chicago Press.

Moran, R. T., Harris, P. R., & Moran, S. V. 2007. *Managing Cultural Differences: Global Leadership Strategies for the 21st Century* (7th ed.). Burlington, MA: Butterworth-Heinemann.

Wallraff, B. 2000. "What Global Language?" *The Atlantic Monthly,* November, pp. 52–66, vol. 286, no. 5.

Wren, J. T. 2006. "A Quest for a Grand Theory of Leadership." In *The Quest for a General Theory of Leadership,* G. R. Goethals & G. J. Sorenson (eds.). Northampton, MA: Edward Elgar, pp. 1–38.

CHAPTER TEN REVIEW QUESTIONS

1. Using Thomas Kuhn's approach, consider the paradigm of higher education that influences your present course of study. What are the limitations of that educational paradigm? Describe alternative paradigms of learning that could be used by the institution where you now study.

   _____

   _____

   _____

2. Attempt to provide a brief definition of the three contemporary eras—The Cold War, The New World Order, and The War on Terror—that are mentioned in the text. In those definitions, include the paradigmatic ideas that influence the thoughts of those who ascribe, or ascribed, to those paradigms. How is your view of contemporary human leadership influenced by any of those definitions?

   _____

   _____

   _____

3. The taxonomy of seven civilizational identifiers provides a potentially controversial evaluation of the trend in contemporary human relationships, including leadership. Identify the assumptions about human relationships underlying the use of this taxonomy. In what ways do you agree or disagree with these assumptions?

   _____

   _____

   _____

4. What separate assumptions about human nature are contained within the emergence paradigm and the cultural imperative paradigm? Describe how you agree or disagree with any or all of these assumptions.

   _____

   _____

   _____

5. Using the suggested analysis framework for the cultural imperatives model, complete a narrative analysis of the influence phenomenon of leadership that likely surrounds key leaders of Al Qaeda.

   _____

   _____

   _____

CHAPTER TEN SELF-TEST

1. James McGregor Burns has been considered the primary advocate for
   _____ methodology.

2. _____ believes the conflict between human civilizations is based
   on the competing core paradigms of religious belief and historical identity.

3. The mnemonic of _____ provides a simple device for remembering
   and applying the seven elements of civilizational taxonomy.

4. _____ are habitual group patterns of behavior that are transmitted
   from one generation to another.

5. While action motivated by _____ may be fading in Western culture,
   evidence suggests it is an increasingly central motivation for social initiative in
   most other civilizations.

6. _____ far outpaces English in present usage and growth of
   usage worldwide.

7. Samuel Huntington argues that there are at least _____ major civilizations that are in constant conflict.

8. _____ and _____ are two forces of integration that are
   bringing civilizations into closer contact and conflict.

9. An example of pattern is a _____.

10. _____, in his book *The End of History and the Last Man*,
    argued that the history of humanity had progressed to the point that cultural
    system conflicts were at an "end."

Case Studies in
Leadership and Service

3
PART

Leading as They Serve

A Case Study of African American Female Community Leaders

Beverly Wade Hogan

Curtina Moreland-Young

■ INTRODUCTION

African American women have historically been viewed as pillars of strength and are often credited with the survival of African American families, culture, and traditions in the United States, yet, when the story of leadership in the African American community and among African Americans is discussed in historical and contemporary context, it is often from the perspective of the contributions of males.

> [M]ost studies refer to the importance, dominance and pervasions of Black women in family and community life. This implies a contradiction; one body of literature indicates through omission that the role of African American women is insignificant, while the other documents the pervasiveness and importance of the Black female presence. The reality of living and working in the Black community strongly affirms that the leadership and roles and functions of Black women are underemphasized. (Moreland-Young, 1995, p. 49[1])

Nationally, black women comprise 61.1 percent of America's black population, yet of the 100 most influential black Americans and organizational leaders listed in *Ebony Magazine* in 2006, only 35 percent were women, including eleven members of Congress. If the female members of Congress were excluded, black women would represent only 24 percent of the leaders (Edney, 2006, p. 1). These data point to the disparity of African American female leaders of national political and organizational groups. Much of the research focuses on the number of African American women in political roles as a measure of the depth and quality of leadership. However, this misses the "boat" because leaders must be understood in various venues and functions, including appointive positions, the nonprofit sector, business, and educational institutions. Though leadership often may be couched in the number of elected officials, leadership is often beyond those who have political positions of authority.

Indeed, when *Forbes* listed its 100 most powerful women in the world, the highest-ranking African Americans were Condoleezza Rice and Oprah Winfrey, neither of whom has ever held elective office nor was head of traditional civic organizations. However, regardless of one's political ideology, both of these women would have to be considered women leaders who have used their positions as vehicles for service.

Thus, we would posit that one of the methods for understanding African American female leadership and service is to look beyond the traditional elected positions and organizations and beyond national statistics. Hence, it may be instructive to take another perspective by understanding the role and function of African American female leaders who are involved in service and to view them as leaders at the community level in myriad roles and patterns.

The purpose of this **case study** is to present a portrait of the African American female leader that encompasses the diversity of their roles and functions, including their involvement in public service. We will discuss these leaders at the micro, or community, level, looking at the diversity of the roles in which they have served, since much of the literature focuses on the number of women in positions of elected leadership. The African American female leaders we observed seem to be most reflective of community leadership, in that they have served in a number of leadership roles, including positional authority in companies, educational institutions, state and government, and civic and political organizations. Also, these women have been actively engaged in their communities to effect positive change and are involved in various levels of civic engagement; this means that they serve on local boards and committees that have decision-making input into our school systems, cultural affairs, and various issues of public policy.

During the last decade or so, a new conversation about leadership has arisen. It is called **community leadership.** The definition we like best for community leadership is taken from the one most used by the National Extension Task Force on Community Leadership. "Community leadership is that which involves influence, power and input into public decision making over one or more specific activity" (Langone, 1992, p. 23). Each of the African American female leaders selected to participate in this research study personify Langone's caption of community leadership. We also observed that there were traits of the servant-leader concept as described by Robert Greenleaf. As we learned in chapter four, Greenleaf noted that the servant-leader is a servant first. He viewed the servant-leader as one who desired to serve, and the conscious choice to serve brings out the more salient aspirations to lead. As in community leadership, Greenleaf did not think that the servant-leader had to hold a formal leadership position. He further described the servant-leader as one who "encourages collaboration, trust, foresight, listening and the ethical use of power and empowerment" (Greenleaf, 1997, p. 8). As the reader will discover from the information presented, African American female leaders in our study revealed through direct expressions, reflective thoughts, and examples that their own philosophy aligned with Greenleaf's thoughts on servant-leadership and Langone's concept of community leadership.

We believe there has been limited inclusion of the African American female leader in the literature beyond those associated with political leadership. We also believe that this discussion of African American female leaders will provide students of leadership with another reference point against which existing theories of leadership can be tested and new ones developed.

As previously stated, this study focused on leadership and the concept of service from the perspective of African American female leaders. We chose to focus on African American female leaders from Jackson, Mississippi. This site was chosen because it provides an excellent laboratory for the exploration and study of the phenomenon of African American community leadership, and there is a long tradition of female leadership and service in the state and the city. This is expounded on later in the discussion under the "Historical Context" section. Second, Jackson is an administrative, political, educational, and economic center of the Mid-South region. It is also the home of numerous African American women who hold leadership positions in many public service areas. Concomitantly, Jackson has also been the site of at least two fairly current large-scale empirical studies on African American female leaders and this effort provides the opportunity to revisit, and build upon these studies (Moreland-Young, 1995, p. 49). Finally, Jackson is the home base of the authors, both of whom serve and have served in leadership capacities at the local, regional, national, and international levels. Based on the preceding premises, the authors believe that the information generated as a result of this research is generalizeable beyond its narrow geographic environment.

◼ THE THEORETICAL FRAMEWORK

The research approach used in generating information for this essay is mixed methods in that it uses **focus group** methodology, content and historical **analysis.** These methods have produced both qualitative and quantitative data. Qualitative methodology allows one to be spontaneous and flexible and to make observations in a natural environment, while quantitative data allow for precise, controllable information, which is usually expressed in numerical terms. This study is primarily qualitative, but we have relied on some demographic statistical data. We chose focus group **methodology** because we realized from our own experiences and knowledge of the literature that one of the important factors in understanding the character and complexity of African American female leaders is providing a "safe and secure venue" for open communication. According to David Morgan, "Focus groups are fundamentally a way of listening to people and learning from them" (Morgan, 1997, p. 9). We developed a set of questions that were informed by the literature and our knowledge of the history of African American female leaders, and we conducted a focus group of contemporary African American female leaders in Jackson, Mississippi. The research questions were designed to explore and learn more about the nature and complexity of African American female leadership. We do not believe that the complete picture of leadership can be gleaned only from the body of knowledge that focuses on political leadership. We also wanted to understand the implications of leadership personas in the context of essential leadership characteristics, strengths, weaknesses, motivating factors, historical influences and role models, leadership philosophy, personal and professional challenges, and coping mechanisms.

We are using the aforementioned previous studies and knowledge of history to inform the findings disseminated in this chapter; therefore, we have found historical and content analysis useful. As previously noted, our knowledge of African American female history and relevant research on African American female leadership, in general, were utilized to inform the development of the focus group questions. We are aware of the validity and reliability questions relative to the use of qualitative data in general and focus groups in particular. Thus, we used two major mechanisms to address any concerns about **validity** or reliability (Davenport, 2007). First, to support our use of qualitative data, we are using two empirical studies to inform this chapter. Also, we subscribe to the opinions of Shakeshaft, Nowell, and Perry, in which they posit that "research about women and leadership should be conducted from a female-defined paradigm that included a method of inquiry growing out of personal experiences, feelings and the needs of the researcher" (Davenport, 2007).

We selected the participants for the focus group session using the following criteria: a leadership-level public service career and/or a leadership public service career in which the participant was the first or only female or African American to occupy the position and a reputation for achievement at the local, state, regional, national, or international level. Another criterion was a public service career rooted in community activities, although the focus could be beyond that environment.

■ REVIEW OF RELEVANT LITERATURE

There is a significant body of **literature** on African American female leaders in particular and on women in general. However, as previously noted, much of the literature traditionally on African American female leaders discusses the role of African American women as political office holders. Although that literature is quite useful in understanding the role and function of African American women, it presents only one dimension of leadership, particularly as it relates to public service. Some of the most useful literature of this type includes *The Impact of Women in Public Office,* by Susan Carrol; *Black Faces in the Mirror: African Americans and Their Representatives in the U.S. Congress,* by Katherine Tate; and an unpublished paper presented at the American Political Science Association annual meeting in 2003 by Melina Abdullah, "Self Defined Leadership Among Black Women: Proactive Group Centered Activism Beyond the Confines of Liberal Reform."

It is particularly illustrative to read what the authors call "classics," which provide a thoughtful, historical, and theoretical context from which to gain an understanding of the dynamics of being African American, female, successful, and a leader. Of particular note in this category are *Ain't I a Women: Black Women and Feminism,* by bell hooks; *Black Women in White America: A Documentary History,* edited by Gerda Lerner; *When and Where I Enter: The Impact of Black Women on Race and Sex in America,* by Paula Giddings; and *All the Women Are White, All the Blacks Are Men, but Some of Us Are Brave,* edited by Gloria Hull, Patricia Scott, and Barbara Smith.

A fairly recent approach to examining African American public service leaders has been that of analyzing women in public and nonprofit leadership roles or their roles in historical epochs, such as the civil rights movement, black liberation, or women's movement. *How Long? How Long? African American Women in the Struggle for Civil Rights,* Belinda Robnett's controversial discussion of the relationship that gender played in developing the role and function of women in civil rights organizations and the movement, provides an excellent example of this trend. Another unique approach to understanding the nature of African American female leadership is provided by Elizabeth Davenport in an article entitled "Telling Stories: Examining the View of an African–Centered Female Minority Leader." In this article, Davenport does an analysis of the life experiences of one leader as a mechanism for understanding ". . . the ways that race, ethnicity and culture influence administrative behavior and decision–making" (Shakeshaft, Nowell, & Perry, 1991). Positing that historically black colleges and universities (HBCUs) are major bulwarks against oppression in the United States, Gaetane Jean-Marie embarked on the study of African American female leaders of HBCUs (Jean-Marie, 2007). Although the focus of the study is on leaders of colleges and universities, the end result is a discussion of the leadership process on the part of black women who are committed to social justice and service.

■ THE AFRICAN AMERICAN FEMALE COMMUNITY LEADER IN HISTORICAL CONTEXT

Historically, African American female leaders from Mississippi have been at the nexus of social change in this country.[2] Thus, it is not surprising that three of the most important African American leaders in this country have Mississippi roots and were females. They were Ida Wells Barnett, Madame C. J. Walker, and Fannie Lou Hamer. It is also instructive that, although these women were active on the national and international stage, they were also community leaders. Community leadership provided the launching pad for their leadership efforts. The lives of Hamer, Barnett, and Walker provide important historical antecedents to the efforts of today's contemporary African American women. Ida Wells Barnett was a native of Holly Springs, Mississippi. *Crusade for Justice,* her autobiography which was edited by her daughter, is an unflinching analysis of a woman whom some people called a "modern day Deborah." In fact, in the forward of the autobiography, noted historian and social commentator Dr. John Hope Franklin stated, "For more than forty years Ida Wells Barnett was one of the most fearless and one of the most respected women in the United States" (Barnett, 1970, p. xiii).

Wells was born in Holly Springs in 1867 into slavery, of slave parents who remained on the plantation after the Civil War, until her father asserted his right to vote independent of his former master's instructions.[3] Fortunately, Mr. and Mrs. Barnett were skilled in carpentry and cooking, respectively. Mr. Barnett opened up a carpentry shop and became a trustee of the "negro" school, which became today's Rust College. He also was very active in local politics. Wells Barnett's mother was a famous cook and attended Rust College until she learned to read the Bible (Barnett, 1970, pp. 8–9; Lerner, 1973).

African American women have historically been the advocates for social change in their communities. These Women's League board members, of Newport, Rhode Island, were vocal advocates for reform in their city in 1899.

Library of Congress.

In 1876, Wells Barnett was fifteen when her life changed dramatically. Her parents died of yellow fever. She assumed the responsibility of rearing her five younger siblings by enrolling in Fisk University and gaining her teaching qualifications in record time. She left Fisk and established herself as a teacher in the Memphis School System (Lengermann & Niebrugge-Brantly, 1998). However, her teaching career ended in Memphis in 1891 because she wrote an article exposing the condition of education for people of color in the school system (Sally, 1993, p. 115). Ida, in addition to her teaching, had begun a career as a crusading journalist, writing under the name Iola (Lerner, 1973). Subsequently, she had to flee Memphis because of her anti-lynching and political stances. Her newspaper was destroyed and her life was threatened (Appiah & Gates, 2003, p. 1003). Eventually, Wells Barnett became known nationally and internationally as a spokesperson and an activist in the struggle for the rights of African Americans and women.[4] At great peril to herself, she was involved in the efforts to document lynchings and race riots and to end the segregation of public facilities. Wells Barnett was even a founding member of the National Association for the Advancement of Colored People (NAACP), but she was disturbed by what she viewed as the organization's lack of militancy and race pride (Lerner, 1973). She was married to fellow activist, newspaper founder, and attorney Ferdinand Lee Barnett. Together, the couple raised six children (Barnett, 1970).

Like Wells Barnett, Madame C. J. Walker was born a slave in Delta, Louisiana, with the birth name of Sarah Breedlove. Delta is right across the state line from Mississippi, and at an early age Madame C. J. Walker moved to Mississippi to escape a yellow fever epidemic. Just like Wells Barnett, she was orphaned by yellow fever. Married at the age of fourteen, she also mothered her only child at a young age

(Women in History, 2007). She was widowed when her daughter A'Lelia was two years of age, and in 1906 she married Charles Joseph Walker, an erstwhile newspaper agent and sometimes barber. It was while married to Walker that she took the appellation of Madam C. J. Walker. Generally recognized as the first woman to make a million dollars due to her own efforts in the United States, Walker, unlike Wells Barnett, did not have much formal education (Bundles, 2001, p. 57). However, she, like Wells Barnett and later Hamer, had a lifelong commitment to learning and improvement.

In fact, it is this commitment to learning and improvement that became the impetus for Walker's fame. After experiencing hair loss and the humility of not having products that addressed the beauty needs of women of color, she invented a line of hair care products and instruments (Bundles, 2001). From her self-taught efforts and desire for improvement and learning, Walker built a successful career as an entrepreneur. She was one of the first "mothers" of the franchise movement in this country, developing a nationwide network of agents (Appiah & Gates, 2003, p. 992). Appiah and Gates state, "Walker was the first woman to sell products via mail order." In addition, she opened her own beauty school and established a chain of beauty parlors throughout the United States, the Caribbean, and South America (Bundles, 2001).

Of course, if Walker were simply a successful entrepreneur, she would not be included in this discussion of leadership. But Walker's business acumen was a mechanism for public service. Indeed, if one reads the biography written by her great-great-granddaughter, Walker viewed her business as a facilitator of her public service work in uplifting the race and women (Bundles, 2001). She worked to have black World War II veterans given full rights. She donated monies to the NAACP for anti-lynching efforts and made contributions to preserve the home of Frederick Douglass. She tried to organize her workers to civic action, and she donated monies toward the establishment of schools and orphanages in the United States and Africa (Bundles, 2001).

Fannie Hamer inspired African Americans as a leader of the Mississippi Freedom Democratic Party, which challenged the segregated state Democratic Party.

Library of Congress.

Fannie Lou Hamer gained fame at the 1964 Democratic Convention as a leader of the Mississippi Freedom Democratic Party, which challenged the seating of the lily white and segregated state Democratic Party. Fannie Hamer was born into the same type of oppressive agrarian environment as her counterparts, Wells Barnett and Walker. She was born in 1917 in Montgomery County, Mississippi, and at the age of two her parents moved the family to Sunflower County, Mississippi. The Hamers were sharecroppers, and she was the youngest of the twenty children born to Ella and Jim Townsend. Hamer started to work in the fields at age six; by age twelve, she had left school to work full-time in the fields (Appiah & Gates, 2003, p. 337). By the time Fannie married Perry "Pap" Hamer at age twenty-five, she was on her way to demonstrating her usefulness on the plantation where her husband worked, as tractor driver, field worker, and timekeeper (Mills, 2007).

In 1962, she was evicted and fired from the Marlow Plantation outside of Ruleville, Mississippi, where she lived, because of her activities with the Student Non-Violent Coordinating Committee (SNCC) (Lewis, 2007). Eventually, Hamer became such a leader of the civil rights movement that she would be called "the spirit of the civil rights movement" (Lewis, 2007). As a field secretary for SNCC, she exhibited great courage and experienced personal danger as she worked to expand the political rights for African Americans in Mississippi and the rest of the United States. She helped organize Freedom Summer in 1964, became a founding member of the Mississippi Freedom Democratic Party, served as a delegate to the 1964 Democratic National Convention, brought Head Start to Ruleville, and started a local pig bank (Lewis, 2007).

Hamer's community activism had regional, national, and international implications. In a partnership with the National Council of Negro Women, Hamer expanded the pig bank to help at least 300 families (Lewis, 2007). In 1971, she helped found the National Women's Political Caucus. Hamer's influence even had an international focus, as she traveled with a group of SNCC leaders to Africa or as she "hosted visitors from developing nations after an International Women's Year Meeting" (Mills, 2007, pp. 315–320).

■ THE CONTEMPORARY FACE OF THE AFRICAN AMERICAN FEMALE LEADER

In a focus group setting, we interviewed ten African American female leaders. All but one held terminal degrees, (M.D., Ph.D., Ed.D., J. D.) The one who did not hold the terminal degree is a candidate for Ph.D. They identified themselves as middle- to upper-class citizens; only one participant identified herself as a working-class citizen. There was a mixture of marital status, though the majority were married. They identified with the Democratic Party in terms of political party affiliation. Their incomes ranged from $60,000 to above $150,000. Only two of the participants were children of college graduates. The participants held a wide range of positions of leadership, including a physician who leads a major research study, a circuit court judge, head of a national women's political organization, head of a major civic organization, a chief executive officer/president and former vice president of a national and regional foundation, educational leaders at various ranks of university leadership, leaders of an international consortium, founders and chief executive officers of their own companies, and heads of other nonprofit-type organizations. Most of the participants had held leadership positions for at least five years; most had more than ten years of leadership experience.

The interviews with the African American female leader participants involved a discussion of leadership, service, and challenges. A series of questions about leadership and service were posed to the participants. The questions focused on the essential characteristics and effective traits of leadership, the strengths and weaknesses that the participants believed they brought to their leadership position and whether any of them were race- or gender-related factors that motivated them toward service as a leader, their leadership philosophy, their role models, their personal challenges, and their coping mechanisms.

The participants used specific terms to identify the essential characteristics of leadership. They used words and phrases such as *integrity, visionary, persuasive, good listener, an effective communicator, values-oriented and centered, strong sense of balance, self-confidence extending to one's own competency, knowledge of position one holds,* and *well-learned in terms of having a worldview of issues.*

The participants viewed the essential characteristics that they identified as also strengths they brought to their positions of leadership. They also listed as other strengths descriptors such as *trustworthy, flexibility, secure in self and one's ability to lead, commitment, dedication, ability to connect to the whole picture—a type of synergistic thinking, visionary thinking,* and *strategic thinking.* The weaknesses identified were uncontrolled impatience—thinking that there is only one right way to do something, including the common practice of women to think they can do everything themselves; inflexible standards; the "Polly Anna" complex of trusting everyone to a fault; the "Doubting Thomasina" complex of not trusting others to do something right; distrust of the process; psychic and physical burnout due largely to not finding the right balance; and lack of time for self-reflection.

The participants believed that some of the strengths and weaknesses were race- and gender-based. They were particularly aware of the attributions of expectations of the African American female that portray her as "some type of superwoman." This is more myth than reality. We posit that the tendency for this attribution might be historically based relating to an era when many African American females took care of other people's households and children while maintaining the care of their own households. The African American female in our sample has high expectations of what she can do and often feels that she carries the "burden" of her race principally on her shoulders. Hence, the African American females interviewed indicated that they do not want to adversely affect the standing and elevation of her race as a result of her performance in service and leadership roles. They believed that the dominant white society tended to paint all African Americans with the same brush.

The participants were presented with the following self-descriptors in the focus group session: *physical attractiveness, self-control, dominant, extroverted, ambitious, confident, dedicated, self-assured, strong,* and *nurturing.*[5] With the exception of *dominant* and *physical attractiveness,* the self-descriptors received a positive response from the group. The group commented on two descriptors: *physical attractiveness* and *dominant.* They thought that the term *physical attractiveness* needed to be defined. While they agreed that it is useful in a leadership position, they wanted to be clear that from their perspective the term is more defining of factors other that of the traditional concept of being considered "a pretty face." It was clear that the participants, like many females, do not want their physical appearance alone to define their competency or minimize their relevance or competency. However, in contrast, the group did indicate that attractiveness can be utilized as a "tool" in the same way that intellect or other attributes of leadership are utilized.

The participants also believed that the word *dominant* carried some negative connotations and that dominance can be less effective if it is not handled appropriately. They stated the term could easily be confused with a domineering personality. There was an observation on the part of some of the participants that for African American females, the word *dominant* may have historical antecedents that are unfavorable. Particularly, in the African American community, the word *dominant* as it refers to females also indicates a lack or abdication on the part of African American males.

The participants noted that the motivating factors toward service for them included parents and parental figures, such as grandparents, the civil rights movement, the black liberation movement, religious beliefs, and to a much lesser degree the women's movement. Though many of the participants grew up in traditional households where there was a clear division of labor, the parents, especially mothers, tended to encourage the females to go beyond the traditionally defined roles for females. Interestingly, the fathers also tended to encourage their daughters toward nontraditional roles while holding the expectation of a traditional model for their wives. The females observed that, in their households, the men had roles more aligned with taking charge and leading the family, while the females were relegated to roles of service. Service came naturally because they witnessed their mothers and other women serving in the home, community, and church. They described their parents as ones who were always helping their fellow human beings. Those who grew up under the oppression of discrimination and Jim Crow laws were more influenced by the civil rights movement and saw their motivation toward leadership and service connected with their desire to contribute to societal changes and make a difference. For African American females, the women's movement was a much lesser influence. The participants identified more with their status as a race than as a gender; they were more connected with their liberation as a "race of people" than their liberation as women.

When speaking of the historical developments that motivated them toward leadership and service, the participants pointed to their educational settings, churches, and parents. They observed females as teachers; teaching was considered a noble and highly honorable profession in the African American community. They also observed women serving in leadership roles in the church and civic organizations. The participants noted that the women's roles in the church were mainly as ushers, boards of mothers, and missionaries. It was uncommon for women to serve on the church's board of trustees and finance committees when many of them were growing up. Their parents encouraged them toward leadership and service. They were encouraged to excel beyond the achievements of their parents and grandparents. They were taught to be supportive of others and to make a difference in the world.

The participants used the phrase "servant-leadership" to describe their leadership philosophy. This identification led to the discussion that the concept of servant-leadership is not race- or gender-based. They commented that the concept was connected to exposure, socialization, culture, and one's orientation to service and leadership. One participant noted that leading and serving are in the interest of helping others and that which forms the basis of her contribution as a leader. She stated, "As an African American female leader, we are not leading for ourselves but for our people." This comment led to comments on the notion of the "burden" of leadership. Again, the African American leaders in our sample feel that they carry the responsibility of their race in the performance of their responsibilities as leaders. If they fail as individuals, the race fails and is measured accordingly by the dominant society. The positions/professional roles that a person occupies do not make him or her a leader. However, most of the participants felt that there is an "anointing" process in which one "pays one's dues" to facilitate the ascension to leadership in the African American community. It is interesting to note that there was a difference in thought among the participants in terms of their philosophies of leadership. These African American female leaders were not monolithic in their perspectives, nor did they believe African Americans in general are monolithic. The two female participants who were forty years of age and less seemed to express the most divergent philosophies from others in the group. These younger respondents tended to describe themselves as leaders rather than African American female leaders. They do not identify with the same sense of burden of the race and were less influenced by the civil rights movement's notion of "paying one's dues" before being accepted as a leader. They saw their roles as leaders as positions they enjoyed and felt they were qualified to perform. However, there was unanimous agreement that leaders should be change agents.

Shirley Chisholm, the first black woman ever elected to Congress, is often cited as a role model by female African American leaders.

Library of Congress.

Leadership Challenge

Imagine that you are asked to participate in a focus group about leadership in your community. Who would you list as role models for your community and state? Why would you select those people?

The participants identified primarily other African American females as their role models. They included many women whom they considered to be change agents. Fannie Lou Hamer was often cited, along with women such as Unita Blackwell, Marian Wright Edelman, Barbara Jordan, Shirley Chisholm, Angela Glover Blackwell, and Vashti Murphy MacKenzie. Unita Blackwell was the first African American female mayor of a Mississippi town, Mayersville. She played a state and national role in improving race relations. Marian Wright Edelman, the founder and president of the Children's Defense, has been a powerful and unrelenting voice for our nation's children. Barbara Jordan, a United States Representative from Texas, was a great orator and rose to recognized national influence during the Watergate era. Shirley Chisholm was the first black woman ever elected to Congress. Angela Glover Blackwell, a former vice president of the Rockefeller Fund, is currently with the Policy Link. Vashti Murphy MacKenzie is the first female bishop in the 200-year history of the African Methodist Episcopal Church. Others also listed their mothers and grandmothers. One noted her grandmother was a midwife who delivered over 500 babies without one loss during her lifetime. This grandmother was described as a woman ahead of her time. With limited formal education during the time of segregation and before women's liberation, this grandmother took a courageous stand against injustices in her community and opened doors of opportunity for her people.

The participants discussed a number of personal challenges. They had difficulty finding balance in their lives. They experienced health-related problems that impede the level of their activity. They are challenged to establish clear priorities and get control of time for themselves. They noted that tolerance and impatience were challenges and there is a consistent urge to resist feeling as though they are a target for public criticism and scrutiny.

They identified coping mechanisms that they employ. Their friendships with other women, especially those with whom they can share openly and honestly, topped the list. Exercise, massages, and spa treatments were also helpful. Others identified having a sense of spirituality and taking the time to engage in pleasure and inspirational reading.

In discussing the challenges they experience in maintaining personal relationships, the participants did not note any major barriers. They pointed out that they had to be intentional at finding a balance and forming partnerships in their marriages. Those who were not married pointed out that they experienced difficulty in meeting professional African American males who could accept their roles as leaders with professional responsibilities. Quality and quantity of time and commitment were factors that impacted their relationships with others. The participants also noted that their unwillingness to change and adapt to lesser standards of lifestyles was also a challenge in maintaining personal relationships. They expressed that their children and siblings were sources of support and encouragement and they rely on them. Their relationships with girlfriends are important and provide sustaining value. They described their friendships as long-standing—dating back to their college days. Though frequent physical contact with friends was a challenge, they communicated frequently with friends through telephone conversations and emails.

The participants did not think that the challenges they faced were unique or due to ethnicity in any large measure. They reaffirmed their belief that African Americans are not a monolithic group. The varying perspectives among African American females in particular are connected to their socialization, cultural and religious experiences, and parental and societal influences. Within this group, whether male or female, there are diverse thoughts, beliefs, behaviors, and experiences, depending on one's orientation. They do believe that more is expected of African American female leaders from other African Americans and larger groups of society.

Many of the myths that women have to be convinced that they can be leaders did not surface during the conversations with this group of participants. They embraced their leadership and service roles; some of them expressed that they felt there was a calling for them to do what they are doing. The participants in one way or another conveyed that their leadership philosophy and concept of service were grounded in the principle of leading from the heart. They enjoyed and thrived in their roles.

■ CONCLUSION: IMPLICATIONS FOR FUTURE STUDY AND PUBLIC POLICY

Perhaps the most insightful expression of what forms the crux of these African American female leaders' perspectives on leadership and service was the identification of their role models. All of them identified African American women who demonstrated pioneering efforts, encountered resistance to their participation, persevered to make a difference, and served as a voice for those whose voices were often silenced. They associated their role models with changing, innovating, and overcoming challenges. Their role models were also women who served their local communities before ascending the ranks of leadership. They were women who were capable of serving the common good and emerged into leadership to further their beliefs through actions. The African American female leaders' perspectives on leadership and service and those they chose as role models in large measure are reflective of the concepts of servant-leadership and community leadership.

African American female leaders are participating in various aspects of community life. They are not confined to any particular domain. They have vision and values, skills and experiences, commitment, and will, all of which are needed in our world today. Further study is needed to explore the broader dynamics of leadership at the levels that African American women participate. The ways in which they effect change in their community and mobilize their networks to action can inform the literature. Many minorities, including women and African Americans, are leaders at the community levels where activism, decision making, and influence are best evidenced. Bringing new realities to the forefront of discussions in classrooms and other public forums can put new faces to leadership, test old theories against new ones, and create a new and different body of knowledge about leadership and service. Further research can provide the material needed to expand our thinking and break down gender and race biases, moving society toward more adequate public policies. Though much progress has been made in the social constructs and workplace structures to include minorities and women, more progress is needed to more effectively address societal biases, inequalities in family balance, and inadequacies in our social policy.

Women in general face challenges in advancing beyond a certain level of leadership in government and corporate structures, and African American women are more adversely limited. Despite the progress that has been made by women during the last forty years, women still encounter persistent and pervasive barriers. Conversations must continue to generate broader understanding, acceptance, and appreciation of their leadership and service in ways that will inform practice and influence social policy. Equal opportunity is still an ideal—and one that in its fullest measure has yet to be reached.

■ KEY TERMS

Analysis—The separation or dissection of the whole, or complex, into more simplistic and more manageable elements.

Case study—A type of research that involves in-depth observation of individuals, groups, or organizations.

Community Leadership—Leadership that involves influence, power, and input into the community decision-making process.

Focus Group—A group of individuals organized by researchers that participate in discussions as part of the information-gathering process.

Literature—The writings and research conducted by the experts in a given field of study or discipline.

Methodology—A systematic procedure for conducting a study or research.

Validity—The extent to which a study, survey, or test successfully measures or predicts, as designed by those conducting the research.

■ SUGGESTED READINGS

Barnett, I. W. 1970. Alfreda Duster (ed.). *Crusade for Justice: the Autobiography of Ida Wells Barnett*. Chicago and London: The University of Chicago Press.

Cole, J. B. 2003. *Gender Talk: The Struggle for Women's Equality in African American Communities*. New York: One World/Ballantine Books.

Hull, G. T., Scott, P. B., & Smith, B. 1982. *All the Women Are White, All the Blacks Are Men, but Some of Us Are Brave*. Old Westbury, NY: The Feminist Press.

REFERENCES

Appiah, K. A. & Gates, H. L. 2003. *Africana: The Encyclopedia of the African and African American Experience*. Philadelphia and London: Running Press.

Barnett, I. W. 1970. Alfreda Duster (ed.). *Crusade for Justice: Autobiography of Ida Wells Barnett*. Chicago and London: The University of Chicago Press.

Bundles, A. 2001. *On Her Own Ground: The Life and Times of Madam C. J. Walker*. New York: Scribner.

Davenport, E. K. 2007. "Telling Stories: Examining the View of an African–Centered Female Minority Leader." *Advancing Women in the Leadership Online Journal, v. 23.*

Edney, H. T. 2006. "Black Women Leaders Still Pushed to the Back of the Bus," *Washington Informer,* NPPA, News Report (20 July).

Greenleaf, R. K. 1997. *Servant Leadership*. New York: Paulist Press.

Jean-Marie, G. 2006. "Welcoming the Unwelcomed: A Social Justice of African American Female Leaders at Historically Black Colleges and Universities." *Educational Foundations, 20(1–2)* Winter–Spring, pp. 83–102.

Langone, C. A. 1992. "Building Community Leadership," *Journal of Extension, 30(4),* pp. 23–25.

Lengermann, P. M. & Niebrugge-Brantly, J. 1998. *The Women Founders: Sociology and Social Theory, 1830–1930*. Boston: McGraw-Hill.

Lerner, G. 1973. *Black Women in White America*. New York: Vintage Press.

Lewis, J. J. "Hamer, Fannie Lou." http://womenhistory.about.com/od/civilrights/ afannielou_hamer.htm September 9, 2007.

McDonald, E. & Schoenberger, C. R. 2005. "The 100 Most Powerful Women." *Forbes* (27 July).

Mills, K. 2007. *This Little Light of Mine: The Life of Fannie Lou Hamer*. Lexington: University of Kentucky Press.

Moreland-Young, C. 1995. "The Powerful Oppressed: A Study of African American Leaders in Jackson, Mississippi." *Journal of Public Management and Policy, 1(1),* pp. 49–65.

Morgan, D. L. 1997. *The Focus Group Guidebook*. Thousand Oaks, CA: Sage.

Sally, C. 1993. *The Black 100: A Ranking of the Most Influential African-Americans, Past and Present*. Secaucus, NJ: Carol.

Shakeshaft, C., Nowell, I., & Perry, A. 1991. "Gender and Supervision," *Theory in Practice, 30(2),* pp. 134–139.

Women in History. 2007. *Madam C. J. Walker Biography*. Lakewood, OH: Lakewood Public Library. http//:www.lkwdpl.org/wihohio/walk-mad.htm. pp. 1–2.

ENDNOTES

1. The first studies partially funded by the Rockefeller Fund was conducted by Curtina Moreland-Young in 1983 and 1993; a follow-up study was conducted in 1994 by doctoral students in the Department of Public Policy and Administration. One of the publications that resulted from these efforts was "Curtina Moreland Young, The Powerful Oppressed: A Study of African American Female Leaders in Jackson, Mississippi," *Journal of Public Management and Policy,* (Vol. 1, No. 1, Spring, 1995), University of Pittsburg, pp. 49–65.

2. The reason for this is not clear. There is considerable disagreement in the scholarly community, perhaps because of the nature of the slavocracy and the history of resistance that developed.

3. It is interesting to note here that Wells Barnett's father was the son of his owner, whose only children were not of his union with Miss Polly, his wife.

4. Barnett is considered one of the "founders" of the black women's club movement, through which much important community work is done today.

5. These are self-descriptors that were used in the earlier studies on African American female leaders, and they emanate from empirical data that examine the comfort level that women have in using certain words as self-descriptors.

CHAPTER ELEVEN REVIEW QUESTIONS

1. Compare and contrast the role, functions, and challenges of historical African American female leaders with that of the contemporary leaders who participated in this case study.

_____

_____

_____

2. What are the most significant attributes you ascribe to effective leadership? Do your choices differ from the essential characteristics indicated by the focus group participants?

_____

_____

_____

3. Do you agree with the authors that there is a need for further study of community leadership and servant-leadership, especially in minority communities? Why? Why not?

_____

_____

_____

4. Were you familiar with the role of prominent African American women in the history of the United States prior to reading this chapter? What did you learn from the vignettes about Hamer, Walker, and Wells Barnett?

_____

_____

_____

5. Do you agree that African American female leaders share a "burden of race," as presented in the chapter? Discuss.

_____

_____

_____

CHAPTER ELEVEN SELF-TEST

1. According to the authors, the leadership and roles and functions of African American women are _____.

2. In order to understand African American female leadership and service, one must look beyond the traditional_____ positions, traditional_____, and national _____.

3. Community leadership involves _____, _____, and _____ into public decision making.

4. According to the authors, the personal philosophy of the study participants aligned with _____'s thoughts on servant leadership.

5. According to David Morgan, "_____ are fundamentally a way of listening to people and learning from them."

6. Three of the most important African American leaders in this country have Mississippi roots and were female. They were_____, _____, and _____.

7. According to the authors, the focus group participants were more connected with their liberation as a _____ than their liberation as women.

8. Focus group participants said that one of their personal challenges in their lives was finding _____.

9. Focus group participants identified a number of African American females as role models; _____ and _____ were two of the many often cited.

10. _____ was the first black woman ever elected to Congress.

Rendezvous with Destiny

A Collective Case Study in Servant-Leadership

John R.
Shoup

■ SO YOU WANT TO BE A LEADER?

As you have gleaned from the previous chapters, and contrary to many traditional views, highly effective leaders have a servant mentality.

■ SO YOU WANT TO BE A SERVANT-LEADER?

Good intentions are essential. Unfortunately, good intentions are not sufficient to become an effective servant-leader. Acquiring the requisite knowledge, skills, and dispositions is also necessary. Fortunately, though, one does not have to wait for a certificate, degree, or formal title to earn the mantle of servant-leader. Hopefully, it will become evident in this collective study of leaders that exemplary leaders can and often do emerge from the trenches of service. It is often in the trenches of serving that emerging leaders acquire the indispensable competencies that make their leadership exemplary.

For clarification, not every servant is or becomes a leader. Many people are content to follow or maintain the status quo. Many in the service industry and public sector are abrupt, uncaring, and/or minimalist when performing their job. In addition, there are many people who are willing to serve but by temperament or by choice do not take on leadership roles.

There is a leadership shortage in almost every sector, exacerbated by the fact that many competent people are turning down formal leadership roles because "it is a thankless job" and it entails extra work and headaches that they are unwilling to endure. A service orientation is often the necessary first step for individuals to put themselves in the leadership arena. There are egotistical reasons to put oneself in a position of leadership; however, it is not uncommon for such leaders to derail eventually. It is a social and personal tragedy when qualified people shun leadership opportunities. A well-known quote attributed to Edmund Burke is "all that it takes for evil to prosper is for good men to do nothing." It is sobering to think what the world would be like if the good men and women of the past had done nothing.

While not all servants are necessarily leaders, not all successful leaders are servants. There are a continua of leadership types (informal to formal leaders; novice to expert; *laissez-faire* to autocratic; self-promoting to selfless; foolish to wise; mean-spirited to gracious and kind; minimally skilled to competent; tyrants to benevolent rulers; unprincipled to ethical; etc.). Leadership roles often attract people who are drawn to the limelight or positions of power, which runs counter to the servant aspect of exemplary leadership. Service, although critical, is but one component of the complex phenomenon of exemplary leadership. However, as will be evident in this chapter, servant-leaders appear to leave a greater legacy.

■ BECOMING A SERVANT-LEADER

In this chapter, we will briefly examine the life of several individuals who started out with relatively average abilities and big hearts to emerge eventually as exemplary leaders, whose sacrificial service to their respective causes led them to the world stage. In our quest to be servant-leaders, it may sound overly ambitious to strive for a national or global impact. It may even sound quixotic to strive to make a difference at the local or state level. The men and women of this collective case study did not start with the foresight that their initial acts of service would lead to future opportunities of a global scale.

The servant-leaders of this case study did not make it their initial ambition to be famous or achieve notoriety, but rather their aspiration was to meet an immediate need. Early in their careers, people such as Theodore Roosevelt, Franklin and Eleanor Roosevelt, Catherine Beecher, Gandhi, Jane Addams, Abraham Lincoln, George Marshall, Booker T. Washington, Harry Truman, Margaret Thatcher, Martin Luther King, and Colin Powell set out to make a difference in their immediate context. This eclectic list of servant-leaders and countless others is the subject of this collective case study. Brief vignettes of exemplary leaders who demonstrated service on a global scale will yield lessons, encouragement, and principles that may serve as a guide for emerging leaders with servant hearts.

The list of role models selected for this case study may appear random and inchoate. This collective case study is in the tradition of the writings of Plutarch (circa A.D. 46–120), Samuel Smiles (1812–1904), Charles Horne (1870–1942), James MacGregor Burns (1918-) and countless other leadership self-help biographies and autobiographies that line library and bookstore shelves.

Plutarch wrote *Parallel Lives,* described by Ralph Waldo Emerson as a bible for heroes, so that the readers "may also be improved" by imitating lives worth emulation (Plutarch, 2001, p. 201). Plutarch compares the lives of twenty-three pairs of Roman and Greek leaders and four unpaired individuals to provide lessons on virtue from fifty brief philosophical biographies. Plutarch was informative in shaping the resolve and character of several initial presidents of our country, as well as President Truman (McCullough, 1992). C. S. Lewis states that "Plutarch's *Lives* built the heroic ideal of the Elizabethan age" (Lewis, 1954, p. 305).

Samuel Smiles first wrote *Self Help with Illustrations of Conduct and Perseverance* in 1859. Smiles provided insight into character and determination based on lessons from over 270 individuals referenced in his book. As one of the first self-help books published, Smiles later regretted the title as misleading in suggesting that it contains a "eulogy of selfishness: the very opposite of what it really is" (Smiles, 1881, p. vi). Smiles goes on to state that the purpose of the book

> is to stimulate youths to apply themselves diligently to right pursuits—sparing neither labour, pains, nor self-denial in prosecuting them—and to rely upon their own efforts in life, rather than depend on the patronage of others, it will also be found, from the examples given of literary and scientific men, artists, inventors, educators, philanthropists, missionaries and martyrs, that the duty to helping one's self in the highest sense involves the helping of one's neighbours (p. vi).

Hundreds of editions in several languages and millions of copies of *Self Help* have been published around the world as the book was a best-seller in several countries. It was also pivotal in reinforcing the Protestant work ethic in England and even in Meiji, Japan. Cummings (2003) correlates the book's impact as "no accident that Japanese pedagogy came to place near total reliance on effort as opposed to ability as the key to learning" (p. 180). Smile's book reminded people and political leaders that hard work and character are keys to individual success and nation building.

Charles F. Horne wrote *Great Men and Famous Women: A Series of Pen and Pencil Sketches of the Lives of More Than 200 of the Most Prominent Personages in History* (1894). Similar to Plutarch and Smiles, Horne found biographies to be powerfully didactic, not only for general purposes of understanding history but also for specific lessons on shaping character. James MacGregor Burns, a Pulitzer Prize–winning presidential biographer, a pioneer in the study of leadership, and an author of over a dozen substantive books on leadership, examined the leadership styles of various political, religious, and social leaders. Burns (1978), in his book *Leadership*, developed his seminal work on transformational leadership based on the life stories and political lessons from a wide assortment of leaders, including Wilson, Gandhi, Hitler, King, and Napoleon. Burns believes biographies are essential for students of leadership.

This chapter is a synthesis of previous and ongoing research on leadership development and borrows heavily from a study titled *A Collective Biography of Twelve World-Class Leaders: A Study on Developing Exemplary Leaders,* in which are documented and discussed seven formative influences behind the life experiences and background of a select list of exemplary leaders (Shoup, 2005). This chapter is also informed by wisdom from twenty-seven interviews with various university senior leaders and exemplary university presidents across the United States on principles for leaders to finish well and avoid derailment (Shoup, 2007). Data from approximately 500 brief email correspondences with various university scholars and university presidents on the facets of exemplary leadership (Shoup & Reeder, 2006) and a plethora of biographical studies on a assortment of leaders (various US presidents, social and educational reformers, military and business leaders) are also included.

There are several common themes from the variety of sources previously cited that offer invaluable insights and principles for becoming a servant-leader. At one level, the insights are not necessarily new but provide a useful model around which to organize one's life in the quest to be an exemplary servant-leader who finishes well and achieves his or her destiny.

Four themes or principles influencing the emergence as exemplary leaders will be addressed in this chapter:

- Inherit a calling.
- Find a niche.
- Secure prodigious patrons.
- Be humble and ethical.

Each of these principles is embedded with both the servant and the leadership motifs. Selected vignettes, while highlighting specific leaders, are selected for their vividness to reflect common themes and principles at work in most exemplary servant-leaders.

Inherit a Calling

A **calling** is work that brings satisfaction, a sense of purpose, and meaning to one's life. Humans long for a sense of purpose and meaning and they feel lost without a purpose in life. This desire for a calling can't be quelled by money and fame, but following your calling can lead to great satisfaction in knowing you made a difference in the lives of others.

Prior to contracting polio in 1921 at the age of thirty-nine, Franklin Delano Roosevelt (FDR) served as a state senator in New York from 1911 to 1913. He then diligently served as the Assistant Secretary of the Navy for the United States until he resigned in 1920. In 1921, FDR was diagnosed with polio, which left him paralyzed from the waist down. In spite of the crippling disease, FDR remained active in politics and went on to serve as governor of New York from 1928 to 1932. He was elected to four terms as the thirty-second president of the United States. FDR was the longest serving president (1933–1945) in America. He helped restore prosperity through various progressive reforms and new deals during one of the harshest economic depressions in the America's history, and he played a strategic role in ending WWII.

FDR experienced a privileged childhood associated with wealth. While many of his contemporaries chose to live a life of leisure with limited responsibilities (similar to the images surrounding many socialites in today's media), FDR did not, even though he had sufficient means to do so. If any adult had a legitimate excuse to retire from the rigors of public service, FDR had one, yet FDR overcame the limitations of his disability and gravitational pull to a life of leisure to serve his country faithfully up to his death at the age of sixty-three.

At the risk of reducing something as complex as individual motivation to a simple cause and effect, there was one recurring theme in FDR's development that instilled in him a propensity to serve. FDR's parents, Sarah and James, took great pains to instill in their only child the concept of *noblesse oblige*—with privilege comes responsibility. A curriculum of nannies, private education, and travels abroad was intentionally structured to groom FDR for a life that involved some component of service.

At the age of fourteen, FDR was intentionally sent to Groton school because of its emphasis on public service. The reputable headmaster, Endicott Peabody, was known for saying, "If some Groton boys do not enter political life and do something for our land, it won't be because they have not been urged" (Freidel, 1990, p. 8). While the sense of duty FDR inherited from his parents was cultivated under the tutelage of Endicott Peabody, it was Eleanor Roosevelt who ignited and sustained his moral passion and compass. As distant cousins, FDR and Eleanor were married March 17, 1905. It was Eleanor, more aware and involved in social causes, who introduced FDR to "witness conditions that he said he had never known existed" (Freidel, 1990, p. 12). "At eighteen in New York City she [Eleanor] was already committed to the social justice movement, teaching at the Rivington Street Settlement House and investigating women's working conditions for the Consumers' League" (Freidel, 1990, p. 12). Eleanor continually educated FDR on the plight of those less fortunate and nurtured many of the sensitivities found in FDR's humane social policies.

Similar to FDR, Eleanor grew up in the context of wealth. But, unlike her husband, Eleanor's childhood was less than idyllic. Her harsh mother died when she was eight, at which point she went to live with her stern maternal grandmother. Eleanor's endearing but alcoholic father died when she was ten years old. It was in the context of suffering in her early years that Eleanor developed a "sympathetic interest in fellow suffers that she was never to lose" (Burns, 1956, p. 27). Prior to her marriage to FDR, Eleanor was considering a career in social service or teaching (Freidel, 1990, p. 12).

It was while teaching on Rivington Street, one of the poorest and most congested sections of New York City, that Eleanor Roosevelt found her calling to fight for social justice.

Library of Congress.

From her marriage to FDR until her death on November 7, 1962, Eleanor led a remarkable life of service, as a zealous formal and informal political helpmate to her husband; as a social reformer for children, minorities, and women; as the United States delegate to the United Nations General Assembly from 1946 to 1952; and as a prolific speaker and writer. Like her husband, she was listed in *Time*'s 100 persons of the twentieth century with a feature article accurately titled *America's Most Influential First Lady Blazed Paths for Women and Led the Battle for Social Justice Everywhere* (Goodwin, 1998).

Like countless other servant-leaders, Franklin and Eleanor internalized a sense of obligation, a calling, and a mission in life that involved serving others. Their commitment is evident in that their leisure time was devoted to political and social causes versus pursuing idle comforts associated with wealth. This sense of calling focused their energies and talents accordingly.

While their respective inherited wealth may have given FDR, Eleanor, and even Theodore Roosevelt (the twenty-sixth president of the United States and Eleanor's uncle) an advantage or a head start for a life of service, they had to overcome the seduction of a comfortable life of leisure, free from the hard work and headaches associated with public service. At the same time, people such as Gandhi, Martin Luther King, Harry Truman, Margaret Thatcher, and Colin Powell, while not poor, were individuals of modest backgrounds. In addition, Theodore Roosevelt (TR) had to overcome frail health as child, including chronic headaches, fever, stomach pains, and the most serious of them all, asthma (Brands, 1998). TR was admonished as a young boy by his father that, if he was ever to to make the most of his mind, he would have to make his body well. At that point, TR committed to a regular regiment of rigorous physical activity that would characterize the rest of his life, aid him in conquering many of his childhood frailties, and enable him to pursue an active and vigorous public life (Brands, 1998).

Destiny is an individual's chosen path and purpose in life. One's position in life does not determine one's destiny. Samuel Smiles in his *Self Help* book astutely observes, "Great men of science, literature, and art—apostles of great thoughts and lords of the great heart—have belonged to no exclusive class nor rank in life. They have come alike from colleges, workshops, and farmhouses—from the huts of poor men and the mansions of the rich. Some of God's greatest apostles have come from the ranks. The poorest have sometimes taken the highest places" (1881, p. 27).

Leadership Challenge

The average traditional college graduate will spend more than forty years in the workplace. Is the major you chose to study in college one that is your calling or was the determining factor the possibility of money or fame. Will employment in your chosen field of study bring satisfaction, a sense of purpose, and meaning? If not, what would you study if money were not an issue and failure were not a possibility?

Just as a journey of a thousand miles begins with a single step (Confucius), servant-leadership often begins with a single resolve. It may sound daunting to take on the additional responsibilities and thankless job one inherits when one volunteers to be a servant-leader, but, as it is often said, "to whom much has been given, much is required." Now it may be easy to think that you have not been given much, compared with the Roosevelts, yet chances are if you are reading this book you are in an undergraduate or a graduate university program. When you realize that approximately only 28 percent of the population in America have an undergraduate degree and approximately 8.1 percent have a master's degree, your education gives you an elite head start relative to well over two-thirds of the population in America (National Center on Educational Statistics, 2006).

Choose to get involved in service and see where it takes you. As you resolve to be a servant-leader, take courage and comfort from the following inspiring, and sobering, words from a lecture titled *Citizenship in a Republic* that TR delivered April 23, 1910, on a university campus in Paris.

> It is not the critic who counts; not the man who points out how the strong man stumbles, or where the doer of deeds could have done them better. The credit belongs to the man who is actually in the arena, whose face is marred by dust and sweat and blood; who strives valiantly; who errs, who comes short again and again, because there is no effort without error and shortcoming; but who does actually strive to do the deeds; who knows great enthusiasms, the great devotions; who spends himself in a worthy cause; who at the best knows in the end the triumph of high achievement, and who at the worst, if he fails, at least fails while daring greatly, so that his place shall never be with those cold and timid souls who neither know victory nor defeat (Auchincloss, 2004, pp. 781–782).

Welcome to the arena. Answering the call to serve puts you in good company. Now that you are committed to being a servant-leader, the next questions are whom you will serve (family, friends, colleagues, neighbors, and strangers); what context you will serve in; (business, education, home, politics, public administration, military, non-profit organizations, and/or social services); and how you will serve (with time, talents, and/or treasures).

Find a Niche

A position or role best suited to a person who occupies it is called a **niche.** Given that the needs are so many, in what arena does one choose to invest one's time, talent, and treasures? Part of the answer involves finding your niche.

Interestingly enough, many exemplary leaders did not anticipate their initial accomplishments. In other words, when they were young, they did not know what they wanted to do when they grew up. It was through selective trial and error and a series of formal and informal mini-apprenticeships that exemplary leaders not only discovered their niche but also were groomed for future opportunities.

General Colin Powell, by his own admission, stumbled into a military career, which eventually led to opportunities to serve as the chairman of the Joint Chiefs of Staff (1989–1993) and as the first African American secretary of state (2001 to 2005). As a freshman at City College of New York, Powell came across the Army ROTC in drill practice, which immediately piqued his curiosity (Powell, 1995, p. 20). Powell acknowledges that, prior to his involvement with the army ROTC, he "had not yet excelled at anything" (Powell, 1995, p. 20). It was in the army that Powell discovered his niche and excelled as he went through the ranks to serve a distinguished and reputable career of public service that did not end after his retirement.

Between his retirement from the army and his appointment to secretary of state, Powell served as the founding chairman of America's Promise Alliance for Youth (founded in 1997). According to the Alliance's web page, America's Promise describes who they are:

> Building on the legacy of our founder, General Colin Powell, we are the leader in forging a strong and effective partnership alliance committed to seeing that children experience the fundamental resources they need to succeed—the Five Promises (caring adults, safe places, a healthy start, an effective education and opportunities to help others)—at home, in school and out in the community (America's Promise Alliance, 2007, Mission).

Powell documents how each level of success opened additional doors of opportunity for greater success. As a Distinguished Military Graduate, Powell received a full commission rather than a reserve commission, making him a full-time military officer. Graduating first in his class at the Infantry Officers Advanced Course led to him be assigned as an instructor for the school. With each new opportunity and additional successes, Powell continually appeared on the radar of his superiors.

George Marshall, the reluctant but ultimate example of a servant-leader who earned the respect of the world, had a journey similar to that of Colin Powell. George Marshall, contemporary of General Douglas McArthur and General George Patton, rose to become the Army Chief of Staff (1939–1945). After retiring as a five-star general, Marshall served a brief term as head of the American National Red Cross (1949–1950) and on several diplomatic missions for President Truman prior to being appointed secretary of state (1947–1949), only to be called out of retirement again to serve a brief tenure as the secretary of defense (1950–1951) during the Korean Conflict. George Marshall was the first soldier to receive the Nobel Peace Prize in 1953 for his efforts in what is known as the Marshall Plan.

Similar to Powell, Marshall did not initially excel in school. Marshall was actually considered a poor student. After a relatively unremarkable and notably undistinguished childhood, by default, Marshall chose to enroll in the Virginia Military Institute (VMI), only to find a sense of belonging (Stoler, 1989). Marshall was able to distinguish himself by sheer resolve at VMI and eventually earn a commission in the army, a credit to his character and competences (Stoler, 1989). Between 1902 and 1916, Marshall served in fourteen different posts, yet with stagnation of promotions at that time and much to his disappointment, he did not receive his promotion to captain until 1917, in spite of high praise from his commanding officers (Mosely, 1982). George graduated first in his class from the Army Staff College in 1908. The subsequent series of experiences groomed Marshall for future positions to eventually get him recognized by General John J. Pershing, commander of the American Expeditionary Forces in Europe during WWI.

Because of his reputation in military tactics, Marshall was eventually transferred to general headquarters to work with General Pershing. Marshall was hoping for his own field command at the time but was considered too valuable a staff member to lose, so his request for transfer was denied. Marshall emerged as one of General Pershing's chief tactical advisors (Mosely, 1982) to serve eventually as General Pershing's aide, which was a catalyst for Marshall's development as an officer. As Pershing's aide, Marshall was "introduced to the highest level of military and political leadership and would receive an education in politico-military affairs unavailable in another position" (Stoler, 1989, p. 42). General Pershing spent the rest of his life as a mentor and surrogate father to Marshall.

Marshall's trajectory was, like the path to leadership for many exemplary leaders, difficult to predict. There was nothing in Marshall's youth to suggest that he was born to command or to succeed. Marshall was a late-bloomer, emerging only gradually from a potentially unpromising VMI cadet to become, according to Truman, "the greatest living American" (Cray, 1990).

Both Marshall and Powell found their niche while in college and relatively young. It took Mahatma Gandhi a bit longer. Also a mediocre student, but determined, Gandhi eventually set out to be a lawyer. Barely passing the matriculation examinations for college and following a failed attempt at Samaldas College in India, Gandhi went to London for three years to study to become a barrister at law. On his return from England, Gandhi was unable to succeed in establishing a career practicing law. He was even denied a teaching position at a local school because he was not a university graduate. In the interim, Gandhi secured a tertiary role in a litigation case with a shipping company that had interests in India and South Africa. Gandhi's initial involvement in the case representing Indian perspectives opened doors for representing Indian rights in South Africa. After a series of small victories, he established a reputation as an effective mobilizer and guardian of oppressed Indians. Gandhi's reputation in South Africa preceded him on his return to India as he went on to lead various local reform movements in India. As Gandhi's regional successes as a social reformer drew national attention, his crusades for peaceful reform took on a larger stage in the eventual and ardous nonviolent battle to secure India's independence from Great Britain in 1947.

The leaders studied did not find just any cause to which they gave their time and energy. They gravitated to those things for which they were passionate about and best suited. Given there are more needs than one person can satisfy, it behooves emerging servant-leaders to enter those arenas in which they are gifted. Through a process of trial and error, these leaders discovered what they were good at. Not only were they good at what they did, but the Roosevelts, Marshall, Powell, and Gandhi pursued their causes with passion (partially fueled by their service orientation), and they found a level of enjoyment and fulfillment that sustained them through the difficult times.

Individuals need to be selective about the niche in which they will eventually serve. Finding a good match among one's current level of knowledge, skills, interests, and the immediate context of leadership is essential for success. This obvious yet liberating principle was reinforced by interviews conducted with nine exemplary university presidents who had served an average of twenty-five years in their current formal position, as well as by their respective vice presidents. The presidents and their immediate colleagues repeatedly emphasized that a healthy fit between the president and his or her institution was a key to the president's longevity. The presidents confessed that, if they were at another type of institution, their success and/or longevity would not be what it was. The good fit between the leader and the institution energized not only the leader but also the institution (Shoup, 2007).

Individuals are gifted differently and as a result have different passions. Finding a niche that aligns with those gifts and passions is a key to success and longevity. The diversity of humanity encourages individuals to judiciously pursue a niche versus indiscrimately joining any worthwhile cause. When you talk to specific servant-leaders about why they do what they do, they will reply that they have a specific passion and enthusiasm that sustains them that is unique. Passionate nurses really want to help the sick and seem to have an extra measure of mercy that sets them apart. Teachers have a passion toward learning and liberating society at the individual level. The prospective nurse is somewhat incredulous that adults would elect to spend seven hours a day with kids, while the prospective teacher is equally amazed that adults would elect to be around sick people all day. Gandhi, Marshall, Powell, the Roosevelts, and countless others emerged as great servant-leaders, in part, because, after a period of discovery and a series of formal and informal apprenticeships, they found a niche in which they could excel.

Along the way of discovering their niche, the emerging leaders acquired a breadth and depth of substantive experiences in the form of formal and informal apprenticeships. It was in the context of a series of evaluated mini-apprenticeships that respective leadership attributes and skills were developed and refined. The series of apprenticeships prepared each of the leaders for the next level of leadership. The initial and emerging successes developed and honed their gifts and talents, all the more, along with developing confidence in their abilities. In addition, the mini-apprenticeships showcased their success, resulting in their being noticed for additional opportunities.

Gandhi's serendipitous involvement in civil rights in South Africa became an apprenticeship for similar work on his return to India. FDR's service as a state senator prepared him for his role of governor of New York, which in turn prepared him for his role as the Assistant Secretary of the Navy during WWI. His apprenticeship as the Assistant Secretary of the Navy groomed him for his role as commander-in-chief of the Armed Forces role while president during WWII. As president, FDR was known for his fireside radio chats (he delivered a total of thirty between 1933 and 1944), which helped endear the nation to him, a practice he started and refined when he was governor of New York. For Powell and Marshall, subsequent placements and field commands all prepared them for the next level of challenges associated with each promotion. David of the TaNaK (the Jewish scriptures and the Old Testament of the Bible) was able to slay the giant Goliath after several successful "internships" with his sling shot protecting his sheep from lions and bears. Let the work of your youth and subsequent experiences hone you for the giants that will come later in life.

The application is to judiciously identify through selective trial and error what you enjoy and are good at, so that your servant-leadership is energized to an "nth" degree more. The second application is to continually groom yourself to become a leader through a series of formal and informal apprenticeships. In other words, get as many leadership and service experiences as you can in contexts consistent with your passions and talents. As a result, your leadership skills and attributes will have the opportunity to mature.

Now that you have decided to serve, and are in the process of discerning the context in which you will serve and developing your leadership acumen, the next step is to solicit and endear the strategic help of others to groom you accordingly.

Secure Prodigious Patrons

Any leader who has served successfully for a long time, unless he or she is egotistical and/or deluded, will share one of the key reasons for his or her success has been various people.

Powell reflected that his life was "a story about the people who helped make me what I am. It is a story of my benefiting from opportunities created by the sacrifice of those who went before me and may be benefiting those who will follow" (Powell, 1995, p. viii). When Powell discovered an Army ROTC unit, he found not only his niche but also a role model who would be one of many who would nurture his leadership abilities.

Powell (1995) wrote:

> One Pershing Rifles member impressed me from the start. Ronald Brooks was a young black man, tall, trim, handsome, the son of a Harlem Baptist Preacher and possessed a maturity beyond most college students. Ronnie was only two years older than I, but something in him commanded deference. . . . Ronnie was sharp, quick, disciplined, organized, qualities then invisible in Colin Powell. I had found a model and a mentor. I set out to remake myself in the Ronnie Brooks mold.
>
> My experience in high school, on basketball and track teams, and briefly in Boy Scouting had never produced a sense of belonging or many permanent friendships. The Pershing Rifles did. For the first time in my life I was a member of a brotherhood (pp. 27, 28).

Ronnie Brooks served as Powell's best man at his wedding and as a continuous source of encouragement and inspiration throughout Powell's career. Like many exemplary leaders, Powell acknowledges the role his spouse played in his success. Early in their marriage while departing for his first Vietnam tour, Powell (1995) realized "that she [his wife] was going to make the perfect life partner for this soldier" (p. 76). She remained loyal and a constant support and anchor, providing Powell the stability of a family in the context of a mobile military life. Celebrating their thirtieth wedding anniversary, Powell (1995) wrote, "When the guests were gone, Alma and I sat amid the festive debris knowing we were richly blessed. And in the lottery of love and marriage, I knew that I had been the big winner" (p. 557).

Powell credits the influence of various mentors and lessons he learned during his White House Fellowship as preparing him for his work as the Chairman of the Joint Chiefs of Staff. He states, "The people I had met during that year were going to shape my future in ways unimaginable to me then. But first I was off to Korea, where an old soldier would teach me a unique brand of military leadership" (Powell, 1995, p. 178). His new mentor in Korea and subsequent others played invaluable roles in honing Powell's leadership abilities.

Marshall benefited tremendously from General Pershing's mentoring. Stoler (1989) documents how "he [Pershing] clearly did become Marshall's mentor, protector, supporter, and booster, and a powerful and influential one at that" (p. 44). In 1924, Marshall reported, "No words can express the regret and loss I feel at the termination of my service with you. Few ever in life have such opportunities and almost none, I believe, such a delightful association as was mine with you" (Stoler, 1989, p. 44). They remained strong professional and personal friends until Pershing's death in 1948.

Franklin Roosevelt credited Endicott Peabody, the rector at Groton School, as one the major influences of his life. It was Peabody who performed the marriage ceremony for FDR and Eleanor and was a continuous source of encouragement to FDR until his death in 1944. Forty years after graduating from Groton, Roosevelt wrote to Peabody, "I count it among the blessings of my life that it was given to me in formative years to have the privilege of your guiding hand" (Burns, 1956, p. 16). After Peabody's death, Roosevelt wrote Peabody's widow that the "whole tone of things is going to be different from now on, for I have leaned on the Rector in all these many years far more than most people know . . ." (Burns, 1956, p. 468).

It was the work of Louis McHenry Howe (Roosevelt's primary political advisor) and Eleanor Roosevelt that helped FDR get reelected to the state senate. Freidel (1990) recounts the details:

> The illness [typhoid fever] made the odds against Roosevelt's reelection to
> the state senate seem insurmountable. At this point a remarkable figure
> came to Roosevelt's rescue and became thenceforth his alter ego. This was
> Louis McHenry Howe, a resourceful, cynical newspaperman. . . . Further,
> Howe was a firm believer in the role of the great man in history. When
> Roosevelt, bedridden for the duration of the campaign, turned to him,
> Howe responded with enthusiasm, attaching his aspirations to the future
> of the handsome, charming young man (p. 22).

It was in part the work of Louis Howe and Eleanor Roosevelt that kept Franklin prominent in politics during his seven-year respite and recuperation after he was first diagnosed with polio in 1921 to being elected governor of New York in 1928. Even though the Roosevelts' marriage evolved to be a marriage of convenience, Eleanor remained a great political partner to FDR. Freidel (1990) states that, "whatever the deficiencies in their intimate relationships, they became the greatest husband-and-wife political partners in American history" (p. 36). She was Roosevelt's moral conscience, serving as a frequent, albeit unofficial, advisor and strategically placing books in front of Roosevelt for him to read. Freidel observed:

> Eleanor Roosevelt herself, with her own entourage, served much of the times, as she had in New York State, as her husband's eyes and ears. She was also his conscience, prodding him on social justice matters such as the need to help black people in their plight. She had much influence on him, and also developed into something of an independent political force of her own right (p. 123).

Gandhi also benefited from the kindness of many in his ascent and grooming for global leadership. Gandhi's brother and extended family sought financial aid for Gandhi to study law in England. Once in England, Gandhi relied on the aid of Dr. Mehta, a friend of the family. Dr. Mehta made housing arrangements and was a source of frequent advice. The following is an example of how one kind person may have changed the course of Ghandi's life as an unknowing catalyst for social change:

> The kindness of a stranger made it possible for Gandhi to arrive in South Africa in a timely fashion. On the day he was to sail, due to an error, no cabins were available for Gandhi. The chief officer, hearing of Gandhi's plight, availed an extra berth in his cabin to Gandhi. This act of kindness prevented Gandhi from being stranded in Bombay for one month and missing his rendezvous with the chain of events to be set in motion in South Africa (Shoup, 2005, p. 49).

Chadha (1992) describes how another stranger acted on Gandhi's behalf at a critical time to save him from a mob that almost killed him:

> The crowd was cursing and shouting, and Gandhi was in danger of his life. Stones, brickbats, mud and rotten fish were being hurled at him. Someone dislodged his turban; someone else struck him with a riding whip. A burly fellow came up to the Mahatma-to-be, slapped him in the face and then kicked him hard. He was gripping the railing of a house nearly unconscious. 'I had almost given up the hope of reaching home alive,' he wrote. . . . At that moment Mrs. Alexander, the wife of the police superintendent, saw what was happening. She advanced into the fray with an open umbrella to keep off the flying missiles and stood between the crowd and Gandhi, protecting him at least against hard blows until the constables arrived to accompany him to the house where his family was waiting (p. 80).

In addition to relying on others for grooming or creating windows of opportunities, once successful leaders reach a position of influence, they recruit reliable colleagues to help them excel all the more in their local, national, or global agendas. Successful leaders hire and empower competent people. Several university presidents who have served exemplary long terms in office explained that the key to their success was hiring people smarter than them and letting those people do their job.

As Roosevelt assumed positions of authority, he surrounded himself with excellent people. Burns (1956) states:

> Outside his family and personal staff were a host of advisers, political associates and correspondents. These men provided something of a measure of the President-elect's ideas and purposes. Two things were remarkable about the men around Roosevelt in 1932: the variety of their backgrounds and ideas, and the fact that not one of them dominated the channels of access to Roosevelt's mind. It was a varied group because Roosevelt's test of a man was not his basic philosophy, or lack of one, but the sweep of his information, his ability to communicate, and his willingness to share ideas. Without any plan, a "brain trust," as the reporters came to call it, grew up around him (p. 153).

Collins (2001), in a highly acclaimed and quoted study titled *Good to Great: Why Some Companies Make the Leap . . . and Others Don't,* analyzed the histories of twenty-eight companies to ascertain what facilitated some companies going from good to great. A key finding Collins and his research team discovered was that highly effective leaders recruited and empowered the right people. Instead of the leader being a "genius with a thousand helpers" who implements the leader's vision (p. 47), the most effective leaders (which he calls Level 5 leaders) develop a superior executive team. Level 5 leaders hire extremely competent people and lets them "figure out the best path to greatness" (p. 47). Exemplary leaders are on the lookout for potential leaders to groom and recruit that enable success.

The wording *prodigious patrons* is intentionally used over the concept of mentor to reflect the range of roles that a series of different people would eventually play in respective leaders' rise to the top and ability to finish well.

> **Prodigious patrons** are people who, almost with a providential timing, and unwittingly at the time, become strategic catalysts for the leader to make it to the next plateau of success. . . . Throughout the leader's career, there was a steady stream or supply of advisors, financial backers, encouragers, kind strangers, and colleagues so that without such involvement, the leader's story may well have had a different outcome. . . . The "prodigious patrons" serve a substantive or monumental role in shaping and maintaining a leader's success and influence. The term "prodigious" is used because it means monumental or consequential effect or outcome from a particular influence at a particular time. Prodigious also has the connotation of providence and fate, reflecting that timing of the influence was an essential factor in the eventual outcome. The prodigious people played such a role that, one is left to wonder, if that person had not acted when he or she did in the manner he or she did, the outcome of the specific sequence of events would have been significantly altered.

A "**patron**" is someone who does something on behalf of another and, hence, is a supporter of the person. The range of supporting activity is from a simple form of encouragement or advice to financial backing. Various people, whether a mother, father, sibling, teacher, spouse, peer, colleague, mentor, acquaintance, or stranger, appeared at the right time and right place to prevent each leader from quitting, taking a different career path or missing fortuitous junctures in their rise to positions of prominent influence (Shoup, 2005, p. 42).

It should be noted that, while every leader had supporters in his or her corner, he or she also had his or her share of critics and, in some cases, adversaries. One university president commented on the nature of leadership in which "friends come and go, but enemies accrue." Many exemplary leaders, instead of getting defensive, benefited from the process of the conflict as a means to refine their views, establish priorities, identify personal or organizational weaknesses. Successful leaders, as noted in the TaNaK, recognize "iron sharpens iron" (Proverbs 27:17) and "faithful are the wounds of a friend" (Proverbs 27:6).

A classic example of the unknown ripple effect that encouragement and sponsorship can have is found in an individual by the name of Barnabas of the New Testament of the Bible. It was Barnabas who first welcomed the converted Paul to a cautious church (many were skeptical that Paul's conversion may have been a ruse to identify and persecute the early church). It was Barnabas who retrieved Paul from exile and involved him in the church at Antioch (Acts 11:25, 26). As Paul's work in establishing the early Christian church flourished, John Mark joined the work. Partway through the journey, John Mark either got homesick or lost interest in the work and decided to return to Jerusalem (Acts 13:13), upsetting Paul. When it came time to revisit the churches Paul and Barnabas established in their previous journey, a disagreement arose whether to take John Mark, who was expressing a renewed interest. Paul, questioning John Mark's fidelity and usefulness, separated from Barnabas. Barnabas took John Mark under his wing to pioneer work in Cyprus while Paul continued west (Acts 15:36–40). Barnabas' investment paid off in Paul's life in that Paul went on to establish much of the early church and write just over half the books in the New Testament. Barnabas' investment in John Mark's life paid off as well. Paul later testified that John Mark was useful to Paul for service (2 Timothy 4:11). John Mark also went on to write one of the New Testament gospels—the Book of Mark.

The application is to intentionally and subtly seek out people to help you grow personally and provide opportunities to experience service and leadership responsibilities. Hang out with the type of people you want to become like and occasionally initiate feedback from your friends, professors, colleagues, parents, and employers on what you can do to improve and see if there are any additional responsibilities that you can assume. In addition, think, feel, and behave like the person you want to become and you will subtly endear prospective mentors and prodigious patrons to yourself and eventually become the servant-leader you aspire.

A second application is to become a prodigious patron yourself. You never know what your acts of kindness and investment in others will reap in the long run. Become a Barnabas to as many people as you can.

As you cultivate your passions for service and hone your leadership abilities through various "apprenticeships," how do you increase the probability that you will finish well, both in the short term and long term? While there is no guarantee that you will not derail in your trajectory (many servant-leaders have been unjustly martyred) or become sidetracked because of circumstances out of your control, many servant-leaders have unexpectedly sabotaged their own legacy because of pride and/or compromised ethics.

Be Humble and Ethical

Lord Acton, as a historian, observed in a letter to Bishop Mandell Creighton in 1887 that "power tends to corrupt, and absolute power corrupts absolutely. Great men are almost always bad men." Acton observed that many people after reaching positions of influence and formal authority become corrupted. Funny things can happen to people on the way to the top that are often the antithesis of servant-leadership. Unfortunately, many emerging servant-leaders reach a level of unequalled success, only to derail because of pride and/or ethical lapses.

As leaders experience progressive levels of success and prominence, they experience a new set of temptations. Successful leaders receive varying degrees of preferential treatment as they move up the hierarchy, so that it becomes easy to start thinking "I am special." In addition, as various successes bring on appropriate accolades, emerging leaders may start to believe, "Wow, maybe I am better than I thought and without me these things would not have happened." When leaders begin to think highly of themselves, several problematic attitudinal and behavioral patterns surface, which, unless corrected, become the beginning of the end for the leader.

Successful leaders often begin to become concerned about impressions versus substance. They want to continue to look good in order to retain the accolades and position of authority. It is too easy for successful leaders to become socialized to believe that their achievements and hard work get them entitlements that others do not (e.g., liberal expense account, longer lunches, hedging decisions in their favor). Small compromises or self-promoting behavior begins to surface as leaders think some unethical decisions are justified (the end justifies the means) or that colleagues should defer to them. Many promising leaders who derail at some point begin to embrace a mindset that the organization is there to serve them and their agendas instead of the organization's agenda. Exemplary leaders are able to finish well when others have derailed because of their commitment and diligence to remain **humble** and ethical.

Encouragingly, power and authority do not have to corrupt, as evidenced by the legacy of countless leaders, especially George Marshall. Throughout his military and political service, Marshall was known for both his refreshing humility and his strong personal ethics. Marshall's humility stands in vivid contrast to General Douglas MacArthur's and General George Patton's flamboyant and arrogant personalities. While Patton and MacArthur were both brilliant military leaders, they had a penchant for self-promoting behaviors and for seeking the limelight. MacArthur's egotistical ambition and maverick mentality eventually resulted in his being relieved of duty by President Truman in April 1951. Mosely (1982) rightly observes that, "in the world of overpaid heroes and untrustworthy officials," Marshall made it to the top and maintained his principles (p. xiii).

Even though he was its primary architect, George Marshall refused to call the European Recovery Act the Marshall Plan. Marshall headed the US delegation to the coronation of Queen Elizabeth II. As the delegation approached their places in the front of Westminster Abbey, Marshall noticed "that the throng of richly clad and bejeweled princes and princesses, lords and ladies, and envoys from all over the world rose to their feet as if to pay homage to someone among them" (Mosely, 1982, p. 509). Perplexed, the unsuspecting Marshall whispered to his fellow delegate, General Bradley, "Who are they rising for?" only to hear General Bradley's answer, "You." When many of his postwar contemporaries were writing their autobiographies, Marshall turned down a $1 million book offer from the *Saturday Evening Post* on a matter of principle. The decision was made, at least in part, out of respect for the privacy of some of his contemporaries who had committed potentially embarrassing foibles and mistakes during the war (Mosely, 1982).

Gandhi was another archetype of humility and ethical living, evidenced by his nonviolent responses to correct social wrongs and to the unjust beatings and imprisonments he endured. Truman helped establish the NATO alliance, the Marshall Plan (or European Recovery Act to restore economic prosperity to war-torn Europe), and the Truman Doctrine (to provide timely and critical postwar resources and aid to Greece and Turkey) under his motto "It is amazing what you can accomplish if you do not care who gets the credit." Humility is a prized virtue even among successful business leaders. Collins (2001) found that great companies were run by Level 5 leaders who "build enduring greatness through a paradoxical blend of personal humility and professional will" (p. 20).

Humility and service go hand in hand. A service mentality requires thinking of others and the organizational mission and values as more important than yourself. You can't have true servant-leadership without a healthy sense of humility. Servant-leaders ask what they can do for others and the organization, not what others or the organization can do for them.

Like humility, a commitment to ethics is a logical extension of servant-leadership. Many exemplary leaders had a strong moral compass that helped them do the right things in the right way. The source of the moral compass for many of the leaders was a range of prodigious patrons, often starting with their parents. Powell documents how his parents' example and extended family provided a solid foundation (Powell, 1995). Even though FDR had his character flaws, FDR had Eleanor and Endicott Peabody as surrogate consciences for many of his dealings and policies. Gandhi's and Powell's religious traditions were an important source of guidance and courage that established them as moral exemplars. Marshall took seriously the code of conduct of a soldier and demonstrated tremendous fidelity to his country, which earned him his reputation as a highly principled man.

Individuals who adhere to a strict moral and ethical code of conduct are said to have **integrity.** Integrity is the number one characteristic people look for in their superiors (Kouzes & Posner, 1995). People want and need ethical leaders. Unfortunately, accounts of ethical failings of leaders abound, in part, because power associated with formal authority socializes unsuspecting leaders to believe with responsibility comes privilege (rather than with privilege comes responsibility).

In high-stakes positions, such as university president, exemplary leaders work hard to remain grounded and maintain an ethical reputation.

Photo courtesy of Diana Goldammer.

Many exemplary university leaders reported that they had colleagues experience a level of success only to derail because they let success go to their head by becoming self-promoting and self-serving, with a percentage acting unethically. In high-stakes positions, such as university president, the temptation to take shortcuts (whether by misrepresenting or withholding critical information, indiscriminately reallocating resources) to produce results is profound. The exemplary university presidents reported that they had to work hard to remain grounded, which they did by several means. One president had his office lined with placards of inspiring quotes to keep him humble and accountable and rotated cards to and from his desk, depending on which quotes were more germane to the issues at hand. Several other presidents kept their religious faiths central to their character through practicing the spiritual disciplines, such as reading of religious texts, prayer, and participation in a religious community. Others revealed that they had colleagues whom they could discuss a range of issues with and sort through the moral complexities they faced. One university president shared that it is hard work and necessary work to establish an ethical reputation, while it takes only one *faux pas* to ruin that reputation and, hence, one's credibility as a leader. Many exemplary university presidents revealed that their success was in part predicated on their trustworthiness (Shoup, 2007).

It may be premature to talk about finishing well when this text is designed for those who are just starting on their servant-leadership trajectory. At the same time, it is never too early to lay the foundation for humility and ethical courage. Remember that, without other people supporting and cheering us on, our successes are bound to be limited. In addition to your competences, remember that ethics and character will set you apart as a leader.

▪ CONCLUSION

Not all servants are, or will be, leaders. Not all leaders are, or will be, servants. However, if you take service to the extreme and leadership to the extreme, the two paradigms are logical extensions of the other.

Becoming a servant-leader is not easy. Service and leadership are already difficult by themselves without combining both roles into one. However, as paradoxical as it sounds, merging the two paradigms into a servant-leadership model yields tremendous influence and greater legacies than service without leadership and leadership without service.

An annotated collective look at various leaders renowned for both their service and leadership has not only, hopefully, inspired a servant-leadership orientation for you but also has revealed a few key themes, lessons, and principles for servant-leaders to emerge and finish well. The world desperately needs individuals who are willing to assume a calling of service and leadership. The world desperately needs discerning servant-leaders in a variety of domains in the local, state, national, and international arenas who have been developed and honed through a series and variety of leadership and service experiences. The world desperately needs a steady stream of prodigious patrons who facilitate opportunities for individuals to emerge as servant-leaders. The world desperately needs people of integrity and strong ethics to lead in the right direction and by the right means.

No one knows where your journey will take you, or what will be your destiny. Serve others, discover your niche, remain humble, maintain your integrity, and let the experiences and your patrons groom you for leadership and service opportunities in your future. In addition, take the role of prodigious patron for the multitude of individuals who will parade through your life. Who knows if you, or someone you encourage, will be among the next Roosevelts, Gandhi, King, Marshall, Powell, Thatcher, and countless other exemplary leaders. It may be you, or someone you encourage, who will be among the future exemplary leaders who will change the world. The choices that you make will determine your destiny.

▪ KEY TERMS

Calling—Work that brings satisfaction, a sense of purpose, and meaning to one's life.

Destiny—An individual's chosen path and purpose in life.

Humble—An absence of vanity and self-importance.

Integrity—Adherence to a strict moral and ethical code of conduct.

Niche—A position or role suited to a person or thing that occupies it.

Noblesse Oblige—The concept or belief that with privilege brings certain responsibilities.

Patron—Someone who does something on behalf of another and provides regular support for that person.

Prodigious Patrons—Persons who serve as catalysts for leadership success.

■ SUGGESTED READINGS

Collins, J. C. 2001. *Good to Great: Why Some Companies Make the Leap . . . and Others Don't*. New York: Harper Business.

Kouzes, J. M. & Posner, B. Z. 1993. *Credibility: How Leaders Gain and Lose It, Why People Demand It*. San Francisco: Jossey-Bass.

Kouzes, J. M. & Posner, B. Z. 1995. *The Leadership Challenge*. San Francisco: Jossey-Bass.

Maxwell, J. C. 1998. *The 21 Irrefutable Laws of Leadership: Follow Them and People Will Follow You*. Nashville, TN: Thomas Nelson.

■ REFERENCES

America's Promise Alliance. 2007. *Our Mission and Vision*. Retrieved December 8, 2007, from http://www.americaspromise.org/APAPage.aspx?id=6516.

Auchincloss, L. (Ed). 2004. *Theodore Roosevelt: Letters and Speeches*. New York: Library of America.

Brands, H. W. 1998. *TR: The Last Romantic*. New York: Basic Books.

Burns, J. M. 1956. *Roosevelt: The Lion and the Fox*. New York: Harcourt, Brace & World.

Burns, J. M. 1978. *Leadership*. New York: Harper Touchbooks.

Chadha, Y. 1992. *Gandhi: A Life*. New York: John Wiley.

Collins, J. C. 2001. *Good to Great: Why Some Companies Make the Leap—and Others Don't*. New York: Harper Business.

Cray, E. 1990. *General of the Army. George Marshall: Soldier and Statesman*. New York: Norton.

Cummings, W. K. 2003. *The Institutions of Education: A Comparative Study of Educational Development in the Six Core Nations*. Oxford, UK: Symposium Books.

Freidel, F. 1990. *Franklin D. Roosevelt: A Rendezvous with Destiny*. Boston: Little, Brown.

Goodwin, D. K. 1998. "Eleanor Roosevelt." *Time: The 100 Most Important People of the Century,* April 13, 122–126.

Horne, C. F. 1894. *Great Men and Famous Women: A Series of Pen and Pencil Sketches of the Lives of More Than 200 of the Most Prominent Personages in History*. New York: Selmar Press.

Lewis, C. S. 1954. *English Literature in the Sixteenth Century*. Oxford, UK: Clarendon Press.

Maxwell, J. C. 1998. *The 21 Irrefutable Laws of Leadership: Follow Them and People Will Follow You*. Nashville, TN: Thomas Nelson.

McCullough, D. 1992. *Truman*. New York: Simon & Schuster.

Mosely, L. 1982. *Marshall: Hero for Our Times*. New York: Hearst Books.

National Center on Educational Statistics. 2006. *Highest Level of Education Attained by Persons 25 Years Old and Over, March 2006* (no. 2007-017). Washington, DC: Author.

Plutarch. 2001. *Parallel Lives* (The Dryden translation). New York: Random House.

Powell, C. L. 1995. *My American Journey*. New York: Random House.

Shoup, J. R. 2005. *A Collective Biography of Twelve World-Class Leaders: A Study on Developing Exemplary Leaders*. Lanham, MD: University Press of America.

Shoup, J. R. 2007. *Leadership Longevity: Principles for Finishing Well.* Presented at ILA Annual Conference.

Shoup, J. R. & Reeder, G. 2006. *Meta-Metaphors and the Essence of Leadership.* Presented at ILA Annual Conference.

Smiles, S. 1881. *Self Help with Illustrations of Conduct and Perseverance.* Chicago: Belford, Clarke.

Stoler, M. 1989. *George C. Marshall: Soldier—Statesman of the American Century.* Boston: Twayne.

CHAPTER TWELVE REVIEW QUESTIONS

1. What do you think are your gifts and talents? List a minimum of three. If you are not sure, ask your friends, your parents, and your teachers.

   _____

   _____

   _____

2. What is your calling? What do you really care about? What do you enjoy?

   _____

   _____

   _____

3. For what arenas of service do you have a particular affinity? List a minimum of three. Some clues are what you care about and those things you enjoy.

   _____

   _____

   _____

4. Whom do you admire and why? Name a minimum of three persons. What can you do to become like those you admire?

   _____

   _____

   _____

5. Why should anyone follow you? If someone asked, what would you say is the source(s) for your moral compass? What things can you do to develop humility and moral character?

   _____

   _____

   _____

CHAPTER TWELVE SELF-TEST

1. Samuel Smiles, in one of the first self-help books ever written, reminded readers that hard work and _____ are keys to success.

2. The four themes or principles that influence the emergence of exemplary leaders that are addressed in this chapter are

   a. _____

   b. _____

   c. _____

   d. _____

3. According to the author, leaders are successful because they surround themselves with _____ people.

4. List three individuals who, according to the author, can provide feedback on what you can do to improve your life and become a better person.

   a. _____

   b. _____

   c. _____

5. While it is common for successful leaders to be derailed by pride and ethical lapses, according to the author, _____ and authority do not have to corrupt.